PELICAN BOOKS
Powers and Liberties

John Hall was born near Manchester in 1949. He was a
Stapledon Scholar in Modern History at Exeter College,
Oxford, before studying sociology at the Pennsylvania
State University and the London School of Economics.
Since 1975 he has been lecturer in Sociology at the Univer-
sity of Southampton. He has lectured widely in Europe
and the United States and has twice taught at Frankfurt
University.

He gained his Ph.D. for work on the character and
nature of the British intelligentsia; he has published
many articles in this field and intends eventually to write
an analytic history of British ideas since Hume. He is
the author of *The Sociology of Literature* (1979), *Diagnoses of Our Time* (1981), *Raymond Aron* (forthcoming)
and *Liberalism* (forthcoming), and editor of collections
on the state, the rise of the West and the neglected
political theorists of the period 1848 to 1945.

John A. Hall

Powers and Liberties
*The Causes and Consequences of
the Rise of the West*

Penguin Books
in association with
Basil Blackwell Ltd

Penguin Books Ltd, Harmondsworth, Middlesex, England
Viking Penguin Inc., 40 West 23rd Street, New York, New York 10010, U.S.A.
Penguin Books Australia Ltd, Ringwood, Victoria, Australia
Penguin Books Canada Limited, 2801 John Street, Markham, Ontario, Canada L3R 1B4
Penguin Books (N.Z.) Ltd, 182–190 Wairau Road, Auckland 10, New Zealand

First published by Basil Blackwell 1985
Published in Pelican Books 1986

Made and printed in Great Britain by
Richard Clay (The Chaucer Press) Ltd,
Bungay, Suffolk
Typeset in Ehrhardt

908.08

Contents

Preface   1

1 Patterns of History   3
The Necessity of Philosophic History   3
Three Views of Our Social Condition   9
Presuppositions and Definitions   17

Part I   Occidental Dynamism

Prologue: the Sociology of Agrarian
     Civilisations   27

2 Imperial China   33
The Origins of the Empire   35
Class, State and the Dynastic Cycle   38
Bureaucracy and Capitalism   45
Expansion without Development   54
Conclusions   56

3 The Land of the Brahmans   58
The Aryans and Caste   59
Buddhism and Empire   64
The Classical Pattern of Hindu India   70
Economic Stagnation   78
Conclusions   83

4 Islam and Pastoralism   84
Monotheism with a Tribal Face   85
The Sociology of Ibn Khaldun   91

The Economy in Classical Islam   99
The Gunpowder Empires   103
Conclusions   109

5 **The Rise of Christian Europe**   111
The City of God   112
The Early Growth of the European Market Economy   121
The Organic State in the State System   133
Conclusions to this Chapter and to Part One   140

Part II   The Modern World

Prologue: a Logic to Industrialism?   147

6 **Liberal Polities inside Capitalist Society**   158
Commerce and Liberty   158
The People, War and the Revolutions of the
    Twentieth Century   163
The Rise and Decline of Keynesianism   171
Splendours and Miseries of the Pax Americana   179
Conclusions, Pessimistic in Tone   186

7 **Beyond the Soviet Model?**   189
Social Origins of the Soviet Model   190
Stalinism and Socialism in One Country   195
State Socialisms   197
Liberalisation   203
The Soviet Union and the Arms Race   210
Conclusions   213

8 **The Third World**   215
The Birth of Nations   217
Capitalism and Imperialism   223
Varieties of Development   231
Conclusions   245

Conclusions: Options and Constraints   249
Progress and its Discontents   250
The Decline of the West: a European Perspective   256

Bibliographical Essay   261

Index   265

Preface

Whilst an undergraduate at Oxford studying history, a close friend was asked to write an essay on the social origins of the Third Reich. He spent a week reading about unemployment, working-class authoritarianism, inflation, reparations, lower middle-class anti-communist attitudes and the like, and produced an essay with these factors very much in mind. His tutor pounced, delighted that his deliberate hoax, designed to teach a lesson, had worked so well. What was the lesson? There *were* no social origins to the Third Reich, the tutor insisted, merely particular moves made by specific actors, especially Von Papen, and these political manoeuvrings were the real cause for Hitler's accession to power.

I was a history undergraduate at Oxford myself, and can vouch that this episode neatly captures the intellectual bias of Oxbridge historians, generally so prone to dismiss out of hand analyses of social structures, blind to their reality. As a result my encounter with Barrington Moore's *Social Origins of Dictatorship and Democracy* amounted to, as the French so nicely put it, 'la scène de séduction'. Here was a book, aware of social forces yet historically informed, which sought to understand our social condition with a view to gaining control of our destiny. Moore sent me back to other great historical sociologists – Durkheim, Weber, Adam Smith and Marx – all of whom proved so exciting that I became a sociologist. In contrast, modern sociology proved to be a terrible disappointment. It was a desert of arid concept-chopping where some sort of multiplier ruled; among various theoretical recipes to our ills and supposedly as guides to social reality were ethnomethodology, structuralism, structuralist Marxism, hermeneutics, phenomenology, functionalism, exchange theory, phenomenological Marxism, hermeneutics plus Marxism, linguistic philosophy, network analysis, and so on, and so on. Poincaré's observation, that natural scientists discuss their results, social scientists their methods, seemed horribly true. This theoretical extravagance scarcely advanced the subject at all for the banal but forceful reason that theories *can* only develop in the process of trying to explain reality. It came as some surprise to read Malcolm Bradbury's *The History Man*: sociologists could control very little, and most of their work was desperately innocuous as well as being awfully boring.

This book leaves behind such recent ephemera and engages, as happily others are now doing, classic questions of historical sociology. I attempt three tasks: to offer an account of the rise of the West in comparative perspective, to characterise our own world, and to reflect upon certain options that face the modern world, and in particular Europeans in that world. It is worth pausing to be explicit about this. Does the author really mean what he says? The claim *is* made consciously and seriously, although with considerable humility considering the range of sources involved, in the belief that any general view encourages thought more than a vacuum does. In the nature of things, it is impossible to be right about the sorts of issue raised, but the effort seems to me worthwhile given that, as Aquinas says somewhere, some light on large topics is better than analysing trivial ones *ad infinitum*.

The model offered is, and is meant to be, eclectic. It is an up-to-date, sociologically informed, philosophy of history, a record of results achieved by, rather than methods canvassed for, social science. In this connection I have a vast debt to acknowledge. For five years Ernest Gellner, Michael Mann and I ran a seminar at LSE entitled 'Patterns of History' dealing with classical questions in historical sociology. I learnt a great deal from the speakers, but infinitely more from my two friends. My general view, from which I suspect they dissent (objecting, however, to different parts), could not have been constructed without borrowing arguments from their work, sometimes in ways of which I am no longer conscious. My debt to Ernest Gellner's work is obvious. I read a manuscript version of *Sources of Social Power*, a work sure to make Michael Mann famous, and the publication of the book by the Cambridge University Press will make my indebtedness to him equally clear. But as the present book was written in adverse, indeed tragic circumstances, my greatest debt to them is personal. Their passion for their work kept mine going.

Patricia Crone read an early version of the first half of the book, tore it apart but believed in the project sufficiently to recommend lines of reconstruction. My debt to her is very large. Many other friends and colleagues have offered criticism and support, and I must name at least some of them: Jackie Butler, Susan and David Gellner, Colin Morris, Marianne Hämäläinen, Sammy Finer, John Roberts, Doreen Davies, Graham Crow, Gay Woolven, Colin Platt, Ursula Gress, José Merquior, Sue Burrett, Peter Carson, Stephen Shennan, George Butterworth, George and Birgitte Speake, the members of the Wednesday Evening Historical Sociology Society and Caroline Thomas.

1

Patterns of History

The Necessity of Philosophic History

This book is an essay in philosophic history. Its concern is with distinguishing different types of society and explaining the transitions from one type to another in order thereby to reflect systematically on the nature of power and human life chances. The term 'philosophic history' was coined by the brilliant thinkers of the Scottish Enlightenment, and both David Hume and Adam Smith have been intellectual influences on this work – but so too have Karl Marx and Max Weber. I am interested, as were all these authors, in trying to establish the broad outlines of our social condition and believe that a necessary element of such under-standing is an historical account explaining from whence we came, not least in order that we may lay bare what it is about us that is truly different and novel.

It is as well to be honest and to admit that, to say the least, philosophic history is currently out of favour. This is strange given the centrality of the subject in previous ages, and stranger given the massive social transformations of the twentieth century, among them the historical dramas that have characterised recent European history. The distaste for the whole enterprise of philosophic history doubtless owes something to the intellectual specialisation that has turned historians into a separate profession. Some among that profession are wont to jibe that philosophic history is more philosophy than history. By and large, however, the most intelligent of that fraternity do *not* make this accusation since they are only too well aware that particular studies involve some general frame of reference, and are fully cognisant that pattern seekers among their own number – Pirenne and Tawney spring instantly to mind – have fertilised whole areas of study, even though their work has subsequently come to be much questioned.

However, the fundamental reason for the current distrust of philosophic history is different. A set of passionate authors deeply marked by personal experience, most notably Raymond Aron, Isaiah Berlin and Sir Karl Popper, argued the simple and clear case that the practice of the philosophy of history is *dangerous*.[1] Such authors were hugely successful in establishing in the public mind a close link between the search for historical laws and the practice of bloody, totalitarian politics. Clearly these thinkers had in mind such twentieth-century ideologies as Marxism, nationalism and Nazism, those revolutions which had put, to use Arnold Toynbee's phrase, history on the move. They argued that the philosophy of history led to 'ideological politics' even though – or, rather, especially *because* – the supposed historical laws were in fact mistaken or spurious. 'Historicism' stressing 'historical inevitability' diminished the role of human action, and in so doing encouraged political stupidity – such as the famous occasion when German Communists supported the Nazi Party in the belief that this was a necessary stage to be passed through on the road to socialism! Further, those who accepted such historical laws were judged by Sir Karl Popper to be morally craven in committing the 'naturalistic fallacy', that is in jumping on the historical bandwagon rather than seeking to ground their morals independently.

Behind this general equation lies a series of more technical arguments against philosophic history, and four of these deserve distinguishing. Firstly, it was claimed, particularly by Popper, that the growth of human knowledge is unpredictable and that this 'defeats' the patterns supposedly established by the most determined philosophies of history. Secondly, historical prediction is said to be defective because social life is so complex that nothing can ever be held to occur for certain. This type of argument often stresses paradoxes of rationality which disrupt social expectations. A classic paradox of this type is that of capitalist behaviour as envisaged by Marx which sees individual entrepreneurs maximising and rationalising, unaware of the fact that collectively such competitive action leads to disaster. The third argument, made much of everywhere today, seeks to stress differences between the field of social and natural science. In particular, social life is seen as the realm of social meanings, and this is held to make it immune from pattern-making or prediction. The final, rather sophisticated, argument is related to this. A. J. Ayer was once moved to summarise what he had learnt from the philosophy of history in four propositions:

1 R. Aron, *Introduction to the Philosophy of History*, Weidenfeld & Nicolson, London, 1961; I. Berlin, *Historical Inevitability*, Oxford University Press, Oxford, 1954; K. Popper, *The Open Society and its Enemies*, Routledge & Kegan Paul, London, 1945.

1 We have had a history.
2 We have now had the history that we have had.
3 We cannot now have any other history than the history that we have had.
4 We ought to be grateful.[2]

As it happens, Ayer's summary is rather misleading, For perhaps the main formal argument against the philosophy of history seems to suggest that we could have had other histories! This argument owes something to Hegel who insisted that we could only have proper history provided that we knew what the end of history in fact was, a matter on which Hegel himself had regrettably few doubts. For history is made up of events, and the significance ascribed to events depends upon their place within a larger story. Those opposed to the philosophy of history, bereft of any Hegelian props, naturally chose to insist that no firm historical knowledge was possible, that each age wrote its own history, and that the very notion of historical laws or pattern-seeking was misguided.

It is as well immediately to allow three limitations to the philosophy of history, to admit certain truths established by the authors mentioned, since this book is self-avowedly an essay in this genre. It *is* impossible for the social sciences to produce laws upon which absolutely unquestioned action can be taken, and it is easy to see why this should be so. There were but *four* major civilisations, and it is simply impossible to produce a general theory or law on the basis of only four cases each of which varies in a whole series of particulars from the others. The same is obviously true for the key event in recent world history, namely the rise of the West. Autonomous economic development can, by definition, only happen once. It is impossible to generalise from a single case.

A second limitation lies less in our knowledge than in the world itself. There are two very silly doctrines about knowledge and the world: that we can do whatever we wish, and that everything is completely determined. There is no one-to-one correspondence, to consider the Marxist case, between a 'mode of production' and a particular social and political organisation, although there is much to be said for the negative notion that once one of these economic stages has been reached certain social practices are thereby ruled out. Agrarian society allows for different institutional options, as does industrial society. A further complication is that there is, as we shall see, no necessary economic mechanism leading from one stage to another: such transitions, especially original transitions, result from a complicated mixture of economic, ideological and

2 I am indebted for this story to Raymond Plant.

political factors. But the key point is that we are faced with options as to the ways in which we can run these 'modes of production', and one key task of contemporary thought must be to spell out and highlight the nature of choices possible.

Finally, we must accept a central Popperian point. It will be argued later that human advance has had a great deal to do with competition of various sorts. Nevertheless, we may now be at a stage at which, understanding this, we wish to put a stop to it. (It is doubtful whether this *is* in fact desirable, and it is hugely improbable that it is possible.) To say this, however, is not to indulge in the fantasy whereby it is suggested that our morals can be detached from the historical process and become free-floating. On the contrary, we are free only in so far as we understand our historical situation.

Beyond these limitations to philosophic history there is very little to be said in favour of the technical arguments against it, and even less to be said in favour of abandoning the enterprise of philosophic history altogether. Something will be said later about the crucial and essentially contested notion of 'social meaning', but criticism of all the other arguments attacking philosophic history can be given immediately.

To begin with, it is mistaken to move (as do thinkers who stress paradoxes of rationality) from demonstrating that the best laid plans come to grief to insisting that as a result we can have no social scientific knowledge. For there is no inherent reason why a social scientist should not be able to discover, and to do so before the event, that there is an imbalance between the goals of individual actors and the goal they might choose were they able to act as a collective social unit. Indeed, one striking tract in political economy, Mancur Olson's *The Rise and Decline of Nations*,[3] tries to specify the exact moment at which the particularistic interests of groups will start to undermine the social whole; this fairly 'hard' knowledge allows him to suggest institutional changes to prevent it.

There is also every good historical reason to be suspicious of Popper's contention that the future is unpredictable because we cannot foretell what the growth of knowledge will bring in its train. One of his forebears in this sort of view was Francis Bacon, who declared that European society had been changed beyond recognition by the technological holy trinity of compass, gunpowder and printing. Yet these inventions came from China and singularly failed to change *that* civilisation. Similarly, as we shall see, the heavy plough and the windmill, two inventions absolutely crucial in the rise of Christian Europe, were known to, but not generally adopted by the Romans. There are very good reasons, in other

3 Yale University Press, New Haven, 1982.

words, to believe that technique is at the mercy of social relationships. Marxists are right to speak of the sin of technicism. We are apt to forget this in the West precisely because we live in an innovating, technically conscious civilisation based on social change. But even here there are limits. Daniel Bell's *The Coming of Post-Industrial Society* argues a version of the Popperian thesis, and adds to it the Saint-Simonian belief that scientific knowledge, and thereby scientists, may become more powerful. Yet it is a striking merit of this book to give us the detailed case study of the occasion on which American nuclear scientists, led by Robert Oppenheimer, tried to lay down policy on scientific grounds rather than to simply accept the dictates of the military-political machine. As is well known, this attempt at autonomy was completely and humiliatingly defeated. Knowledge was not power.[4]

But what of the original equation posited by the thinkers mentioned, that the philosophy of history equals danger? This equation probably only proved persuasive because of the moral authority which these thinkers, themselves of Jewish backgrounds, gained from confronting the appalling events of twentieth-century European history. Nevertheless this argument, essentially one from emotion, seems to me very largely wrong; and in so far as it is not wrong, the authors may be accused of drawing the wrong conclusions from their reflections. For the character of twentieth-century history is not simply the direct product of the unleashing of historicist philosophy. The fundamental fact of recent world history has been, and remains, the sea change between an agrarian and an industrial way of life. It was always likely, probably inevitable, that a change of this proportion would involve massive social disruption. Nation-building and the various solutions to the peasant problem required for an industrial society are bound – and this is designed as something like a law-like statement! – to engender extraordinary social upheaval. While we may not wish to celebrate this, we can at least recognise it. Structural changes lay behind the upheavals of the twentieth century in a way in which these thinkers, prone to be obsessed by the power of ideas, sometimes forgot. To say this is to admit a further point of their case, namely that intellectuals do have great salience during great social upheavals. But we should not stop there; instead we must ask *why* this should be so. In this matter it is possible to reverse the moral opprobrium directed against philosophic history. A refusal to try and spell out one's basic historical position can lead to a type of social passivity, or at least leave the fastidious at the mercy of those – for all are unlikely to follow such a dry argument – who do possess some historical

---

4 For a full analysis of this tension in Bell's work, see my *Diagnoses of Our Time*, Heinemann, London, 1981, ch. 4.

vision. The Ayatollah Khomeini has such a vision, derived from religion, and it is simply an abrogation of duty on the part of Western intellectuals not to oppose it with an alternative. The automatic quality of the equation can be further diminished by noting that the philosophic history of Adam Smith and David Hume, to take but one example, in no way advocated anything other than a cautious and pragmatic blending of liberal politics with a market economy.

It is as well to be open and to say clearly that two further fundamental reasons lie behind my advocacy of philosophic history. Firstly, though the matter is highly complex, it seems that a measure of philosophic realism about history is justified; changing interpretative systems will not alter the sheer facticity of some major events. We may come to downplay the importance of particular battles, or stress events over a longer period of time, but the world historical significance of the discoveries, the invention of gunpowder and so on will surely *not* disappear however different our judgements about these matters may become. Secondly, and centrally, philosophic history may as well be practised openly since otherwise it is practised covertly. Even in 'normal' periods of history, political action is guided and constrained by implicit views of our social condition. Only a few examples are needed to make it quite clear that there is no escape to a presuppositionless world. It matters a great deal, for our political behaviour, whether we consider our own society to be capitalist, industrial, industrial capitalist, liberal, democratic, or some sort of mixture of these; the same is, of course, true of the manner in which we conceive Eastern European states. Perhaps a still more pertinent example was provided by the 1982 conflict between Argentina and Britain over the Falkland Islands. Was General Galtieri a fascist, or just another tinpot Latin American dictator? Or was he, as some of the best informed assured us, in fact trying to liberalise his country, not, à la Karamanlis, at the point of failure, but as a result of a signal success? Such conceptions matter. There is probably much more to be said, for example, for detente with the regime under Raul Alfonsin which followed Galtieri's downfall than there was for the same policy under the generals. All in all, it is best to be as open and as explicit as possible; if not we tend to be at the mercy of half-baked versions of older historical views. And it is an interesting fact that a great number of current political assumptions still rest in a rather automatic and unquestioned way upon classical political economy and upon Marxism. One of the purposes of this book is to spell out the key ideas of both Adam Smith and Karl Marx, to admit certain of their virtues and yet to isolate weaknesses, sometimes shared, that should lead us to go beyond them.

All these points can be summarised briefly. The conclusion drawn by

Aron, Popper and Berlin that the philosophy of history is too hot to handle seems to me mistaken. Surely there is sense, especially as we do and must have some conception of our historical position, to an alternative reaction which insists that we can improve and create a more accurate philosophic history? Of course, it would be the height of vanity to ignore the limits to our knowledge that the complexity of social life occasions. But it is possible to take this as a challenge rather than to parade it exultingly as a cheerfully worn badge of despair. It is a problem not a solution. In this matter it is as well to be blunt. Despite caution, I do actually believe that certain patterns in social life *can be, indeed have been, discovered*, and this book will list some of them.

Three Views of Our Social Condition

Two warnings are in order. In this section, three philosophies of history are pillaged for the purposes of the general argument; they are not discussed fully in their own terms, but only in so far as they advance the argument. For analytic purposes, I extract from each a type of social power. One central claim of this book is that these three types of power are *the* crucial ones in human history, and they correspondingly appear throughout. Secondly, given that my flesh is weak and my knowledge consequently limited, this book does not cover all of human history; attention focuses instead on world history since the emergence, between 600 BC and AD 700, of the world religions and ethics. This means that no sustained attention is given to classic questions such as the emergence of literacy and coinage, and the origins of the state. Though there are reasons for taking this breakpoint, it can be admitted immediately that it will provide certain problems when studying the rise of the West.

Human societies have conceived of history in many different ways. Classical Hinduism asserts that human history is, despite partial cycles of renewal, witness to a long process of deterioration. More usual has been the view shared by thinkers as diverse as Machiavelli and Ibn Khaldun that history goes in cycles with periods of corruption eventually being followed by eras of renewal. The rise of the West induced a key change in the philosophy of history by giving it an evolutionary turn. All the thinkers considered here shared this basic assumption.

The first philosophy of history is that of Karl Marx, and it requires the most attention since its characteristic weaknesses in effect explain why the other two theories are needed. Karl Marx was, as is realised increasingly, very much a mid-nineteenth-century thinker, and in no way was this more true than in the matter of social evolution. Marx's theory of history remains the boldest ever produced, and its core doctrine can be summarised diagramatically:

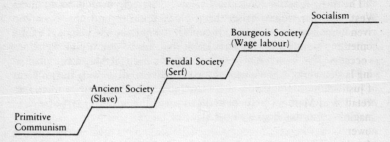

The tenets of Marx's theory are implied in the simple model but deserve to be listed separately. Firstly, his contention is that each type of society is held together by a particular form of economy. But, secondly, each of these modes of production is seen as internally unbalanced and out of joint since it is the field in which different social classes battle. Thirdly, it is claimed that a lower class, bearer of a new mode of production, eventually wins the class struggle and thereby sets the society on a higher course.

This magnificent theory amounts in principle to a secular religion. It suggests that a period of innocence is to be followed by three ages of travail before salvation can be reached. These periods of purgatory are the result of the key characteristic about this theory that I wish to emphasise, namely that evil is seen as the result of one factor alone, economic exploitation by class. This is a theory of definite clarity and essential simplicity which is superbly designed as an instrument of popular appeal. It is perhaps worth contrasting Marx's own theory with more academic Marxisms currently on offer in the West. Most of these try and add to Marx's essential economic determinacy relative autonomies for various other realms of social life, most notably politics and ideology. The trouble with such additions is that they are neither clear nor convincing. Once art, law or the means of violence are considered as part of the base of society, what then is left of the original vision? This criticism should not be misunderstood. My contention is *precisely* that an understanding of economic actors needs to be complemented by an understanding of intellectuals and state functionaries. This appreciation of the role of ideology and politics is designed to complement that of Marx in order to produce a better-balanced social theory which recognises that these actors in social life can, at times, be *completely* autonomous. We are driven to complement Marx in this way *only* in so far as we keep in view the elegant simplicity of his original theory, and are then forced to realise certain weaknesses that derive from it.

The interpretation of Marx is by now a notable growth industry in the West, and there are certainly those who would object to the exposition given here. But there are good reasons for believing that Marx did intend something simple and comprehensible, and many recent interpretations – occasionally considering marginalia to be 'the real Marx' and dismissing larger works as mere propaganda – have their own weighty problems of justification. Nothing in the general argument hangs upon the interpretation of Marx himself; all that matters is that it is at least possible to imagine a theory which does see the economy as the principal source of power. Nevertheless, three important general points must be made about Marxism. Firstly, there is an ongoing debate inside Marxist theory as to exactly what makes up a mode of production: should this be seen in essentially technological terms or should the state of class war be given independence over technology? Does a mode of production fundamentally, to use technical Marxist terms, derive from the forces or the relations of production? Throughout this book I shall simply separate these general meanings of the economy by distinguishing between a productive system and socio-economic extractive relationships. The former can allow several different types of the latter. Secondly, the author is cognisant of the sea-change that took place between Marx and Lenin: where the former was essentially democratic and rather naïve about power relations, the latter was elitist and thoroughly in tune with the harsher realities of power. Thirdly, Marxism as a universal and unilinear theory suggested that each society had to go through every stage specified. Modern Soviet Marxists have begun to argue that there is no real reason why Marxism need have unilinealism as one of its tenets. This is to recognise, for example, the obvious fact that some ex-colonies in Africa are attempting a direct transition from 'feudalism to socialism'. A society, in other words, usually operates with knowledge of the possibilities revealed by other societies. But the actual transition from one mode of production to another must be made, if Marxism is to make sense, as a result of class war. One of the principal contentions of this book is that factors other than economic ones played a role in the rise of the West.

All that has been said to this point is broadly sympathetic to Marx's general position. It is now time to turn to a fundamental flaw, consideration of which leads to the other general views to be discussed. Marx himself recognised, and in some regrettably racist remarks welcomed, the fact that Western imperialism would push stagnant Eastern societies onto the ladder of world history. Implicitly, but not theoretically, he thereby recognised that social evolution could result, not from internal class factors, but from inter-societal comparison, force and competition. However, his view of Asian societies presents Marxism with a problem which is insoluble within its own theoretical terms, and this merits a moment's digression.

When Marx and Engels tried to explain the stagnant nature of Asian societies they often did so by reference to the type of state required by the water-control systems of such societies. This view was fully developed by K. O. Wittfogel, whose *Oriental Despotism*[5] discusses a bureaucratic state placed 'above social classes', possessed of 'total power'. If this theory is accepted, the essential appeal of Marxism goes by the board for East becomes East, West becomes West, and the unity of mankind is thereby destroyed. As crucial is the damage done to the Marxist conceptual apparatus. If the state is free-floating it either has an autonomous role functional for the whole society (the end of the concept of class society), or it is a source of power in its own right (thus adding a second source of travail to human history). Marxists have long realised the dangers of accepting the thesis, and it has been declared invalid on conceptual *and* historical grounds in both Russia and Western Europe. How do such Marxists seek to preserve the theoretical intention of Marx *malgré lui?* All argue that Asian society is in fact composed of classes, that irrigation is, in other words, provided by the state in the interests of particular classes. In so doing it is necessary to abandon certain statements of Marx, but these are variously ascribed to the needs of propaganda, the evil influence of Hegel or straightforward immaturity. Beyond this strategies vary: some Soviet authors consider the Asian stage a sixth one in world history, whilst others seek to conflate it with slave-owning or feudal society. But there is an impasse as powerful as that affecting the hydraulic society thesis. If the great emotional appeal of Marx's schema of world history is its escalator-type quality, its sensation that we are being carried to salvation, then it is extremely disturbing to discover that Chinese society was stuck in the same stage for over two thousand years, while Europe, in comparison, progressed like a champion hurdler. Class *is* a useful concept to help understand agrarian civilisations, including those of the East. But if classes in Asian society do not create social evolution, then the emotional aura associated with the Marxist concept of class must be abandoned. This is a very grave loss.

All this deserves summary. Asian societies defeat Marxism since they present a fork on one prong of which the doctrine is bound to perish. If

5 Yale University Press, New Haven, 1957. Cf. E. Gellner, 'Soviets against Wittfogel', in J. C. Galey (ed.), *Différences, valeurs, hiérarchie*, L'Ecole des Hautes Etudes en Science Sociales, Paris, 1984.

the hydraulic society thesis is accepted, Marxist universalism perishes, political power becomes autonomous and class does not play its proper part – all points which are anathema to Marxism. But the alternative view, stressing that Asian society is class society, falls before the brute fact that Asia did *not* autonomously develop, and lands Marxism with the unexplained and theoretically equally horrific fact of modes of production bereft of an internal motor. Marxism is caught on a fork which refutes it.

Marx's work remains vital since it directs our attention to economic factors. Criticisms made of it already point to the second philosophy of history to be discussed – or rather *used* since the intention is to isolate a factor, on this occasion politics, which must be theorised if we are to understand human history. No single thinker dominated this philosophy of history, but various parts of it were articulated by Montesquieu, David Hume and Adam Smith, and it represented many of the more general hopes of the age. One particular tenet of the theory was neatly summarised by Samuel Johnson's famous dictum that a man is never so innocently employed as when he is making money.[6] This represents a strikingly different appreciation of the new commercial order than that of Karl Marx since it implies that other passions, envy and the love of power above all, are far more dangerous than is money-making. To this author at least, this seems patently obvious. Endemic conflict between human beings means that the necessity of regulation by politics is a permanent task of complex social life. But politics enters into the work of these eighteenth-century thinkers in two more substantive ways.

Firstly, such thinkers, above all Hume and Smith, and most brilliantly in the third book of the latter's *Wealth of Nations*, possessed their own theory of history. It is traditional to stress that commerce, in the eyes of the Scottish moralists, is the *consequence* of *laissez-faire* politics. However, recent scholarship has made it clear that commerce was also seen as the *cause* of the respect for law that characterised all Europe – in this matter Hume and Smith refused to see the Settlement of 1688/89, which they endorsed, as sufficiently important to rule France out of the bounds of civilised society.[7] The crucial role in the emergence of the rule of law is held to be the relative weakness of the medieval monarch who, in order to gain revenue and to balance baronial power, allowed towns to purchase their independence. This small change was held to have had an enormous impact on the feudal nobility. The king alone could not tame them and so install a respect for law. What the king could not achieve,

6 This element of the approach has been evocatively discussed by A. O. Hirschman, *The Passions and the Interests*, Princeton University Press, Princeton, 1977.
7 D. Winch, *Adam Smith's Politics*, Cambridge University Press, Cambridge, 1978.

however, was managed by the taste for luxuries provided by the productive, autonomous city. The feudal lords suddenly had something on which to spend their money. Instead of simply buying retainers, the lords, selfish to a degree, could buy *things*, and so live ostentatiously and gratify their pride. Thus as soon as the lords lost their retainers, the rule of law became a possibility.

Some points are worth making about this ingenious theory. Smith had his own view of Asian stagnation, and *Wealth of Nations* as a whole suggests that the effectiveness of the European market depended both upon the underclass being by no means as poor as that of Asia, and upon the habit of investment rather than conspicuous consumption on the part of the landlord class. As we shall see, both these presuppositions have truth to them. Smith's account implies some general considerations as to the emergence of the market in European history, namely that it came into being as the result of political fragmentation. There is something to this as well, although we shall have to add to it an understanding of the consensual capacity of the Latin Christian church. It is worth spelling out then that the theory of Smith and Hume, interestingly linking commerce with freedom, is not naïvely economically determinist in character: on the contrary, military and political factors play crucial roles in social evolution. This points to a difference with the schema of Karl Marx and it generates in turn a further such contrast. Hume and Smith had the clear belief that the rise of commercial society was more or less the result of luck, of a fortuitous coincidence of circumstances planned by nobody.

The second general point about politics that we can gain from this school is implied in this comment by Gibbon:

The division of Europe into a number of independent states, connected, however, with each other, by the general resemblance of religion, language, and manners, is productive of the most beneficial consequences to the liberty of mankind. A modern tyrant, who should find no resistance either in his own breast or in his people, would soon experience a gentle restraint from the example of his equals, the dread of present censure, the advice of his allies, and the apprehension of his enemies. The object of his displeasure, escaping from the narrow limits of his dominions, would easily obtain, in a happier climate, a secure refuge, a new fortune adequate to his merit, the freedom of complaint, and perhaps the means of revenge. But the empire of the Romans filled the world, and, when that empire fell into the hands of a single person, the world became a safe and dreary prison for his enemies . . . To resist was fatal, and it was impossible to fly.[8]

What is most obvious here is the distrust of empire, and the awareness of its negative impact on social evolution. Yet something much more impor-

8 E. Gibbon, *The Decline and Fall of the Roman Empire*, Everyman, London, 1905, vol. 1, p. 93.

tant is at issue. The contrast being drawn is not between an empire and a nation-state, but between the former and a state system. There is, in other words, a larger international society in which states play their part. However, international society was not conceived in wholly political terms by eighteenth-century thinkers. Competition by means of war was not the only point at issue. Hume and Smith were also well aware of international economic competition, and indeed participated in a debate about the likely consequences of such competition. Hume argued that rich nations would eventually, by means of high wages, price themselves out of the international market. This did not worry Hume who believed that decay need not occur; production for an ever-increasing home market could take the place of international trade. In contrast, Smith insisted that there was nothing wrong with high wages; rather such wages, if they increased productivity, were the secret to maintaining one's share of international trade. This is not to say that Smith was a total optimist; his *Wealth of Nations* was, after all, a pessimistic account of the way in which the merchant interest was making Britain less flexible, and thereby debilitating its response to the changing international context.[9]

The implications of this position are so vital as to require some amplification, and to do so it is necessary to try to go beyond our traditional conceptual apparatus. These thinkers in effect argue that there were different levels to their society, the national and the international, and that the interaction between them, largely of a competitive nature, brought in its train human progress. It is worth highlighting that they insisted that the national level could respond to the international context, although there was no guarantee of this occurring.[10]

All this seems a clear advance on Karl Marx whose conceptual categories presume that capitalist society will be simply transnational. This obviously ignores the continuing presence of nations, capable of making wars and so changing patterns of social evolution. Further, nations are

9 I. Hont, 'The "rich country–poor country debate" in Scottish classical political economy' in I. Hont and M. Ignatieff (eds), *Wealth and Virtue*, Cambridge University Press, Cambridge, 1983.

10 A key definitional point is being implied here, and can usefully be brought into the open. That there is an international context means that every state is involved in larger social processes. But I distinguish rigorously between this international *constraint* and full-blooded international *control* or dependency. When a state does not respond to international political or economic constraints, this is often the result of internal social inertias, and this should not be blamed on external forces. Dependency does, however, result from external interference which prevents a nation from acting autonomously. A modern example may be helpful here. The West, and in particular America, is to blame in countries such as the Honduras or El Salvador, where its policies prevent the emergence of strong states, able to modernise and develop. In contrast, the key limits on Indian development can now be ascribed to internal social inertias, notably those of caste and patterns of land-holding.

also economic actors, indeed are often driven to be because of international political competition, and an account concentrating solely on capitalism fails to realise that social development has involved a complex dialectic between capital and nation. There will be much to say about these matters in what follows, but it is as well to disassociate oneself from the optimism that Hume and Smith shared, despite their different positions as to international economic competition. There have been many examples which prove the validity of Hume's contention that capitalism is mobile, not least among them being the decline of Holland in the eighteenth century and Great Britain in the twentieth. These nations are not, however, able to feed themselves and are, *pace* Hume, ineluctably involved in international commerce. Moreover, there is a pessimistic case to be derived from Smith. There may be a beneficent cycle whereby rich nations, by means of economic growth, are able to keep themselves socially flexible and thereby to become richer. However, rich nations which develop social inertias may equally be consigned to a vicious cycle whereby a loss of growth makes flexibility that much harder to achieve.

The third philosophy of history of interest here is that of Max Weber. This universal thinker had very great insight into both economic and political forces in history, but he remains celebrated as *the* thinker who stressed the importance of ideological factors in world history. Weber is however a hugely complex figure and so for our purposes a distinction at this point between Weber's *Problematik* and Weberism is apposite.

Weber, like Smith, believed that the rise of the West was a unique and perhaps fortuitous event. But he did not believe that the transition to industrial society was from a single agrarian type. On the contrary, he recognised that agrarian societies had been turned into separate civilisations by the emergence of the world religions and ethics, an event as crucial in his mind as the neolithic or industrial revolutions. Some of these civilisations were destroyed, such as Zoroastrian Persia and Byzantium, and he therefore concentrated his attention on the four classic world civilisations of Confucian China, Islam, Latin Christendom, and Hindu India. He was of course interested in explaining the rise of one of these, and his definition of the problem has everything to recommend it.[11] His solution is a much more dubious matter.

It is in fact exceptionally difficult to disentangle from his writings on the impact of world religions exactly what sort of causal process Max

11 There is a point to be made against this view. W. H. McNeill's various books on world history make much of the interrelationships between the world civilisations, particularly in terms of the movement of people and disease. Whilst not wishing to deny the force of these factors, they seem to me less important than institutional factors. In any case, I am concentrating on explaining the pattern of such factors.

Weber felt was at work. So rather than in any way distort his thought, let us analyse the Weberist notion to which he subscribed at least some of the time and with which his name is popularly associated. Weberism asserts that economic development was either hindered or helped by the actual tenets of belief encoded in the world religions. Thus Protestantism encouraged capitalism because it was at once ascetic *and* this-worldly. This encouraged thrift and accumulation. In contrast, other world religions or ethics were either other-worldly or non-ascetic, and sometimes both. It *is* probably correct to say that Protestantism did provide a more suitable ethic for fifteenth- and sixteenth-century capitalists than did Catholicism. Nevertheless this association does not explain the origins of capitalism nor is it *the* secret to the rise of the West because, to mention but one point, the unique dynamism of this civilisation was already in place well before the fifteenth and sixteenth centuries. Perhaps still more importantly, Weber did not properly appreciate the character of the other world religions. Islam, in particular, was and is as suited for economic development as is Calvinism, being rigorous, ascetic and universal. The failure of that civilisation to develop autonomously cannot be blamed on the inadequacies of the tenets of that particular religion. I shall *on occasion* agree with Weberism that the actual tenets of the world religions and ethics do substantially matter, especially in terms of political theory which in turn affected economic development. We need a rather different understanding of ideology, however, if we are on the one hand to accept Weber's problem, yet on the other to suggest that on the whole Weberism is wrong.

Presuppositions and Definitions

As the scope of this book is large and ambitious, it is as well to try and be as clear as possible about certain presuppositions and definitions, and the former may usefully be tackled first. The diagram on page 18 at once incorporates Weber's *Problematik*, improves upon Marx's scheme, and gives some hints – what diagram can do more! – as to the real shape of human history. This scheme claims that history is structured by productive systems and by the world religions, that the civilisation of one of the latter invented modernity, albeit accidentally, and that history is fundamentally progressive and evolutionary. Some amplifying and qualifying comments are very much in order.

In the prologue to part I, a qualification will be offered concerning hunters and gatherers. Barring this qualification, however, the evolutionary claim made here is meant to be a strong one. Some pockets of hunters and gatherers exist in the world even today, but the development

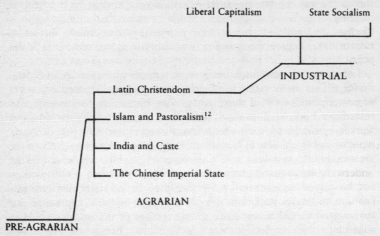

Liberal Capitalism   State Socialism

INDUSTRIAL

Latin Christendom

Islam and Pastoralism[12]

India and Caste

The Chinese Imperial State

AGRARIAN

PRE-AGRARIAN

in the sources of social power noted means that adaptation is generally the price of survival. Thus the creation of industrial capitalism forced the rest of the world into a new social era. State socialist societies have managed the transition to this new era, and the fate of the underdeveloped countries, which include China, India and much of Islam, remains the central issue of contemporary world politics. There is clearly progress in terms of the growth of the powers of the economy, and the state. Progress can also be seen in ideology. Social evolution can be seen in the fact that the world religions and ethics, in the final forms, share one great similarity: they hold open the possibility for salvation to everyone and are thus quite unlike the primitive religions of, for example, Sumer and early Egypt. Such doctrines all evolve towards some form of monotheism, although certain types of monotheism are much more rigorous than others. Progress is, however, much more general. The modern world sees the entry of the people onto the political stage for the first time, while in world historical terms modern societies do witness a drive towards equality: we know that the differentials inside Pompey's army were as great as 67–1 and the division of booty even sharper, and

12 Adam Smith's theory of history is superior in one way to the schema provided by Karl Marx. Smith recognised that pastoralism represented something of a mode of production in its own right, and this, as we shall see when discussing Islam, is essentially correct. But pastoralism has not been conceived here as a separate stage or type for one reason other than pictorial simplicity. Most pastoralists in human history, probably because they have been accustomed to a certain standard of living, have depended upon trade with towns in agrarian civilisations. They are thus symbiotic with, and not a true alternative to, agrarian society.

this is typical of pre-industrial civilisations, Finally, the industrial machine is capable of creating affluence such that certain blights – disease and famine – are at least potentially removable. This is an extraordinary achievement and it is no wonder it still structures world politics.

Let us turn our attention more systematically to the nature of power. So far, the economy, polity and ideology have been considered as sources of power[13] and each of these realms can be usefully personalised by restating the argument in terms of landlord/peasant/capitalist/industrial worker, in contrast to state servants and intellectuals. The first two such types of power are easy to grasp, but matters are much more tricky in the area of belief; this area still presents the greatest problems for the understanding of human behaviour, and, though all such problems cannot be solved here, there is everything to be said for clarifying the position to be adopted. The test of this position is less in its formal suggestiveness and much more in the fertility of the questions that it allows.

It was noted earlier that those opposed to the practice of the philosophy of history make much of the importance of social meanings in defeating any law-like science of history. There are two general arguments to be made against this position. Firstly, it is by now a truism that belief does not exist in a vacuum, that there is (to use the chemical expression used by Goethe to name his masterpiece, and thence by Weber to sum up the link between belief and social situation) an 'elective affinity' between one's social situation and the belief one chooses. This general view of human belief does not lend great weight to the argument of those critical of the philosophy of history. For this view, while it does not deny the force and necessity of norms in human society, nevertheless insists that they can be explained in other more structural terms. Secondly, we can again note the insistence of Weberism that the actual tenets of doctrine, and especially the absence or presence of key alternatives, structures human action thereafter. Once the commanding heights of our conceptual apparatus are conquered, Weberism seems to say, human conduct must follow certain paths. There *is* some truth to this, albeit much less in the matter of economic doctrine than in the basic political theories of the world religions. Yet there are good general reasons to be wary of too easy an extension of this view. Most belief

---

13 I differ here from Michael Mann (*Sources of Social Power*, vol. 1, *From the Beginning to 1760 A.D.*, Cambridge University Press, Cambridge, 1986) who treats military power as a fourth category, whereas I include it amidst political power. There is an empirical justification for this difference. Gunpowder was a vital change in military technology but it was only in the European state system that it came to prominence: a very different state structure, that of Imperial China, tried to do without it.

systems are adaptable, and change considerably over time. Moreover, the world religions and ethics are fundamentally *similar*, as argued, in their promise of salvation for every individual. More importantly, these belief-systems are loose and baggy monsters, full of saving clauses and alternatives that can be brought out by an interested group when occasion demands. This process needs to be explained in traditional social structural terms. In other words, we are returned to the position that there is an affinity between people's beliefs and their circumstances.

These general comments are negative in spirit and designed to counteract the tendency in modern thought to lend too great weight to the power of 'ideas', especially when no attempt is made to examine why a particular belief system has a specific content, why it spreads and why its hold is maintained over time. But these negative comments should not mask the clear contention here that there have been two great moments of ideology in human history, namely the period of the world religions and the modern period concerned with the speedy exit from the agrarian age, nor should they obscure the claim that in circumstances of confusion and chaos intellectuals tend to have great salience. It is possible to go some way beyond these remarks to highlight propositions which can advance the understanding of ideology, and which structure comments made about it throughout this book.

The 'idealist' view of autonomous ideas so far considered can be contrasted with an extremely down-to-earth 'materialist' view according to which we see intellectuals as a self-interested group in society along with any other, keen to improve its own social status. There is a long line of debunking theorists, from Edmund Burke to Georges Sorel to George Orwell, who see intellectuals in this manner. There is undoubted truth to this approach, and we shall have particular cause to note the social impact that the land hunger of the Latin Christian church, perhaps the most organised of all the world religions, had upon its larger society.

Nevertheless, this view is not sufficient by itself for it gives us the impression of intellectuals manipulating belief at will. Belief involves a larger credence in society, and thus often derives, especially in formative moments, *from a realisation and appreciation of concrete services performed by intellectuals*. In agrarian civilisations, such services often revolve around the control of literacy; the manner in which such control gells with other elements in the elite, that is, whether the intellectual is priest, bureaucrat or servant of an independent church organisation crucially affects these civilisations. There is an important point to be made here. In conditions of crisis intellectuals can assume great power, less because of their ability to explain to fellow citizens some confusing situation than on account of their ability actually to *create a society in the first place.* Indian, Islamic and Latin Christian civilisations were, in differing ways, to differing extents and at different times, held together by shared cultural unity. In the modern world, the role of nationalist and Marxist intellectuals in actually forming governments is so obvious as to need no comment. This ideological power is worth characterising. Such power derives from the capacity to organise actors over space, and the conceptual approach we need to understand this is a type of organisational materialism. This capacity to create societies shows ideological power at its most potent and autonomous; the power to create civilisations places Islam, Hinduism and Christianity in marked contrast to Confucianism, a much more passive product of the imperial state. This approach to ideological power has rather little to do with the general spirit of Weber's sociology of religion. The great German thinker was very much a high intellectual who considered that religion was concerned with ultimate meaning between God and man. As a matter of fact, it is usually only experts who are drawn to such matters. It is altogether more mundane reasons – above all, the creation of a *community* – which influence the creation and spread of religions.

However, there is no reason why we should be tempted to abandon the Weberist enterprise altogether. The historic record on occasion does require attention to the actual doctrine of belief systems. That there is sufficient room inside belief systems to justify most actions has already been noted; but we must add to this an insistence that certain doctrines can possess a core, abandonment of which is almost impossible. This is particularly true of those visions which are clear and simple, above all Marxism and Islam. Further, ideological residues can have some influence on future behaviour and this is so whether the doctrine was the creator or the product of a specific civilisation. However there is very little to be said, at least in so far as the first emergence of modernity is concerned, for Weber's insistence that the crucial set of ideological residues at issue were those stressing attitudes to work. In so far as there is force to Weberism, it must be found in attitudes to politics encoded in the world religions. We need, in other words, a politics, rather than an economics, of the world religions.

Perhaps the most damning and dangerous criticism of classical Marxism is that, to adopt a phrase of David Hume's, the economy does not have a distinct existence from other social relations since it depends upon and involves, for example, prior legal understandings. Underlying this attack – which can easily be extended to undermine the idea that polity, economy and ideology can be distinguished – is the cogent observation that power, especially in more primitive societies, tends to come in packages. Those who are powerful seek and gain money and ritual legitimation. It is not necessary to accept everything that is implied in this criticism, and especially not the notion that is often prevalent that consensual agreement underlies all other social relationships. Norms are often passive in society, that is, they are created by and reflect other power sources. Further, it is possible to theorise about the changing capacities of the power types mentioned. Thus ideology is, in the long run, likely to be less powerful in the modern world than it had previously been, ultimately in so far as literacy, the typical resource of intellectuals, becomes widely diffused. This is seen in the fact that whereas intellectuals in history held some agrarian civilisations together for long stretches of time, their modern counterparts, who take over modern states, tend to be replaced quickly by economic or political elites. But the essential point to be made is that *it is possible to occasionally distinguish moments in which one or other power source is the leading one, and when it sets the pace for others*. Such moments are those of real autonomy and they can sometimes be prolonged. Typically such a moment of autonomy will quickly draw to it, and become involved with, other social relationships. How could it be otherwise? Thus religious power, as Weber realised, has to tell people how to conduct their economic affairs in this world, and to that extent compromises the purity of its stance. Nevertheless, in so far as any resulting social *form* in which other social relationships take place and continue to operate depends upon this initial moment, it is crucial to consider it. This often involves asking historical questions to which clear answers, due to lack of evidence, cannot be given. Yet the questions themselves are worth asking; certainly the success of a social theory does depend upon its capacity to isolate variables from each other.

A final definitional point must be made about the nature of power. In social and political theory there have always been two rival definitions of power. One stresses coercion or command, the ability to get someone to do something against their will; another view sees power as a capacity created by social agreement. It is worth emphasising that the latter type of power, here termed enabling, can generate a greater sum of energy since interaction is not a zero-sum game in which one person's will triumphs over the other. Thus in studies of the family one may distinguish precisely between those studies of power which discuss, say, the husband's decision of resource allocation from other studies which concentrate on families in which shared goals can create greater energy. Similarly the senescence of nations is often characterised by social inertias, that is, by a power stand-off between groups that have had time to organise themselves; greater social drive seems to be possible in earlier periods when this rigidity is absent. This again forces us to note that agreement can lead to a greater sum of social energy. All this is extremely relevant for the types of power distinguished so far. Where ideological, political and economic power move in the same direction, it is extremely likely that great social energy will be created. In contrast to such enabling power stand those situations of *blocking* power in which a power stand-off between, say, landlords and the servants of the state prevents the release of social energy.[14]

A large part of this book is concerned with the relationships between these types of power, political forms and social development and some of the arguments can be briefly hinted at by noting changes in the meaning of the word 'liberties'. In Western Europe liberties has principally meant rights, and it is of the utmost significance to realise that these rights were widespread. This played a great part in creating a political system in which pluralism was openly recognised. In a nutshell, Europe was quick to develop a strong civil society by means of groups which were not only powerful but also *autonomous*. A crucial argument to be made is that this type of liberal polity encouraged and allowed the co-operation of various groups, thus generating the kind of energy seen in the political and economic dynamism characteristic of European history. In contrast, the despotic policies which often characterised the polities of the other world civilisations encouraged powerful groups to create a power stand-off resulting in the loss of social energy – not just because of their own sheer selfishness but also by preventing the full emergence and participation of other social groups.

One key finding of the first half of this book is then extremely positive. Liberal politics were linked with liberties and with economic development. It is hard to be quite so sanguine about the modern world. As is well known, forced development is possible, indeed required in modernity. This commonly entails the initial suppression of pluralism and clearly has no elective affinity with liberal politics. Nevertheless, social development will itself increase and strengthen pluralism, and one can hope that this will lead to demands for greater autonomy which may in turn help soften political habits. There is no guarantee that this will happen for a strengthening of pluralism may result in some sort of power stand-off, a lessening of the dynamics of social development and consequent political difficulties. For liberties has changed its meaning in Western society in a disturbing manner, being currently used to describe privileges, akin to those of powerful groups in ancient empires, which are held against the public interest and thereby resulting in a power stand-off. This gives rise to fears for the future of Western society. But before we reach such fears it is time to turn to a full explanation of the original European miracle.

14 Suggestive arguments aware of this distinction have been made by Olson, *The Rise and Decline of Nations* and L. Thurow, *The Zero-Sum Society*, Penguin, London, 1982.

Part I

Occidental Dynamism

Prologue

The Sociology of Agrarian Civilisations

For some time now we have become accustomed to realising that the hunting and gathering societies of the pre-agrarian world were, if not the most affluent, then certainly the most leisured in human history. Such peoples historically (and contemporaneously too, albeit in small, often adulterated pockets) had to work for perhaps three hours a day in order to sustain themselves but were otherwise quite free from labour. It seems very likely that hunters and gatherers always knew about agriculture but simply did not choose to adopt it. However, the neolithic revolution *does* represent an enormous and irreversible step in human destinies, even if it is not strictly an evolutionary one. Nobody is quite sure why this step was taken. Probably hunting and gathering depends upon low population, and therefore ultimately upon the exposure of children. As hunters and gatherers failed historically to control their population, the adoption of agriculture became necessary. Perhaps only those hunters and gatherers with social resources which encouraged delayed returns, the middle-class members of this world, actually made this transition successfully. This is an interesting idea since it suggests that even the pre-agrarian productive system was capable of supporting different forms of social organisation.[1]

Agriculture varies in its social effects. In Africa the bountifulness and extent of the land makes for a mobile peasantry, necessarily therefore poor material on which to build states. Something like this is probably true of all slash-and-burn agriculture. In contrast the great river valleys necessitated continuous occupation of the land so that full advantage could be taken of the investment made in simple irrigation channels which opened up rich alluvial soils. There is thus something to Wittfogel's concern with the great river valleys: they forced the peasantry

1 J. Woodburn, 'Hunters and gatherers today and reconstruction of the past' in E. Gellner (ed.), *Soviet and Western Anthropology*, Duckworth, London, 1980.

to settle and thus made them, as did olives in certain parts of the
Mediterranean, decent material on which states could be built. Thus the
origins of warfare, the state and record-keeping are all associated with
the neolithic revolution.

The concern of the first part of this book is not with *all* early agrarian
states and societies, but with the classical agrarian civilisations. Amongst
the latter, only those which were in existence as rivals to Latin Christendom, i.e. that had the chance to develop autonomously, are analysed;
consequently Zoroastrian Persia and Greek Christendom are put to one
side. By agrarian civilisation is meant the combination of the agrarian
productive system with one of the world religions, or perhaps one and a
half in the case of India and China, both heavily influenced by
Buddhism. The world religions do represent some sort of evolutionary
step in human history; in their final forms, they offer salvation to the
masses in one way or another, while their eventual monotheism represents a sea-change in religious history. Nevertheless, it is often more
practical matters about the world religions that make their impact on the
shape of world history so important. What is most notable here is that
they represent the insertion of organised intellectuals/priests/bureauc-
rats, often gaining power as monopolists of literacy, into the agrarian age.
The forms that this insertion took go a long way to describing the
characteristic patterns of the four civilisations to be studied.

The first part of this book is concerned with the way in which
economic, ideological and political power worked in the agrarian age,
and it seeks to explain the combination of circumstances that enabled
one agrarian civilisation to develop autonomously in a broadly capitalist
manner. The argument can be highlighted throughout by grasping the
general model of the 'agro-literate polity' offered by Ernest Gellner.[2]
This is most helpful, and its implications need to be spelt out. But a word
of warning must come first. There can be no *single* model for agrarian
civilisation: the fundamental point is that the differences between these
civilisations, the differences allowed by the single productive system, are
vital. As a result, the following four chapters will offer models which are
variations on the theme of Gellner. Perhaps this is slightly overstated.
The proverbial Martian visiting the world in A.D. 1000 *would* probably
have produced a model akin to Gellner's, and with every reason, since
similarities almost certainly outweighed differences. My interest, therefore, is in the small but crucial institutional differences which mattered in
the long run. With this reservation out of the way, however, three
implications can be stressed.

2 *Nations and Nationalism*, Basil Blackwell, Oxford, 1983, p. 7.

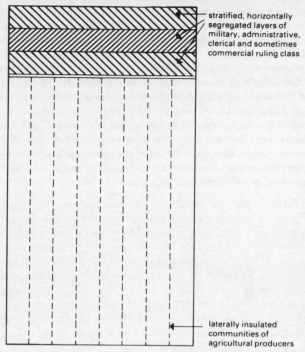

stratified, horizontally segregated layers of military, administrative, clerical and sometimes commercial ruling class

laterally insulated communities of agricultural producers

Model 1: The agro-literate polity

1   Agrarian civilisations are not 'societies'. Our sense of society, derived from Durkheim and Weber, depends upon the sharing of a set of norms by all citizens of a geographically bounded space capped over by a single source of authority, the state, which monopolises the use of violence. This sense of society reflects the conditions of European nation-states between, say, 1870 and 1945; this view was mistaken even then since conflict between states was, to some degree, regulated by being members of a state system within a shared culture. This concept is quite useless when seeking to understand modern societies and perhaps even more so when seeking to understand agrarian civilisations. The model makes this quite clear by showing that peasants typically belonged to their own 'societies', sometimes in historical cases not knowing they were part of this or that empire. Something important for social theory follows from this. Those theorists, and particularly those idealist theorists indebted to the *Geisteswissenschaften* tradition, who emphasise the importance of shared social beliefs are very largely wrong because the sharing of norms

is an exception in history. Perhaps these nineteenth-century German thinkers made so much of the matter because their nation *had* just been born. In agrarian civilisations, the elite sometimes did not even bother itself with the magical rubbish that the masses believed, and such 'tolerance' characterised much of Chinese and Roman imperial history; in other cases, such as those of Latin Christendom and Islam, there remained a massive difference between the 'Great' tradition of the educated elite and the 'Little' tradition of peasants and pastoralists. In the medieval Pyrenean village of Montaillou everybody did think of themselves as Christian; but the peasants regarded the Bishop of Pamiers as a feudal exploiter.[3] It is hard to explain social developments in 'Weberist' terms when religions allow options by means of which different groups can articulate their interests.

2   As Gellner stresses, politics in agrarian civilisations concerns the elite. Thus an interesting book on the enemies of the Roman order spends more time discussing senatorial plots than it does peasant revolts; soothsayers proved dangerous because they had their own non-official and horizontal means of communication.[4] Without equivalent itinerants, usually *déclassé* members of the mandarinate, the vertically segregated sets of Chinese peasants would never have been able to join together, as they sometimes did, in peasant revolts. Finally, it must be stressed that the possible coalitions of various elite groupings can be very complicated indeed, and it is upon this that much of the variety in agrarian civilisations hangs.

3   Elites in the model sit on top of various peasant communities, unable to penetrate far into the societies beneath them. In consequence, though their government may look impressive, it is a mere holding operation. The size of their bureaucracies is puny, and taxation is only done via the acquiescence, often reluctant, of local elites. Such social organisation, unable to mobilise the people, could generate a small sum of social power.

Two important qualifications must be made to the way in which the above paragraph is phrased. Firstly, one must be wary of the term *government* as used above. The Chinese did have an imperial state, but Latin Christendom, Islam and Hindu India functioned and survived as civilisations throughout crucial periods in their history without proper state regulation. Secondly, differences existed in the penetrative capacity of the elites of the world civilisations, and three such differences can be

3 E. Le Roy Ladurie, *Montaillou*, Scolar Press, London, 1978.
4 R. MacMullen, *Enemies of the Roman Order*, Harvard University Press, Cambridge, 1966.

highlighted immediately. Firstly, the Brahmans were able to organise social life to a much greater extent than could the mandarins, the Ulama and the priests of Christian Europe. There is an amusing paradox here. Brahmanical power was achieved largely through systematically compromising with local beliefs, rather than insisting upon some tightly organised central creed of its own. In contrast, the jealous monotheisms of Christianity and Islam sought in theory to create genuinely universalistic societies, but were in large measure incapable of so doing in pre-industrial conditions. (Their universal drive may, however, be very significant in modern conditions, as the revival of Islam demonstrates.) Secondly, the European feudal landlord had a much greater capacity to affect social life than did his counterpart in the other world civilisations. Thirdly, a clear contrast must be drawn between the weak polities of China, India and Islam, and the organic states of the West which, slowly but surely, sent deep roots into their societies. This situation can be characterised in terms of the comments made about the two faces of power. China, Islam and India created polities which acted in a zero-sum manner, being arbitrary and incapable of providing many services, and this reflected certain blockages in society. European civilisation, in contrast, produced a state which was less arbitrary and which provided a great measure of social infrastructure, and this will be explained in terms of the absence of social blockages. The former states produced, as we would expect, less total energy than did the latter.

There is nothing in the approach taken that is designed to rule out in an a priori manner the use of certain Marxist concepts, and some words indicating the position taken here in connection with Marx's concepts – his shape of history has already been rejected – may usefully conclude this prologue. The slave mode of production is not taken seriously as a stage of universal history for the solid empirical reason that there have been only five slave-based societies in human history, namely those of Greece, Rome, the *ante-bellum* South, Brazil and the West Indies. Geoffrey de Ste Croix's sophisticated analysis of slavery in the ancient Greek world argues that, though never widespread, it was vital in providing profits for the landlord elite. This may be so, but it does not detract from the fact, willingly admitted by de Ste Croix, that Roman society came to be characterised by a landlord class confronted by 'humiliores', a class very much akin to the feudal serf.[5] What is generally striking about agrarian civilisations is the similarity of productive systems. This is not to deny for a moment that socio-economic extractive relations varied from one place to another, and that this variance was extremely important.

5 G. de Ste Croix, *Class Struggles in the Ancient Greek World*, Duckworth, London, 1981.

Class, in other words, is a useful concept for understanding the pre-industrial world. Nevertheless, class conflict did not occur in the requisite dynamic Marxist manner. Furthermore, non-economic actors proved to have a certain sway over economic ones; the form of class relationships was often dependent upon these actors, or, in other words, was at least part of a package deal that combined other actors, and without which that form could not have existed.

2

Imperial China

The Chinese empire was first securely founded in 221 BC and it lasted until AD 1911. Imperial unity was not, however, preserved throughout this 2000-year span. Thus the dynasties of Ch'in, and former and later Han were followed by a long period of disunity from 220 to 589, often compared to the situation in Western Europe at the fall of the Roman empire. Throughout this period of disunity there tended to be different states in North and South China, each of which was able to base itself on a 'key economic area', namely the Yellow or Yangtze river valleys. However, imperial unity was recreated by the Sui and the Tang, and when a second period of disunity occurred between 907 and 1279 it was neither as serious nor as long lasting. Thereafter China was united by the Mongols, the Ming and the Manchu. Nevertheless, imperial control varied considerably during the lifetime of a dynasty, each being, for reasons to be examined, stronger at the start than at the end. Thus the control exercised by the Tang was considerably undermined after the An Lu Shan rebellion of the 750s, although the dynasty itself struggled on until 907.

A second reservation is also in order which makes the picture of a 2000-year-old unchanging monolith somewhat complex. Throughout Chinese history there was considerable economic advance. This is popularly regarded as the result of Chinese inventions such as the casting of iron, the wheelbarrow, gunpowder and paper. Probably of more importance to the Chinese themselves were crucial agricultural innovations such as the adoption of double-cropping rice and the expansion and colonisation of the lands of South China. Despite all this *the* fundamental fact about Chinese history remains its continuity and stability. Whatever political troubles there were, it proved impossible to invent an alternative political form. Similarly, such economic development as there was did not prove to be capable of creating a dynamism such that self-sustaining economic development occurred. There was, to use the expression of the American economist Walt Rostow, no 'take-off'.

The argument of this chapter can, as a result of these comments, be stated now in a nutshell: economic dynamism was curtailed by the imperial form. In other words, politics played a crucial blocking role in Chinese history. This claim obviously places me in direct opposition to mainstream Marxism, and I shall correspondingly be in debate with various Marxist attempts to downplay the importance of the politics of empire. A general view of the sociology of empires underlies my own interpretation of Chinese history, and it is useful to highlight this approach immediately. However, the full positive characterisation of the mechanisms of the Chinese empire will take the whole of this chapter, not least because there is undoubtedly *some* truth to certain contentions of the more sophisticated Marxists.

The image to the forefront of our minds when we think of empires is that of great strength. This is in part surely due to modern representations, to the impact of Cecil B. de Mille upon our minds. However, it is also due in part to the sheer size of empires and the character of the monuments that they have left behind: notably the Forbidden City, the Pyramids, the Taj Mahal. Moreover, the records which have been left to us also speak of massive armies and of the potency of the central administration – and we do know that emperors (and empresses!) *did*, at a whim, have those who offended them whipped or killed. Yet it is always dangerous to take written records at face value, and this is especially true of pre-industrial empires whose records often consist largely of court chronicles designed to shower praise on the emperor. They are often exercises in myth, in royal propaganda, rather than reliable empirical reports. Further, we can take with a very considerable pinch of salt, thanks to the brilliant logistical exercise of Engel,[1] the oft-repeated claim of great military strength. Such military might simply was not available in pre-industrial civilisations, and we can conclude as a result that the rule of empires was nowhere near as strong and cohesive as is often claimed. Finally, even a cursory reading of modern historians on various empires quickly shows a series of ways in which the powers of the emperors were limited. In the later Roman empire, for example, the emperor was quite incapable of seeing every paper sent to him. He threatened all administrators who prepared or submitted illegal rescripts. 'But he openly admitted his impotence by declaring invalid in advance any special grants in contravention of the law, even if they bore his own signature.'[2]

Those who have written about empires have tended to stress either strength or weakness. But *both* were present, and the paradox (for it is not

1 D. Engel, *Alexander the Great and the Logistics of the Macedonian Army*, University of California, Berkeley, 1978.

2 A.H.M. Jones, *The Later Roman Empire*, Basil Blackwell, Oxford, 1973, p. 410.

a contradiction) of empires is that their strength, that is their monuments, their arbitrariness, their scorn for human life, hides, is based
upon, and reflects social weakness. They are not able to deeply penetrate, change and mobilise the social order. Empires have, in our terms,
strong blocking but weak enabling powers, and I shall eventually characterise the Chinese empire as that of successful capstone government,
incapable of generating a large sum of social energy. This became clearly
and cruelly apparent in 1840 when the empire had to accept the opium
trade imposed upon it by the barbarian British. Those 'Orientalist'
philosophers of history prone to criticise the centrality of the Western
story in world history in that it suggests that other societies were 'failures'
have much on their side in the case of the high civilisation produced in
China, although they probably underestimate the very great human costs
of that achievement. But they have little to recommend their position
when they suggest that, but for the West, a dynamism might have been
discovered in the Far East. Western powers did play a role in the demise
of the imperial state, but that state was already moribund and the whole
tenor of the social formation was one which ruled out the creation of any
real dynamism.

The Origins of the Empire

If we recall Marx's scheme of history, then it can be seen that the
classical pattern (based, as noted, on European history) sees the move
from an empire to feudalism, itself in turn the progenitor of capitalism.
China represents an obvious problem for Marxists in comparison to this,
since feudalism *precedes* the creation of an imperial unity from which no
self-sustaining capitalism emerged. Nevertheless, there are interesting
Marxist attempts to deal with this matter which will advance our general
argument. In order to understand them, however, it is necessary first to
say something about the origins of the empire.

   Ancient Chinese historians, particularly the great Han historian
Su-ma-Ch'ien, argued that there was an early period of Chinese unity
under the Shang. Archaeological findings have corroborated a surprising
number of previously discredited notions about the Shang but, despite
this, general historical sociology would tend to suggest that the Shang
were merely the leading members of a confederacy of tribal groups.
Fortunately, our knowledge of the post-Shang period is much more
firmly based. In this period the Chou, first in the West and then in the
East, maintained some sort of supremacy over the other princes. This
collapsed, leading to the period of warring kingdoms, highly reminiscent
of medieval Europe. There was, however, one difference from the

European scene. Successful feudal princes – the *Wangs* – were those whose military prowess had been proved in the fight at the borders of Chinese settled life against the nomads, and who then used this prowess when turning back inwards to control their fellow Chinese. Chinese feudalism was thus not based upon a type of ethnic superstratification, nor did it come from the collapse of a civilisation, but rather from the periphery of one which was expanding.[3] Eventually, as was not the case in Europe, one such highly militaristic kingdom, that of the Ch'in, making use of large citizen armies and acting with brutality of Assyrian intensity, united all China in 221 BC. The first dynasty perished quickly as the result of military defeat in combination with peasant revolt, and the Han dynasty, founded by peasants, inherited the unified empire ready made. They consolidated the work of the first emperor by joining together various small walls of different kingdoms to create the first version of the Great Wall, designed to keep the nomads out and the tax-paying peasants within. Crucially, they set a pattern for later Chinese dynasties by reducing the land tax, first to a fifteenth and then to a thirtieth of the yield, in the belief that a strong and prosperous peasantry would provide soldiers and taxes.

Although the full workings of the empire will become apparent only later, the origins of the empire occasion some systematic reflections, the first of which is negative. The positive theory at work in Wittfogel's *Oriental Despotism* is that which sees a systematic link between despotism and the maintenance of hydraulic works, whether to prevent flooding or to control irrigation. There is almost no truth in this proposition. 'Despotism' originated at the western borders of China where there was no water control to speak of; indeed the empire was firmly in place before much advantage was taken of the loess soils of the great river valleys. The bureaucracy *never* managed or planned irrigation works, although it did plan the logistically vital Grand Canal that was to bring rice from the South to the troops at the Great Wall in the North. It could not do so for the simple reason that it did not have the requisite manpower. The only connection between imperial government and water control seems to be much more tenuous. Imperial peace meant that investments in water control were not destroyed, as happened quite generally during the first period of disunity.

But certain properties are implicit in the creation of the empire. Most obviously, we can add to Gellner's diagram a scheme of Owen Lattimore's, recently made much of by Michael Mann.[4] Lattimore asks

3 O. Lattimore, *Studies in Frontier History*, Oxford University Press, Oxford, 1982, p. 548.

4 Ibid.; M. Mann, 'States, ancient and modern', *European Journal of Sociology*, vol. 18, 1977.

how it is possible to integrate large areas in pre-industrial civilisations. He suggests that the economy can integrate the smallest area. This is almost *necessarily* so in the agrarian age, given that an ox pulling a cart of grain would have eaten its load within a hundred miles. There is obviously likely to be a great difference if an empire is situated around an internal sea such as the Mediterranean, but even this did not much alter the inherently segmented nature of the Roman economy. In contrast, Lattimore and Mann argue that military organisation is capable of integrating a much larger area. Certainly, the Chinese empire was created by military means, and the limit of that empire was marked by the Great Wall, the consolidation of which was a priority of the first Chinese emperors.

The blunt contrast between economic and military means of integration introduces a set of significant problems. There is a standard Marxist answer to those who seek to allow some independent autonomy to military and political factors in history, namely that soldiers are inherently parasitic on the producers of wealth. There are two obvious objections to this rather easy formulation. Firstly, an empire could be created 'cost-free' since booty was capable of financing much military expansion. Secondly, the peace brought by imperial rule was not entirely exploitative; a lessening of warfare and banditry combined with the diffusion of knowledge and coinage typically makes for greater productivity within empires than without. Nevertheless, neither of these objections is sufficient to hide the great merit of the Marxist question. Empires are not just created by the sword; if they wish to survive then they must also *continue* to possess military might. This means that it is necessary to ask questions about the intermediate range of integration identified by Lattimore, namely that of political integration. How was it possible to raise sufficient revenues to maintain the army over time? Some part of the answer lies in the increasing productivity of agriculture within imperial boundaries, but fundamentally it is necessary to confront the question of the relationship between state and society.

Pre-industrial empires confront a problem when trying to extract taxation. Typically, they do not themselves possess large enough bureaucracies to administer taxation, and are thus forced to do so via local notables. A great deal of the politics of pre-industrial empires revolves around the form which the relationship between the government, seeking fuller autonomy, and the local landlords, seeking to minimise such autonomy, takes. Pre-industrial empires aim at full autonomy but cannot possibly attain it, and are instead reduced to a series of measures – the systematic rotation of offices, the prohibition of serving in one's own locality and so on – designed to prevent too close a collusion between government agents and local notables. It is at this point that we can redeem the promise made earlier to note a sophisticated Marxist defence against the charge that the political form in Chinese life really mattered. The Polish sinologist Witold Rodinski puts the defence with meritorious bluntness:

> The political structure of the Chou era clearly and unambiguously deserves to be referred to as feudal; confusion ensues when some historians, who restrict the meaning of this term to political phenomena, see in the creation of a centralised, absolute monarchy, beginning with Ch'in and Han, an end to feudalism in China. In reality, in its socioeconomic sense, it was to be presented up to the middle of the twentieth century.[5]

This is a very bold statement which says, in effect, that the fact of empire has no fundamental importance at all – something, it can be noted in passing, at odds with the explanations offered in the rest of Rodinski's history of China. His point can be put in a slightly more subtle form. What is really being claimed is that the state did not manage to achieve any real autonomy, and that the history of Chinese civilisation is correspondingly to be written in terms derived from Karl Marx. What justice is there to this claim? What exactly were the relations between state and society? The elucidation of these crucial questions deserves to be considered separately, but the reader may well be helped by a brief anticipation of the argument: there is considerable justice to the view that the Chinese state, in its normal workings, had little autonomy apart from the leading social class, but this does not mean that the fact of imperial form is without explanatory force in understanding Chinese history.

Class, State and the Dynastic Cycle

It was suggested above that pre-industrial empires *typically* must tax through local notables since they lack sufficient bureaucracy to penetrate society to any great degree. But was China different? Its most distinctive social institution was that of the mandarinate, examined in the classics and comprising a professional bureaucratic strata. Is there not *some* truth to Wittfogel's thesis about the 'total control' of society, which reflects his background as a professional sinologist, even admitting that his general picture of hydraulic society is deeply flawed? In order to answer *this* question it is necessary to examine the mandarinate at some length.

Perhaps the most famous invention of the Han was the creation of a civil service based upon Confucianism, and we must begin by saying something about this doctrine. Confucius himself died in 479 BC, having lived throughout the period of Warring States. The sage apparently

5 *The Walled Kingdom*, Fontana, London, 1984, p. 23.

considered himself a conservative, harking back to the good practices of the period of Shang unity, and this certainly marked the doctrine that he developed. The key notion is that of *Chün-tzu*, the stoical notion that stresses that one's duties, especially towards the family, should be performed in a courteous, gentlemanly fashion. There is no room for great individualism, nor for passion in this doctrine; what is called for instead is respect for social conventions. In this Confucianism can be distinguished from the many other doctrines that were developed during this intellectually fertile period. Moism stressed the need for and possibility of universal love, whilst Taoism tended to see the world as nothing but a sphere of illusion. Confucianism was far removed from this. Nor would it have anything to do with Legalism which argued that only force held the state together. Confucianism placed a much greater stress on the need for the observation of ritual, by the emperor and throughout society, in the belief that this could create just order. Only in so far as the emperor behaved towards his subjects as a father would harmony prevail. Perhaps all this reflected the fact that Confucius and his followers were younger sons of the aristocracy, bereft of employment. They sought this in government service and probably provided an ethic of such service. Perhaps vitally, the fact of their being *younger* sons encouraged that ethic to be meritocratic. To be a gentleman required spiritual accomplishments, that is, personal merits rather than just good birth. This injunction was, of course, poorly observed, yet Confucianism would not have been so ideologically successful but for this. The situation is reminiscent of America where the belief in openness *matters*, that is, is a social fact, despite evidence that class mobility is no greater than in other industrial societies. One final point must be further stressed. The ponderous expression 'the world religions and ethics' has been used above in order to accommodate Confucianism. This intellectual class served as bureaucrats to the government rather than as priests, perhaps in this reflecting the fact that the Shang rulers had performed rituals *themselves* without the aids of priests. Its great capacity lay in integrating the elite, and this elite did not even seek to control nor understand the beliefs of those below them, in this perfectly corresponding to the shape of Gellner's model. There was an organised dissociation between the culture of the elite and that of the masses. To some extent this situation changed historically. Perhaps Confucianism always had some sort of background conception of religion, although this clearly became much enhanced with time. By late traditional China, a very curious mixture of Taoist mysticism, Buddhist personal salvation and Confucianism, now with its own temples, had come into being, and most of the population would not have been able to clearly distinguish the elements in a mixture which now allowed salvation for the masses.

What can be said in summary about this doctrine? It would be interesting to know more about the original ideas of Confucius himself since this would enable some light to be thrown on the Weberist contention that Chinese civilisation somehow resulted from the ideas of the great sage. But we have very little that is original, although much that resulted from later codifications. This is tremendously revealing and leads to the conclusion more or less adopted by Weber himself in his *Religion of China*, namely that this ethic was created by the state. Confucianism was thus passive and reflective in character rather than truly creative, although, as we shall see, this is not to deny a certain autonomous power to this ideology. Interestingly, however, the doctrine was not perhaps the one most perfectly suited to imperial rule. Legalism had been preferred by the first Ch'in emperor, but his brutalities, especially the burning of Confucian scholars together with their books, ruled this doctrine out of court thereafter. As it is, Confucianism supported the state but did so only as long as it was successful: the withdrawal of the mandate of heaven could be proclaimed, as most emperors realised.

It is very important to note one distinctive element in Chinese civilisation that lay behind the extraordinary cohesion of the scholar-gentry class as a whole. This was the morphemic style of lettering, that is a non-phonetic, largely non-alphabetic, pictorial language. This placed controls on the radicalising potential of literacy. In Europe a simple phonetic and alphabetic language meant that literacy was constantly, especially with the invention of printing, slipping out of the control of the state. To master a great number of symbols required years of practice, not to mention considerable skill in brushwork, and this was a notable barrier in its own right. Perhaps a more crucial factor was that the script could be understood by the elite in the whole of SE Asia whatever dialectal differences there were. This helped create, reflected, and certainly maintained China's homogenous, elite cultural unity. Unlike the Middle East, China never saw another culture, whether imperial or mercantile in character, and there was in consequence no equivalent number of cultural modes to encourage social diversity. Few social practices, with Buddhism being the striking exception, crossed into China. Similarly, though with reservations to be noted, China was not faced with inter-state competitors of its own calibre. Once the empire had been founded, warfare always seemed to have the character of civil war; it was unnatural and temporary, and fit to be removed – in this of course providing a marked contrast with the European situation.

What of the social composition of the mandarinate? To pass civil service examinations required years of training, and this meant that a kinship group would often band together in order to subsidise a single candidate for such study. The profits from office were considerably higher than those derived from the land itself, despite the three-year rotation of offices and occasional state investigation. However, such profits were not typically able to establish great estates for the individual. On the contrary, the kin group as a whole benefited; indeed there was a Chinese saying that each such group needed one member in the civil service every three generations if it was not to decline.[6] This was not simply a matter of money with which to buy land. Participation in the bureaucracy established contacts, and a retired scholar would be expected to use such contacts to further the interests of his family, both by treating with government agents and in demanding help in starting, for example, irrigation projects.

How then should we perceive this scholar-gentry class? Was this a bureaucracy *sans compeer*, a model of great efficiency? There were occasional bureaucrats who did loyally maintain Confucian morals, and baulked at the false appropriation of taxes, but they were massively unpopular amongst their gentry colleagues and did not last long. More importantly, there were never even enough mandarins for them to form an efficient governing class, although in comparative historical terms the bureaucracy *was* relatively large. The first Ming emperor in 1371 sought to have as few as 5,488 mandarins in government service. This number did expand, but in the sixteenth century – the last of the Ming dynasty – there were still only about 20,400 in the empire as a whole, although there may have been another 50,000 minor officials.[7] As a very large number of these were concentrated in Peking, an official in one of the 1,100 local districts might well have managed 500 to 1,000 square miles with the aid of only three assistants. Weber's comment remains apposite:

The officials' short term of office (three years), corresponding to similar Islamic institutions, allowed for intensive and rational influencing of the economy through the administration as such only in an intermittent and jerky way. This was the case in spite of the administration's theoretical omnipotence. It is astonishing how few permanent officials the administration believed to be sufficient. The figures alone make it perfectly obvious that as a rule things must have been permitted to take their own course, as long as the interests of the state power and of the treasury remained untouched . . .[8]

Further hugely important figures underline the limited size of the elite in China. Stover's figures for the nineteenth century suggest that the elite comprised only 2 per cent of the society as a whole, that is, perhaps only seven and a half million people, who were supported by about 400

6 The political and economic importance of strong kinship links in India, China and Islam is discussed systematically in chapter 5 on European civilisation, where such links were much more tenuous.

7 R. Huang, *1587*, Yale University Press, New Haven, 1981, ch. 2

8 M. Weber, *The Religion of China*, The Free Press, New York, 1964, p. 134.

million, nearly all of them peasants. In contrast, Le Roy Ladurie suggests that a full 15 per cent of the 40 million inhabitants of France, Germany and England had risen above peasant status by the start of the fourteenth century.[9]

All this deserves summary. The Chinese state did not have the means to obtain the total control envisaged in Wittfogel's fantasy. Of course, it sought, as did other imperial states, to gain such autonomy, and the use of eunuchs, supposedly *biologically* loyal to the state, is one index of this. Importantly, the mandarinate was always jealous of such eunuchs since it was aware that an increase in central power would be at their own expense. When the state was strong, most usually when it had just been founded, decentralising tendencies were strongly counteracted; land was shared out, taxes collected and abuses corrected – to the extent, at the accession of the Ming in 1371, that over 100,000 members of the gentry were executed. Moreover, individual members of the gentry always had something to fear from the arbitrary exercise of state power, and the making of a fortune in state service was best followed by a discreet withdrawal to the country, away from the pressures of court politics, where profits could be enjoyed in peace. Nevertheless, arbitrary action against individuals was counterbalanced by an inability of the state to fundamentally go against the gentry class as a whole. Reformer after reformer tried to establish a decent land registry as the basis for a proper taxation system, but all were defeated by the refusal of landlords to co-operate. Chinese society thus witnessed a power stand-off between state and society, a stalemate which led to the inability to generate a large total sum of societal energy.

The mechanism of this power stand-off can be seen at work in the characteristic process of Chinese history already noted, that is, in the cyclical pattern, well known to the mandarins themselves, whereby disintegration of the empire was followed by imperial reconstitution. Naturally each historical case had its peculiarities, but it is possible nevertheless to detect an habitual pattern. A newly established dynasty sought to create a healthy peasant base both for its tax and military potential. To this end, seeds were distributed and some attempt made, often with striking success, to promote agricultural development, not least through the printing of agricultural handbooks. Yet even without internal or external pressures, the state tended to lose control of society. The power of the gentry locally was transformed into the ability both to increase their estates and to avoid taxation. Other pressures on the empire were

9 E. Le Roy Ladurie, *The Territory of the Historian*, Harvester Press, Sussex, 1979, p. 87, cited in E. L. Jones, *The European Miracle*, Cambridge University Press, Cambridge, 1981, p.4.

usually present as well. Internally, an expansion of population, by no means discouraged by the gentry, eventually caused land hunger and peasant rebellions. Externally, the nomads on the borders found the empire more and more attractive as its prosperity waxed in front of their eyes. There is some scholarly debate as to whether such nomads invade 'of their own will' or whether they are forced into such action by mercantilist type policies of the state itself, keen to keep its riches to itself and loathe to trade with nomads, for whom a trade is virtually a necessity. Whatever the case, nomads do not often, despite what Hollywood representations might suggest, come into empires intent on loot, rape and destruction – although these *were* precisely the aims of the Mongols. Barbarians wish to possess the benefits of civilisation and prove increasingly capable of getting them. They are often employed as mercenaries by empires in their later days; as a result they learn military techniques which, when allied with their inherent military resource of great mobility, make them a formidable force. In these circumstances, the imperial state is, of course, forced to increase taxation rates, and it is at this moment that the power stand-off between state and society proves to be important. For many landlords choose to shelter peasants who refuse to pay such increased taxation, and thereby increase their own local power. The combination of feudal-type disintegration and overpopulation led to a constant decrease in the number of tax-paying peasant smallholders. Rodinski cites as one example of this process the census of 754 which showed that there were only 7.6 million tax-payers out of a total population of 52.8 million.[10] In such circumstances the state is forced to tax even more heavily where it can and is driven to arbitrary actions of all types, and this in its own turn fuels peasant unrest. This situation of breakdown and division could last for a long time, but a new dynasty was established in the long run, usually in one of two ways. Nomads succeeded in establishing only two dynasties which united all of China, namely those of the Mongols and the Manchu, although nomads ruled various segments of northern China on several occasions. Other dynasties resulted from peasant revolt. It is worth noting that peasants were not able to horizontally link their laterally insulated communities, so that successful and non-local revolt often depended upon the help of *déclassé* mandarins, members of millenarian groups or discontented gentry. The leaders of such revolts, when they proved successful, eventually co-operated with the gentry and founded a new dynasty which began again the cycle of Chinese history.

This has been a long paragraph describing the perpetual cycle of Chinese civilisation, and certain points at issue in it need to be spelt out.

10 Rodinski, *The Walled Kingdom*, p. 78.

In so far as nomad pressure ran according to its own logic, it is inappropriate to say that the whole cycle of Chinese history can be seen in internal class terms. The empire, to borrow a famous description of the fall of Rome, was, at least sometimes, 'assassinated' from outside. But Marxist analyses have important points to make, and these have been made with marvellous acuity by Geoffrey de Ste Croix, for a different empire, in his *Class Struggles in the Ancient Greek World.*[11] Such analyses draw our attention powerfully to the thoroughgoing class nature of the imperial state, and to the extreme selfishness of the upper classes in refusing to place the situation of their civilisation above their own privileges. Had this class domination been absent, it is argued, nomadic pressure could have been dealt with since, after all, a mere 10,000 nomads on one occasion overran the Chinese state. It is unlikely that this debate over the primacy of external military or internal class factors, whether in Rome or China, is ever going to be finally resolved, largely because both approaches do point up certain features of social reality. But even were some ultimate primacy to be given to class factors, when considering the fall of empires, it remains the case that the classical Marxist canon would remain badly dented.

At an abstract level Marxist concepts depend upon classes being dynamic; that is, conflicting in such a way as to lead to higher modes of productive relationships. This developmental aspect to class was missing in China and indeed in Rome; in both cases the situation can be captured in the words of Marx as historian rather than theorist – 'both classes went to their common ruin'. This point can be put in more technical terms, borrowed from Mann.[12] Where class conflict in the modern world sees organised groups of owners confronting equally organised groups of workers, the segmented nature of the pre-industrial economy meant that class conflict took on a very different form. Most typically, conflict is avoided by the *disintegration* of society which results from landlords protecting the peasants from the taxing powers of the central state. The theoretical point to be made is simple: it looks very much as if social progress does *not* result only from internal class factors, and, in this manner, the general approach adopted in this book gains further support.

It remains necessary to ask why the Chinese empire was restored time and again. We shall see later that the collapse of Rome led to a type of treason amongst one section of that elite whereby Christian priests came to terms with the barbarians and took civilisation to them. This played a vital role in the rise of the West. The mandarins, in contrast, held together and remained true to the imperial ideal. On a number of

11 Duckworth, London, 1981.
12 Mann, 'States, ancient and modern'.

occasions barbarians tried to rule without them, partly because they wished to maintain their own cultural identity, and partly because the mandarins were wont to stay away from a dynasty that did not respect the fundamentals of Confucianism. A famous example of this was that of the Mongols who tried to turn northern China into pasture for their horses. This phase did not last long. The Mongols wished to be civilised and, in order to become so, they had to adopt and adapt to the imperial form. Any consideration of the rather small numbers of the elite shows that an enormous confidence trick was played on the gentry. They remained loyal to the state, but the paucity of their numbers is evidence that they did not do all that well from it; indeed, a well-known problem in Chinese history was the downward mobility of those members of the gentry who failed in one way or another. Furthermore, there was great insecurity attached to office-holding. This is not, it must be stressed, to resurrect the notion of totalitarian strength on the part of the state. This did not exist, and in most matters and for most of the time the scholar-gentry class could block imperial initiatives, even though *individuals* amongst its number did suffer in one way or another. So the argument being made here is that there is a definite autonomy of the state, of the political, in Chinese history because the state *was* strong enough to force class relations into a particular pattern. Of course, this pattern was maintained by the acquisition of solid profits via state service and by cultural indoctrination stressing imperial loyalty. It is a remarkable fact that this loyalty survived during periods of disunity, and especially during the long first period of disunity about which much too little is known. Perhaps the mandarins were prepared to wait for the material incentive of renewed state profit, but a further part of the explanation may be found in the monolithic nature of Chinese culture. The more cosmopolitan world of the Near and Middle East allowed for different ideological options, but the centrality of Confucianism in China gave it a certain force. Whatever the exact explanation for the loyalty, its importance is clear: it largely explains the power of the empire to reconstitute itself. This returns us to the key question: in what ways, if any, did the imperial form have deleterious effects upon the Chinese economy?

Bureaucracy and Capitalism

A number of theoretical contentions need to be highlighted at the start. If greater taxation and control of landlord classes was one way in which empires could, in principle, have been able to counteract barbarian invasion, another method much discussed by Marxist writers would have been to increase state revenue by means of expanding and improving the

economy. This brings to mind Max Weber's assertion that the bureaucracy of pre-industrial empires killed off capitalist developments (and I
shall have a word to say about 'socialist' developments as well) within
their territories.[13] What truth is there to this?

It is as well to concentrate our attention if much real light is to be
thrown upon this question. It is not just easy but perhaps also tempting to
do so; for there was one highly notable efflorescence of economic
advance in mediaeval China from the tenth or eleventh to the fourteenth
century. There are obvious indices of economic progress in this period.
A striking revolution in water transport occurred, and this was of course
a necessary precondition for greater economic interchange. Overall the
commercial spirit penetrated society, with predictable results for the
nature of business and financial organisation. The government provided
a sound copper currency; as a result, where only 4 per cent of taxes had
been paid in money in 750, about 50 per cent were so paid in 1065.
Perhaps the most impressive achievement is that the iron and steel
industry in Sung China produced at least 125,000 tons of iron in 1078,
thereby easily leading the world in production of this basic commodity.
Further, government servants made some attempt to come to terms with
the needs of an expanding economy by including an understanding of
economics and finance in higher level mandarin examinations. Yet in the
end this fabulous start did not lead to any 'take-off' and we must ask
why this was so.[14]

The first point to note is that the greatest expansion took place during
a period of *disunity*. The Northern Sung did, supposedly, rule all of
China from 960 to 1127, but even in that period they were faced with the
militant nomadic Jurchen who conquered their capital Kaifeng in 1127.
After that, the Southern Sung (1127–1269) were always faced with
competitors to the north, first Jurchen and then Mongol. The fact of
disunity is exceptionally important. It encouraged the Southern Sung to
build a navy in order to man all waterways which stood between them and
their northern competitors. This construction produced techniques and
skills, that is a general infrastructure, which proved beneficial to the
economy as a whole and most spectacularly so for the Chinese voyages of
discovery of the fourteenth century. Further action of this sort was forced
on the Sung by the presence of real competitors. Their dynasty is the
only one in Chinese history to have been founded by a general, and
probably for that reason it distrusted an aggressive military policy. It
preferred instead the passive policy of defending cities and did so by
making especial use of the crossbow; perhaps this policy brought in its

13 *The Sociology of Agrarian Civilisations*, New Left Books, London, 1978, p. 368 and
passim.
14 W.H. McNeill, *The Pursuit of Power*, Basil Blackwell, Oxford, 1982, ch. 2.

train a respect for the market as demand went beyond what government ordnance factories could provide.[15] More generally, the market and cities gained some autonomy precisely during this period of disunity in Chinese history. Thus the quality of coinage provided by states tended to improve during disunity for the simple reason that traders would not themselves return to or trust governments which manipulated the coinage too much for their own ends.[16] The general principle seems to be that 'competition between equals, whether the Southern Sung and the Mongols, or the contestants in the Japanese civil wars, or the states of early modern Europe, is an indispensable condition of progress in military technology.'[17]

There is something like conclusive proof of this point. Much of the interest shown by the Sung in military matters resulted from their nomadic neighbours in fact having the edge over them. The Mongols were the first to use gunpowder, and they forced the Sung into adopting it as well. Yet once China was firmly reunited under the native Ming dynasty, it proved possible for many decades to *downplay* gunpowder. The nomads to the north, even when they continued to use gunpowder, could always be defeated by sheer logistical weight; and it was thought best that gunpowder was controlled since it could all too easily help bring about further disunification of the empire. Such policy is typical of empires:

In other societies, heavy state expenditure on war has stimulated economic growth; the competitive drive to win has promoted creative investment and the military has constituted a very large market for arms, supplies and ships. This also occurred in the Roman empire, in that the exaction of taxes to pay troops was a major stimulus to long-distance trade. But Roman armies never faced an enemy which was significantly superior in equipment, so that war did not act as a spur to imitation or invention. Indeed, because of state power, military demands eventually restricted economic growth. In the Late Empire, military supplies and taxes were removed from the market; military supplies were demanded as taxes in kind; for a time, money taxes were virtually abolished. The response to increased external pressure from barbarians was thus not invention but a tightening of the screws of state repression.[18]

The point being made is this: only an empire free of rivals of equal status could afford this sort of policy. In the Christian West, this policy would have spelt destruction, probably within a single generation.

15. Ibid., pp. 38–9.

16 M. Elvin, *The Pattern of the Chinese Past*, Stanford University Press, California, 1973, ch. 14.

17 Ibid., p. 97.

18 K. Hopkins, 'Economic growth and towns in classical antiquity' in P. Abrams and E. A. Wrigley (eds), *Towns in Societies*, Cambridge University Press, Cambridge, 1976, p. 77.

It is worth recapitulating at this point. Some economic improvements, particularly the distribution of seeds and the diffusion of knowledge, cannot be laid at the door of imperial policy for the simple and banal reason that they took place during a period of disunity. But it is now time to turn to the other side of the coin, namely to the impact of the empire upon the Chinese economy when unity was restored.

It has already been seen that the imperial bureaucracy was not so extensive as to be able to effectively control everything that happened at the ground level of Chinese society. Market exchanges did increasingly characterise Chinese imperial society until its demise. Nevertheless, the fact of empire militated against the full impact of capitalism. The empire supported a traditional status system which was a surer access to money than was commerce.

Trade and other profit-making activities are not necessarily in themselves forces making for liberation – they must be considered within an overall social context – and while the development of commercial capital undermined the pre-existing economic system, it did not prepare in inevitable fashion the way for the appearance of new powers of production.[19]

Trade in large part consisted of the supplying of shortages in one area from another; it rested on price differentials much more than it did on real production. Other sources of profit were safer. This was true of land, speculation and money-lending but, above all, of office-holding, itself not such as to rule out the other activities:

Many merchants and industrialists also sought to buy official status, and it was inevitable that, as the conflict between growing urban economic power and intensifying official control became more pronounced, the upper classes in the cities would attempt to safeguard their wealth by assuming a politically parasitical character. This contributed to the further division of the urban populace into very rich and very poor, and one consequence of this was that it was on the purchasing power not of the majority of the city population but of a minority of rich persons that the control of the markets in the last analysis depended. This in turn imposed a limit on the development of urban industry and trade.[20]

In the Chinese empire, in other words, power tended to concentrate into a single set of hands. Economic relationships tended to be subordinate, and the autonomy of the market correspondingly downplayed.

Imperial government was equally important in urban affairs. Chinese cities had no autonomy in pre-Sung Chinese imperial history; indeed, they were themselves the seats of government where the local magistrate

19 Y. Shiba, *Commerce and Society in Sung China*, University of Michigan Press, Ann Arbor, 1970, p. 2.
20 Ibid., pp. 139–40.

had his office. This imperial presence typically led to the regulation of guilds and markets held within the city. But during the Sung, the growth of market relationships meant both the creation of intermediate-sized cities and the spreading of markets beyond the walls of larger cities, and both led to a diminishing role for the state. However, this interdependence was increasingly at risk, even under the Sung. During this dynasty the Confucian mandarin creed came into its apogee in the codification of Chun-Hsi, and this both allowed and perhaps reflected an increase in the confidence of that class. This confidence left its impact on urban affairs. Early Kaifeng had been bustling and disorderly, but this came increasingly to be seen as an unfitting spectacle for an imperial city. Plans were therefore drawn up designed to achieve the proper symbolic splendour, and these, interestingly, involved displacing market activities. It is as if the large vistas planned by Sir Christopher Wren for London after the Great Fire had not been defeated by commercial and propertied interests. There is another related point of great importance. It is now becoming something of an orthodoxy, *pace* Joseph Needham's *Science and Civilisation in China*, to stress that Chinese science did *not* prove adept at technological-type discoveries *after* the Sung![21] Scientific development was perhaps set back by the great codifications of Confucianism since these were capable of explaining away observed discrepancies in events; elsewhere, the observation of discrepancies led to the recasting of intellectual assumptions. Quite probably this was related to the relative lack of autonomy of cities and of the burgher element; the demand for science-cum-technology was that much weaker.

But if there were *obstacles* to capitalist-type economic advance, we have already seen that it *did* have spectacular success stories to its credit. How did the empire react to capitalist forces? Unfortunately, very little is known about the cause of the collapse, once they were in place, of the iron and steel industries of mediaeval China. It is plausible, perhaps likely, that imperial interference in pricing policy with an eye to revenue gains undermined this spectacular success story.[22] However, there *is* sufficient information available to be fairly definite when discussing the collapse of the other great Sung achievement, its naval power. The navy retained some strength even under the Mongols, but the foundation of a native dynasty which improved the Grand Canal (so no longer necessitating ocean-going transport from South to North) led to a series of edicts that undermined its position. Most obviously, between 1371 and 1567, all foreign trade was banned. This is not to say that trade in fact

21 See the discussion of Needham's work in *Past and Present*, no. 32, 1980.
22 McNeill, *The Pursuit of Power*, ch. 2.

ceased. Instead it was organised by 'pirates', often of Japanese origin, in
conjunction with local gentry who thereby gained considerable profit.
Such a ban must have had a great effect. We know that the ban instituted
in 1430 against the construction of further ocean-going ships led
eventually to technological amnesia – in this case, *pace* Popper, by 1553
knowledge was actually forgotten! Nevertheless, *the* most spectacular
way in which politics could affect the economy concerned the fate of
explorations undertaken by the eunuch admiral Cheng-Ho in the 1540s.
As befitted an empire, these expeditions both to the Pacific and the
Indian oceans, were mounted on a large scale. They were, moreover,
entirely successful and they placed China in a position where she could
have reaped the benefits that were shortly to fall to the Portuguese,
Dutch and British. The character of politics in China, and in this case
largely court politics, determined that none of this was to happen. The
mandarins were always extemely jealous of the emergence of sources of
power that rivalled their own. They were opposed to Cheng-Ho because
he was a eunuch whose cause was promoted by the eunuchs at court.
They had good reasons or, perhaps, rationalisations, for their opposition.
Crucial, perhaps, was sudden renewed nomadic pressure on the
northern frontiers which allowed them to argue that resources had to be
spent to meet a more immediate problem. In a centralised system,
relatively minor conflicts and pressures could have major effects.

Let us return to Max Weber's dictum that bureaucracy killed off
capitalism in the pre-industrial world. Certain reservations must be
made about such a blunt formulation. On the one hand, this view tends
to underplay economic advance within empires, in particular agricultural
advance to which the state did, so far as its limited resources allowed,
sometimes contribute. On the other hand, Weber's formulation occasionally gives the impression that the state was all powerful, and that
bureaucratic interference in pre-industrial and industrial societies is
somehow of the same character. In fact the German sociologist was well
aware that bureaucracy in pre-industrial societies was puny, and that, as
we shall see, a stronger state might have been able to foster economic
advance. Ultimately however Weber's argument gains support from the
Chinese case. It is true that there is one undeniably intangible point. The
Ming were perhaps unusual compared to other empires in stepping
backwards by abandoning coinage and creating a purely natural economy.
Had they continued along the path laid down by the Sung, it is possible
that greater tax revenues could have enabled them to provide the social
infrastructure their society needed for economic take-off. Perhaps the
character of the Ming was historically peculiar and certainly that character was possible only in an extremely isolated geographical surround.
Nevertheless there seem to be plenty of factors at work to suggest that

the habitual character of imperial politics was exerting its sway. Thus the attempts of Prime Minister Chang Chu-cheng at the end of the sixteenth century to reform the state's administration and finances were only possible because of favourable personal relationships established with the Dowager Empress. Once these changed an alternative, and easier, policy was always likely to be adopted.[23] Similarly, the distrust shown of non-official sources of power in China typifies imperial rule. So too does the seeking of career mobility via state service, though in this connection it has been argued that the Chinese state, whatever its weaknesses, had strength enough to instil sufficient loyalty among its gentry to allow own reconstitution.

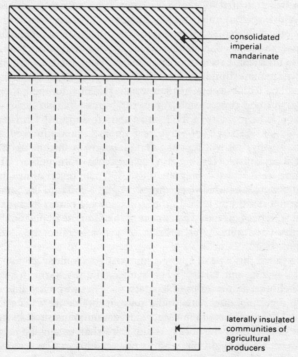

consolidated imperial mandarinate

laterally insulated communities of agricultural producers

Model 2: The Chinese capstone state

The Chinese state can best be characterised by means of a variation on Gellner's model of the agro-literate polity. The mandarins sought to oust other groups seeking to become part of the elite in fear that their own

23 R. Huang's *1587* marvellously captures the tone of court intrigue.

power would thereby be diminished, even though this meant that they themselves were stuck with a single cultural ideal to which, perhaps perforce, they were loyal. Mandarin jealousy of other power sources, is, moreover, something of a constant feature in Chinese history. Although the bureaucracy was not able to penetrate far into society, it could and did prevent other forces from gaining much autonomy. A classic instance of this was that of the suppression of Buddhist monasteries. Buddhism had spread very fast once it had been introduced from India, and its success was seen in the number of Buddhist monasteries established in China. It seems quite likely that such monasteries played a substantial role in trade, and also in production. Certainly some of the most famous of them were situated on the inner Asian trade routes. Buddhism was attractive to barbarian rulers both because it had greater penetration into the society than had Confucianism, and because it represented a counterweight to it. For all these reasons, the mandarin bureaucrats sought to undermine its institutional power. They succeeded during the Tang dynasty, and Buddhism thereafter never regained its institutional position. The Chinese elite, in other words, remained unified; there were to be no further church–state, or priest–bureaucrat, struggles in this civilisation. The inability of the Roman state to suppress Christianity, a matter, as we shall see, of very great import, stands in very striking contrast. Finally, it is worth noting that mandarin suspicion was directed not just at capitalist forces, but also against those of the military. Thus in 1569 there were probably only about 845,000 men under arms (although 3,138,000 were supposedly so); this is roughly similar to the number of troops supported by a single European country, France, by about 1650 and that with perhaps only 15 per cent of the Chinese population![24] The mandarins undermined the position of generals once they were too successful.

I have called this type of Chinese imperial government *capstone*, and it is worth spelling out further what is meant by this term. The united Chinese elite sat atop a series of separate 'societies', which it did not wish to penetrate or mobilise; perhaps the key to its behaviour was its fear that horizontal linkages it could not see would get out of control. Its concern was less with intensifying social relationships than in seeking to prevent any linkages which might diminish its power. This can be seen particularly clearly in Huang's brilliant analysis of Ming taxation. The main task of the administration of the Ming was that of imperial cohesion:

As the Ming administrators saw it, to promote those advanced sectors of the economy would only widen the economic imbalance, which in turn would threaten the empire's political unity. It was far more desirable to keep all the

24 R. Huang, *Taxation and Governmental Finance in Sixteenth-Century Ming China*, Cambridge University Press, Cambridge, 1974, p. 290.

provinces on the same footing, albeit at the level of the more backward sectors of the economy.[25]

Of course, this meant that they would seek their revenue in taxation from the land. The Ming initially sought to have this taxation paid mostly in kind and to that end did not provide sound copper currency. Probably the fundamental reason for this change was once again political. The Ming did not wish monetary supplies and surpluses to be located at any single point where they could be seized and used to support rebellion. 'The empire's fiscal operations were so fragmented as to make them virtually safe from capture, and the mere knowledge of this fact was sometimes sufficient to discourage potential rebels.'[26] It is worth remembering that the empire founded by the Ming, and continued by the Manchu, lasted from 1371 to 1911: this represented the longest period of uninterrupted imperial rule in history. The capstone system *did* remove all alternative bases of power, and there were *no* successful internal revolts for half a millenium. The Ming and Manchu had learnt how to perfect capstone government.

Some final points are worth making, even though they anticipate the discussion of Latin Christendom. Chinese capstone government blocked the fully fledged emergence of intensive capitalist relationships. This is *not* to say that the impact of the state upon capitalism must always be negative. A different type of state, the European organic state, proved capable, once capitalist relationships were established, of providing crucial services for this type of economic system; Chinese capstone government was incapable of providing equivalent services. The aim of the Ming was to create a stable agrarian state based on healthy peasantry. This was based on the traditional Confucian view which considered that the land was the provider of all that was meritorious, and perhaps the origin of the Ming in a peasant rebellion helped cement this view. But the fixing of once-and-for-all tax revenues at the beginning of the dynasty proved to be a terrible mistake, especially given that the administration was initially conceived on such a small scale. The trouble proved to be that the administration was under-financed, and thus too weak to take advantage of the expansion of population. Their image of a *strong* peasantry could only have been achieved had the state been powerful enough to establish decent currency and credit arrangements, instead of allowing the peasantry to be exploited at the will of moneylenders and the gentry. The weakness of the government can be seen in other ways:

It must be pointed out that in the late Ming most of the service facilities indispensable to the development of capitalism were clearly lacking. There was no legal protection for the businessman, money was scarce, interest rates high

25 Ibid., p. 2.
26 Ibid., p. 321.

and banking undeveloped . . . At the same time merchants and entrepreneurs were hindered by the frequent roadblocks on the trade routes, government purchase orders and forced contributions, the government's near monopoly of the use of the Grand Canal and active involvement in manufacturing. On the other hand the security and status of land ownership, the tax-exemption enjoyed by those who purchased official rank, and the non-progressive nature of the land tax increased the attractions of farming to the detriment of business investment.[27]

Nor could the state play much of a role in helping recovery from those natural disasters that so plagued Chinese ecology. The weakness of the government is aptly caught in a dilemma in which it found itself when administering the salt monopoly. Quotas for salt had initially been set without an eye to expanding consumption, and the government simply had no machinery by means of which it could itself increase production, even though thereby it would have made substantial profits. When merchants began new production, it became clear that 'private salt' undercut 'official salt', with a corresponding loss to government revenue. Not surprisingly, the government sought to control the former even at the cost of widespread hardship.[28]

One presupposition of the argument is worth noting. By intensive development I have meant in effect intensive *capitalist* development, and my purpose has been to show how this was stifled in Chinese civilisation. This suggests an objection: could not economic development have occurred in a 'state socialist' manner, that is, by means of a much stronger state, strong not just in terms of arbitrariness but also in its capacity to penetrate and mobilise society? There are two reasons for doubting this. Most obviously, pre-industrial rule simply did not allow such a policy, given the small size of ruling agencies and their poor means of communication. Secondly, societies and civilisations face the problems of their own times, not those we ascribe to them. The population of China doubled or trebled from the sixteenth to the mid-nineteenth century to reach perhaps 450 million, most of whom were, most of the time, able to eat and breed in peace. This is by some standards a sign of success: was it not 'the greatest happiness of the greatest number'? A final consideration of this matter is now in order.

Expansion without Development

Notions of success and failure of civilisations tend to conflate normality with success. This is highly questionable since the success of Europe in civilisational terms was not normal but pathological. Social stability calls

27 Ibid., pp. 318–19.
28 Ibid., pp. chapter 5.

for less explanation. But is this to say that 'success' should be seen in purely neutral, technical and economic terms, bereft of all moral approbation? The situation of late traditional China, where a potential for intensive capitalist development had been blocked, suggests that success should retain some such moral connotation.

The situation of the Chinese elite need not concern us overmuch. But what of the peasantry? Their numbers certainly grew. But did Chinese policy, seeking as it did to protect and encourage them, in fact give them a decent life?

The large quantity of unused labour in these households certainly represented a more substantial loss to the economy than did that of the large landowners, who were far fewer in number. It was indeed basically because of the former that the land tax rates could not be adequately readjusted upwards. The adminstration was undoubtedly handicapped not only by its inability to impose progressive taxation on the large landowners, but also by great concern for the interests of small-scale proprietors. Regardless of misappropriation, taxation in traditional China simply did not generate sufficient revenue to enable the government to carry out all its functions properly, let alone to stimulate any economic breakthrough.[29]

It is a mistake to follow too slavishly the well-known theory according to which Chinese history is to be seen in terms of a dynastic cycle. The mandarins themselves stressed that this cycle moved in moral terms, choosing to stress in particular that in their later periods dynasties tended to overtax. Now this is somewhat too straightforward in the Chinese case since it suggests that the dynasty had been strong and efficient at the start. Modern sinologists see the whole question in more structural terms. The trouble was rather, for the Ming at least, that the level of taxation was set too low from the start, making it impossible to penetrate society, let alone provide it with any services. This is related to the lack of agrarian improvement. Pressure on the peasantry certainly *did* increase in a cyclical manner: 'Since the tax rates were generally low and money was scarce, this combination of circumstances must have created a paradise for agrarian exploitation on all levels and on all scales. In the course of two centuries, the tax-paying capacity of the population was thus severely undercut.'[30] Decent credit facilities, which would have been necessary for the government's dream of a strong peasantry to be realised, were not provided by the government. Instead moneylenders, often themselves members of the gentry, exploited the peasantry by means of very high interest rates. In a nutshell, the peasants were not sufficiently independent to prosper. On the other hand, the gentry was more interested in

29 Ibid., pp. 187–8.
30 Ibid., p. 309.

profits from state service than in those to be gained from commercial farming. The increase in population, perhaps trebling to approximately 450 million from the sixteenth to the mid-nineteenth century, hid a failure to raise the general standard of living. Furthermore, this increase in itself became an obstacle to the creation of any sort of dynamism in the Chinese economy. In the nineteenth century, the size of the population militated against technological improvements which centred on labour-saving devices, especially in the cotton industry.[31] Instead of producing an economic surplus that could be used for investment, Chinese society tended to produce mouths that swallowed up improvements extensively. All this was quite apparent before the arrival of the influence of the Western industrial powers on nineteenth-century China. They brought progress.

Conclusions

It is worth reiterating that China was by no means a stagnant society. Its history saw a long and continuous expansion of agriculture, especially in the South, whilst its polity as a whole experienced a dynastic cycle. By conceptualising the weakness of the empire, we are at last beginning to understand this cycle in structural terms, rather than, as Confucian ideology would have it, as the consequence of moral decay. Despite this, Chinese society did not create a nervous, restless dynamism sufficient to allow it to dominate the world. Very much to the contrary, what strikes time and time again is the immeasurable self-confidence that derives from thinking of oneself *as the world*. Thus the Ch'ien Lung emperor, rejecting trade with George III, chose to ignore the insistence of the English envoys: 'I do not forget the lonely remoteness of your island, cut off from the world by intervening wastes of sea, nor do I overlook your excusable ignorance of the usages of Our Celestial Empire.'[32]

Clearly China never witnessed much competition. The market gained only fitful internal autonomy, few social practices crossed over the frontier, and no political rivals existed capable of putting this civilisation to the test of war. The latter two of these points result in part from geography; they represent conditions allowing the imperial form to continue untroubled. But institutional blockages to the market, consequent upon the fact of empire, played a vital role. My argument has had one particular nuance. The market was not destroyed because the imperial

31 Elvin, *The Pattern of the Chinese Past*, ch. 16.
32 'The Emperor's Decree to the Outer Barbarians' in E. Schurmann and O. Schell (eds), *Imperial China*, London, 1977; p. 104.

state was so strong but rather, at least in part, because it was so feeble. It was in essence a place, an area, and the mandarins often captured it, instituted policies to suit themselves, and thereby prevented any historically autonomous rise of the East.

3

The Land of the Brahmans

Indian civilisation is very ancient. Key contours of that civilisation resulted from the invasion through the North-West Frontier of the Aryan peoples of Persia, and this may have taken place as early as 1800 BC. It will *not* be my argument that the characteristic social physiognomy of India civilisation was permanently fixed as early as this. Very much to the contrary and in opposition to Louis Dumont, the celebrated modern Indologist who is a very strong practitioner of Weberist principles,[1] I shall insist that caste, unquestionably the most distinctive Indian social institution, became stronger and more effective only as the result of an historical process to be described. Perhaps the term description heralds too much; certainly a word of warning is immediately in order. We lack written records of early Indian history, and the historiography of India is likely to remain the weakest of all the world civilisations. A part of the power of the Brahman in Indian life has been based on the capacity to memorise and recite rather than to refer to written documents; such written authorities and sources as there were suffered disastrous losses from Muslim invasions into India. Moreover, any laxness or inattention in recopying manuscripts led to the loss of written sources because the birchbark on which they were written decays rapidly in the Indian climate. Hence it is perhaps better to speak of a considered theory of early Indian civilisation since nobody is or ever can be sure of exactly what happened. One final reservation to any picture of unchanging India

1 See *Homo Hierarchus*, Weidenfeld and Nicolson, London, 1957; *Religion/Politics and History in India*, Mouton, The Hague, 1957; *From Mandeville to Marx*, Chicago University Press, Chicago, 1977. There is a good article on Weber's book on India by David N. Gellner, 'Weber, Capitalism and the Religion of India', *Sociology*, vol. 16, 1982. I am much indebted to discussions with David Gellner, most particularly in my interpretations of Buddhism and caste. Interestingly, Max Weber's own account of Indian civilisation, *The Religion of India* (Free Press, New York, 1958), is often not Weberist in tone, indeed at times it is crassly materialistic. These points are discussed later in this chapter.

can usefully be made immediately. Aryan culture took a considerable amount of time to establish itself in the North, and it was much longer before its sway, never complete, extended to the South.

Nevertheless, when visitors from China in the early centuries of the Christian era, intent upon trade and copying the Buddhist scriptures, spoke of the 'land of the Brahmans', when the Arabs labelled this civilisation Hindu, and when the Portuguese coined the word caste, they were essentially correct. Indian civilisation *did* gell into a particular pattern, and this pattern was one which proved extremely inimical to the autonomous emergence of any economic dynamic. It will prove easier to describe the system once in place than to explain its emergence. However, the general argument to be made can be highlighted immediately by recalling some phrases of Karl Marx, used in his newspaper articles on British rule in India.[2] Indian civilisation was united politically only three times: before the Christian era by the native Mauryans, in the Middle Ages in the Muslim Mughal empire, and finally by the British. Typically, Indian history sees a mass of political movements, often involving foreign conquest. Yet these were, in Marx's words, but 'storm-clouds' in the sky, and the fundamental reality is the stability of the social order beneath the political realm. Politics were, to an extraordinary extent, free-floating, a statement not designed to suggest, however, that they were without *any* significant impact. Marx himself occasionally hinted that an explanation for such stability was to be sought in the self-sustaining village, and this view, that India is a land of thousands of autonomous villages, is a common one, not least in Gandhian ideology. In order to understand the uniqueness of the Indian historical pattern, it will have to be decisively rejected.

The Aryans and Caste

Virtually nothing is known for sure about the coming of the Aryans. Nineteenth-century views tend to give the impression of a whole people uprooting itself and moving *en bloc*. To this has been added the argument that the Aryans were responsible for destroying the Indus valley civilisation they encountered, whose greatest monuments, only relatively recently discovered, are the cities of Harappa and Mohenjo-Daro. General considerations cast doubt upon this picture. Logistical reasons would suggest that a mass movement of a whole people is most unlikely to have occurred and may in fact have been absolutely impossible. Far more likely was a series of leap-frogging conquests, further and further into

2 These are easily available in K. Marx, *Surveys from Exile*, Penguin, London, 1973.

India; the idea of searching for a single date for the arrival of the Aryans is simply misguided. This sort of progress would not have been able to destroy the Indus valley civilisation, and the current state of evidence suggests that internal factors were probably responsible for the collapse of that hydraulic society.

Our main evidence for early Aryan society is the series of hymns and chants collected together as the *Rig Veda*.[3] Aryan strength seems likely to have derived initially from the possession of a particular military capacity: they were experts in chariot warfare, and this gave them an edge over those whom they encountered. Furthermore, being pastoralists, they seem to have been opposed to city life, somewhat in the manner of the Mongols, though they herded cattle rather than horses. Nevertheless, it would be a great mistake to see the Aryans in purely negative terms as simply destroyers of the settled life they encountered. For the Vedic hymns make clear that they brought with them the deep plough, pulled by oxen. Vedic hymns and modern archaeology suggest that jungle was burnt and agriculture expanded step by step until the Ganges valley was reached. Early Vedic civilisation sees, then, a striking expansion, both geographically and intensively, of a tribal civilisation based upon notable agrarian improvements.

The *Rig Veda* makes other elements of Aryan society clear. The invaders were not able to rest easily in the land they had conquered since warfare with the native population continued. It may well be that this native population, termed Dasas or Dravidians, was of an entirely different colour. 'Thus although the main issue in the war between the Aryans and their enemies was the possession of cattle, chariots and other forms of wealth, differences in race, religion and modes of speech also seemed to exacerbate relations.'[4] It is worth contrasting this situation with those that faced nomad invaders elsewhere. The barbarians who invaded the Roman empire rapidly bowed before Christian monotheism, and most nomads in history, faced with 'civilisation', tend to be absorbed through intermarriage into the larger world they conquer. The Islamic nomad conquerors of the Middle East were, as we shall see, completely different from this, for they brought with them their own monotheistic religion, and they accordingly felt superior in terms of civilisation to those they conquered. They were not absorbed by a civilisation but rather created their own. Perhaps the situation of the Aryan invaders was in the middle of these extreme positions:

3 A useful selection is available: *The Rig Veda*, ed. W.D. O'Flaherty, Penguin, London, 1983.

4 R.S. Sharma, *Sudras in Ancient India*, Motilal Banarsidass, Delhi, 2nd Edition, 1980, p. 16.

There were a few cities with a little writing, there was agriculture, there were other ruling people and the earliest records of the conquerors show that they were neither much superior nor inferior in civilisation to the people among whom they came. The only advantage they possessed was a great mobility ... The Indo-Aryans were neither submerged nor were able completely to dominate ... they accommodated themselves to a life which allowed a certain separateness together with a certain independence.[5]

This is to offer the beginnings of an explanation of the caste system, the characteristic social and religious organisation of the Aryans, and it is as well to try and confront this complex matter directly.

Most authors agree on what it is that constitutes caste in its full, achieved, modern sense.[6] Caste rests upon three key elements: specialisation of occupation, social hierarchy enforced by the control of marriage, and social and dietary laws designed to prevent higher castes from being polluted by contact with the lower castes. In classical Vedic theory four castes were distinguished, and they remain recognisable today: the Brahman (priest), the Ksatriya (warrior), the Vaisya (husbandman, trader) and the Sudra (servant). This classical Varna or estate system has within it a key distinction between the top three castes, Aryan in origin, each of whom is twice born, and the Sudra, probably initially composed of the native and conquered population, which is held to be only once born. Historically, however, even more important than this was the emergence of the Untouchables – clearly present before the Christian era but perhaps only 5 per cent of the total population in the classical periods of Indian civilisation – since these casteless people brought pollution and were the fundamental justification for the caste system. They were excluded from social life, and tended to live outside the pale of settled life. The process of Aryanization of much of India resulted when the native inhabitants called the Brahmans to help them distinguish themselves from Untouchables forced to move into their areas, from whom they had probably learnt of caste in the first instance. It is very important to realise that all that has been said about caste to this point is in the realms of strikingly pure and well-developed classical theory. The workings of caste on the ground are much more messy and *ad hoc*. Most obviously, locally Jati (i.e. sub-groups of caste) proliferate. The system of division is endlessly extensible, and it allows room for new occupations and sub-occupations, as well as for invaders. Indians themselves were

5 I. Karve, *Hindu Society: an Interpretation*, Deccan College, Poona, 1961, p. 40.

6 On caste in general, see Dumont, *Homo Hierarchus*; J. Hutton, *Caste in India*, Cambridge University Press, Cambridge, 1946; and A.M. Hocart, *Caste: a Comparative Study*, Methuen, London, 1950.

less bound by caste hierarchy than might be suggested by the formal scheme. There is a fair degree of co-operation amongst castes today and this is after the caste system gained vigour under Muslim and British rulers. There was, of course, no link with the casteless, but it has always been possible for a particular Jat to move up in the caste system over time; mobility was also open to an individual able to afford the services of a Brahman. This is not to say that the fact of caste is without vital explanatory power in Indian civilisation, merely to suggest that its impact is not always to be sought in terms of its specialised hierarchy. The other face of caste is often less its hierarchical rules, so often ignored in practice, than the fact that – in theory from the earliest times, and crucially, eventually in reality – much social organisation was achieved by caste rather than by politics.

The social and religious organisation of the early Aryans was in no way as strict as the caste system just outlined, whose theory is very much the product of later Brahman rationalisation. The estates were present, but no bans on commensality or intermarriage were known. It is further noticeable that warriors/kings are seen actively participating in religious rituals, something which suggest that the Brahman had no early, automatic monopoly of religious practices.

With the passing of time, however, a more complex social order did emerge, and this is clear in the literature of the later Vedic age between roughly 800 BC and the creation of empire under the Nandas and Mauryans in the fourth century BC. In the *Brahmanas* it is possible to detect a certain hardening of stratification as more specialised rule took the place of egalitarian assemblies. This probably involved tying the poorest members of the Aryans to the land; perhaps this is to be explained by specialisation in military techniques involving the use of iron weapons. Such a process is historically normal, and had equivalents in other parts of the world, not least in the history of Europe. One development *is* historically unusual. The *Brahmanas* show an increasing hold over religious power on the part of the Brahmans. In China intellectuals at the behest of the state produced a type of Caesaropapist doctrine, and such fusion of religious and political power occurred elsewhere. In India a division took place between secular and religious power from very early times. This is not to say that there is evidence of conscious hostility between rulers and priests; on the contrary, a certain division of labour seems apparent in which each depends upon and supports the other. How could this situation have arisen? Nobody knows, but it is worth putting forward a reasoned speculation. The Aryans felt threatened by the native population, larger in sheer numbers and probably of a different racial composition. It is quite possible that their desire to distinguish themselves was met by the Brahmans who captured and enshrined the Aryan ethnic inheritance in emerging caste-type organisations.[7] The Brahmans provided rituals which enabled the community to survive.

In a brilliant essay, dealing with the kingship in early India, Louis Dumont spelt out some of the consequences of this situation. The *Brahmanas* make it clear that the king depends upon priests for all religious functions and cannot sacrifice by himself. His Brahman adviser and religious specialist, the *purohita*, has a monopoly of the crucial legitimating authority, the king possessing merely political power. Power is disconnected from authority, and held inferior to it.

Through this dissociation, the function of the king in India has been *secularised*. It is from this point that a differentiation has occurred, the separation within the religious universe of a sphere or realm opposed to the religious, and roughly corresponding to what we call the political. As opposed to the realm of values and norms it is the realm of force. As opposed to the *dharma* or universal order of the Brahman, it is the realm of interest or advantage, *artha*.[8]

The contrast with the situation in the political tradition of the Western world is very great. In India, politics are only 'relatively autonomous' and are not seen as the *source* of law and ultimate meaning; those matters are ascribed to the social order and to the duties the individual has within that social order. All this is to emphasise the extraordinary position of the Brahman in Indian civilisation. In the West, in contrast, the state is seen as the fount of authority over the social order, whilst churches, nationalised formally as the result of the Reformation, are left merely with the monopoly of spiritual services.

The documents which we have show Brahmans occupying a key role in society and the source of this power may have been their ability to devise rituals that kept the ethnic heritage of the Aryans alive. Nevertheless it is as well to remember that the *Brahmanas* are *ideology*; they are a claim to power quite as much as a description of actual social practices. This social structure of early India was very flexible, and it would be a mistake to imagine that it was *always* on the cards that the Brahmans' claim to power would be recognised. Ideas do not always translate into reality. We can see this by turning to the challenges that emerged in the later Vedic period to Brahmanical power. Classical Hindu social organisation was born from the fight against challenges to Brahmanical ideas which nearly succeeded.

7 This is suggested by Michael Mann, *Sources of Social Power*, vol. 1, *From the Beginning to 1760 A.D.*, Cambridge University Press, Cambridge, 1986.

8 *Religion/Politics and History in India*, p. 68.

Buddhism and Empire

The later Vedic period was one of intense dynamism in every facet of social life. Something must be said about material, political and intellectual developments, all of which were closely interlinked.[9]

This period saw a marked expansion of economic relationships. A key background development was the growing knowledge of the use of iron, which was itself further facilitated through the use of the bellows. This made the plough more effective and allowed for agrarian advance, particularly in the use of certain types of rice and sugar.[10] Most striking was the rise in urbanisation in this period. We know of the existence of at least 60 towns, and some of these seem to have been large. Their rise was connected with an increase in trade, the monetization of economic relations and the establishment of crafts, themselves increasingly controlled by guilds.

In light of the remarks made when discussing China, it is not altogether surprising that such economic advance took place during a period of political fragmentation. In the river valleys, monarchies arose in which the powers of the king with the Brahman at his side, increased dramatically. In contrast, there was a series of republics, mostly in the hills and often involved in trade, where Brahman/royal power seems to have been considerably less. Certainly popular assemblies, probably derived from traditional tribal meetings, regularly took place. The relationship between these different polities, and indeed within the types themselves, was one of warfare, most notably between Kosala, Magadha, Vrijis and Kashi.

The Brahmans, anchored for the most part at this time to the countryside, were not able to keep pace with these sorts of developments. Their conceptions of religion and social order were derived from a simple kin-based landed society, and these failed to meet the new religious needs created by the more cosmopolitan situation. In particular, the individualism and discipline encouraged by urban life seem to have created some sort of demand for a more rational type of religion, capable of offering the individual a route to salvation.

This intellectual challenge can be seen surfacing in three ways. Firstly, criticism arose within the orthodox Vedic tradition. The *Upanishads*, written sometime during the later Vedic period, describe a much more personalistic religious quest for ultimate meaning; they exhibit a desire for a fully worked out soteriology. These texts also abound with criticisms of the mere ritualism of the Brahmans:

9 N. Wagle, *Society at the Time of the Buddha*, Popular Prakashan, Bombay, 1966.

10 R.S. Sharma, *Light on Early Indian Society and Economy*, Manaktala, Bombay, 1966, p. 60 and ch. 7 *passim*.

Of what use is the *Rig Veda* to one who does not know the Spirit from whom the *Rig Veda* comes, and in whom all things abide? For only those who have found him have found peace.

For all the sacred books, all holy sacrifice and ritual and prayers, all the words of the *Vedas*, and the whole past and present and future, come from Spirit.[11]

Secondly, Mahavira brought together ideas during the sixth century BC which had been present in embryo form for at least a century, and thereby created Jainism. This religion is atheistical in tenor since the existence of God does not affect its doctrine. Everthing is deemed to have a soul, and the purpose of living is held to be that of purifying the soul so that it may then be released into bliss. Such purification cannot, as the *Upanishads* had argued, be achieved through knowledge; rather a balanced, frugal life offers the best hope for salvation. Doctrinally, Jainism emphasised the importance of non-violence, and its adherents took this to the extent of wearing a muslin mask to prevent swallowing even the smallest of insects. This ruled out the possibility of agrarian life, and Jainism thereafter spread amongst merchants. It was, as Max Weber realised, the Indian equivalent of European Protestantism.[12]

But it was the third challenge that proved most significant. It established nothing less than a world religion. Gautama, or the Buddha (that is, the enlightened one) as he is best known, was born in 566 BC in the Sakya republic at the northern limit of the Ganges basin. His father was a leading Ksatriya, and in fact was the leader of his tribe. The Buddha rejected his background and initially sought meaning through asceticism. When this route failed the Buddha entered a period of meditation, on the 49th day of which he finally received enlightenment. He soon began to preach – significantly in popular Magadhi rather than in the Sanskrit used by the Brahmans – the Four Noble Truths (that the world is suffering, that suffering is caused by human desire, that renunciation leads to salvation, and that a method to this end, the Eightfold Path, is available), and that the Eightfold Path consisting in principles of moderate and balanced behaviour, would lead to the blessed state of nothingness, Nirvana.

Buddhism had significant general appeal. In one of the earliest Buddhist discourses it is possible to see that the Brahmanical ordering of society was being fundamentally challenged by a more universalist creed:

... it asserts that a criminal, whether Brahman or Servant, Warrior or Husbandman, would be sentenced by the king of a newly centralised state strictly according to the seriousness of his deed, not according to his estate. This was

---

11 *The Upanishads*, Penguin Books, London, 1965, pp. 91–2.

12 Weber, *The Religion of India*. I have drawn heavily on R. Thapar, *A History of India*, vol. 1, Penguin, London, 1966, especially p. 65, when describing Jainism.

quite contrary to the old view, however, for there the punishment – envisaged as reparation or penance – was to be appropriate to the person, to the estate of the transgressor, not only to the crime. Were Brahmans and Warriors to be treated like common criminals? Were the estates not to be respected? And ... the discourse points out that, in the urban world of the Buddha, it was quite possible for someone born of high estate, a Brahman or a Warrior, to be employed as a servant by someone of low caste, a Servant or a Husbandman. Such an eventuality was wholly inconceivable under the old order: Servants could only serve, Brahmans and Warriors only command.[13]

This is not to say that Buddhism directly attacked Brahmanical religion. Somewhat to the contrary, Buddhism chose to ignore it and sought successfully to spread its message by the creation of monastic communities concerned with the spiritual life. Early Theravada Buddhism thereby became a religion of specialists. Nevertheless, Buddhism fundamentally changed the terms of religious debate.

The argument so far has been that Brahmanical religious practices failed to keep pace with new needs created by a growing complexity of the social order, and that a religious challenge to their position resulted. However, this was not the only challenged that faced the Brahmans' claim to speak for the social order as a whole. The Nanda rulers (354–324 BC), originating in Magadha, united India under a single imperial umbrella for the first time, apparently as the result of the use of larger armies than had hitherto been traditional. Their policy was successfully completed by the Mauryan dynasty (321–185 BC), and in particular by the Emperor Asoka (272–231 BC). We do not know much about the actual political capacities of the empire, but should, for general historical sociological reasons, be suspicious of some of the claims of power made in imperial documents; they are ideology rather than sociology. Nevertheless, what is noticeable about the attempt to create an empire is how similar the measures taken were to those achieved in China and Rome. The state sought to standardise weights and measures and to encourage agricultural advance. A system of taxation was created, based upon an administrative division of the empire, and officials were paid in money rather than in kind. The *Arthashastra*, a handbook for the prince often compared with Machiavelli's famous treatise, was probably written sometime during the imperial period, perhaps by Kautilya, the chief adviser of the first Mauryan emperor. It demonstrates a significant sophistication about political power and the espionage system it describes is evidence of the attempt on the part of the state to control society. Further, considerable efforts were made to try and produce an ethic suited to the empire as a whole. Asoka introduced and generalised the

---

13 M. Carrithers, *The Buddha*, Oxford University Press, Oxford, 1983, pp. 16–17.

idea of *Dhamma*. This was not at all like the Brahmanical view of *Dhamma* which had insisted that one's duties were to the fulfilment of one's position inside the religiously defined and controlled social order. *Dhamma* did not stress religious observance at all and instead actively encouraged an attitude of tolerance towards all religious practices. Such tolerance is characteristic of pre-industrial empires, unable to police the beliefs of their people. Crucially, *Dhamma* stressed, as had Confucianism, social responsibility, service to the state and the virtues of the contemplative life. It also emphasised that the emperor was the father of his people and sought their welfare. In the words of one of Asoka's edicts:

On the roads I have had banyan trees planted, which will give shade to beasts and men. I have had mango groves planted and I have had wells dug and rest houses built every nine miles . . . And I have had many watering places made everywhere for the use of beasts and men. But this benefit is important, and indeed the world has enjoyed attention in many ways from former kings as well as from me. But I have done these things in order that my people might conform to *Dhamma*.[11]

Asoka established officers of *Dhamma*, and it is not too fanciful to see in this the beginnings of the creation of a mandarin-type bureaucracy.

What does all this amount to? the imperial drive tried to create loyalty to the emperor rather than to the social order. It sought to undo that secularisation of power which Dumont considered characteristic of the Vedic system. Power and hierarchy were to be reconciled and the emperor, as the fount of law, was to become leader of the community. It is at this point that an elective affinity was established between the political and the religious threats to Brahmanical control. Asoka became a Buddhist, and it seems likely, we can say no more, that he was attracted by the universalism of a salvationist religion which could combine happily with the universal political order of the empire. He favoured Buddhism materially, and in his edicts poured scorn on useless sacrifices and ceremonies that made up the daily bread of the lesser Brahmans. Importantly, Buddhism, greedy for land, attacked kinship ties, which prevented free donation of land. In the long run this would have helped, as it was to in Europe,[15] the creation of a dynamic economy and a strong state. In principle the situation was flexible enough to allow one of two developments. On the one hand, something like the Chinese imperial system might have emerged, that is Buddhism might have found a way to ally itself with or even endorse an imperial ethic for a bureaucratic elite.

14 Cited in Thapar, *A History of India*, p. 88.
15 As already noted, the impact of kinship is discussed systematically in ch. 5.

Alternatively, Buddhism might have remained a more private source of salvation while nevertheless allowing, perhaps even justifying, universal empire, as did Greek Christendom.

The elective affinity between Buddhism and empire never fully gelled sufficiently to create a stable imperial system. The most obvious reason for this lies in the short duration of the Mauryan empire. The Mauryans made significant mistakes. Insufficient attention was paid to binding the literate elite to the imperial order by the creation of an examination system with a developed system of grades and rankings. The loyalty that Asoka demanded was personal rather than institutional, to him rather than to the state as such. Probably the empire overtaxed itself. There are records of economic hardship, evidence of the debasement of coinage and of the abandonment of cities, and this was all probably occasioned by a top-heavy imperial/military structure. There may be something more fundamental at work as well. India divides ecologically into North and South, and there is dense jungle between these regions; in addition riverine transportation is much less effective in India than in China. All this has made it hard to unite India and helps account for unity being established only three times in the history of this civilisation.

If these answers are obvious and striking they remain superficial. They fail to explain why at some later date the creation of a universal empire, backed by Buddhism, was not attempted and achieved. Why was there no restoration or recreation of something like the Mauryan empire? My answer to this question follows in the next section, but it can be highlighted immediately: the Brahmans responded vigorously and immediately to the Buddhist/imperial challenge, and turned earlier Vedic claims to power into a firm social reality, thus achieving, in vastly different form, many traditional imperial ambitions. Before characterising and explaining this achievement, it is important to reflect upon the nature of the argument made to this point, and to say rather more about Buddhism; this can best be done in the light of a celebrated essay by Louis Dumont on 'World Renunciation in Indian Religions'.

Buddhism, in Dumont's eyes, is but an example of the turn to renunciation within Indian religion as a whole:

... we can see that the developments of renunciation, with all their richness, are contained after all within narrow limits which they were unable to go beyond. Of the success of renunciation, in the place asssigned to it by society, Buddhism is a witness. Situated outside the world but linked to it, the renouncer is impotent against it; if he ventures in that direction his ideas become ephemeral. On the contrary, there is a positive dialectic between his 'discipline' and the religion of the world.[16]

16 Dumont, *Religion/Politics and History in India*, p. 59.

The argument of the French Indologist is that the terms of Buddhism were set by the Vedic tradition, that it was fundamentally a reaction to that tradition and remains best understood within it. The organisation of social life by the Brahmans drove those searching for salvation into other-worldly avenues. The individual could seek salvation in Indian life but only by retreating from the world. The implication of this is clear: it is that Buddhism, being but a movement within a larger whole, never had a significant chance of changing the terms of Indian civilisation, either by itself or in combination with a secular empire. This is an important argument which deserves attention; it forces further reflection upon the character of Buddhism.

Rather mundane arguments ignored by Dumont and alien to the spirit of his general sociology go a long way to explaining the failure of Buddhism to triumph in India. Buddhism, unlike Confucianism in China, grew up amid its rivals, and had that much more difficulty in dominating them; even so it was the main religion of India for several centuries and its hold might never have been broken but for the destruction wreaked upon its monasteries by invading Muslims.[17] Perhaps more importantly, there are at least two ways in which Buddhism did *not* neatly fit with the rule of emperors and kings who with time consequently became suspicious of the movement that they had helped to spread. Firstly, Buddhism in certain ways was not sympathetic to the pretensions of rulers. Their order of monasteries was democratic in tone and this attitude comes across in early Buddhist discourses on kingship: 'The chief message is that kings, no less than anyone else, are subject to the moral order, to considerations of what is morally and socially skilful. When there came to be Buddhist kings these discourses were taken at face value to construct a specifically Buddhist theory of ethical kingship.'[18] In contrast to this the Vedic tradition, especially when it attained its classical form, gave a prominent, indeed a sacred place to kings, even though it did regard them only as the servants of the social order. Secondly, rulers in India may well have become suspicious of Buddhism's relation to the political realm for altogether more material reasons. In time the Brahman may have been welcomed:

... as a counterpoise and a safeguard. The Buddhist monasteries were incessantly enriched by pious donations, and, thanks to their longevity, stability and organisation were powerful institutions, the lords of souls and of vast estates. They checkmated temporal authority and even threatened to destroy it. The Brahman gave it less to fear: he had taken no vow and was bound by no contract; he was free, independent and alone; he could move with the times and he

17 Where there were not invasions, notably in Nepal, Buddhism continued to flourish.
18 Carrithers, *The Buddha*, pp. 96–7.

founded no order; he did not live in a community . . . He did not dream of human brotherhood or universal salvation; he aimed only at his own supremacy, and, as the basis for it the caste system; he carried his institutions, beliefs and laws within himself . . .[19]

These points do not detract from the undoubted fact that a further reason for the failure of Buddhism to triumph over its rivals lay in its total concentration on salvation. It is useful to distinguish two elements to the appeal of religion. On the one hand there is the soteriological concern with salvation, upon which Max Weber concentrated most, but not all, of his attention; on the other hand stand the regulations and practices of daily communal life which Emile Durkheim understood so well. The Judaeo-Christian tradition has fulfilled the requirements of both; in India they are compartmentalized. Buddhism simply turned its back on the Durkheimian aspect of religion: thus it offered no real guidance, until the modern period, for as basic a social need as the regulation of marriage! Buddhism chose to become an anti-society rather than to regulate social relationships. This attitude left the Brahmans sufficient room with which to counterattack in the long run. Does admitting all this entail acceptance of Dumont's contention that Buddhism had no real chance to change the fundamental character of Indian civilisation? Were the commanding heights of the ideology captured before the Mauryans, and was Indian history but a working out of the logic enshrined at that time? There is much to be said for scepticism about this general position. What is striking about early Indian history is the sense of openness, the feeling that the civilisation had yet to gell and could have gone different ways. It *is* possible that Indian Buddhism could have developed, or at least allowed, imperial politics more thoroughly as it did in China. A failure of imagination is at work here rather than the unfolding of some inevitable logic of a pre-established position. Certainly Buddhism showed itself capable of running a polity in Tibet. Nevertheless, lack of interest in organising social life is not surprising given the insistence that life is pain, fit only to be escaped – surely the most pessimistic doctrine propounded by any organised belief-system. *Even so, its concern with soteriology had a fundamental impact on Brahmanism*. It is wrong to imagine that the terms of Indian civilisation were set early on since it was only as the result of an historical process that Brahmanism managed to make good its control of a social order. Where the Buddhist challenge was not very great, as in Ceylon, caste remained much weaker than it became in India. The work of Dumont lacks a sense of history and presents closure on the pattern of Indian civilisation much too early. It is now time to

19 S. Lévi, *Le Népal*, Ernest Leroux, Paris, 1905, vol. I, p. 30. David Gellner drew my attention to this argument and the translation is his.

turn to the manner in which closure was eventually achieved; and the reader can be warned immediately that this achievement depended much more upon substantive social services provided by Brahmans than it did, as Dumont suggests, upon the inner logic of Indian ideas.

The Classical Pattern of Hindu India

The general argument can be advanced speedily by means of a further variation on the initial model of the agro-literate polity. This model sins against caste ideology by placing the political realm above religious order. If we bear this reservation in mind, the model remains useful heuristically in pointing to the key features of Indian civilisation: the 'free-floating' quality of politics, the horizontal and locally penetrative power of Brahmans, and the ability of the social order to work without benefit of proper state regulation. This stability and resilience of the

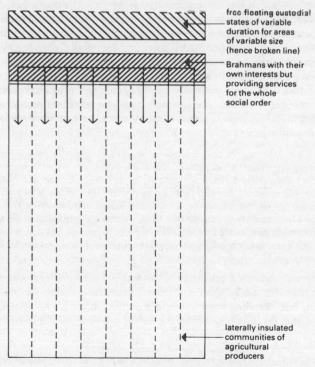

free floating custodial states of variable duration for areas of variable size (hence broken line)

Brahmans with their own interests but providing services for the whole social order

laterally insulated communities of agricultural producers

Model 3: The land of the Brahmans

social order, even in the face of foreign conquest, is very remarkable. This pattern represents, and is probably only made possible by, a *withdrawal* from political power. The Brahman did not support the political order as did the Confucian mandarins, nor did he oppose it as did the Islamic ulama, and neither did he allow, even encourage, the creation of a multipolar state system in the manner of the Christian church in Latin Christendom. This withdrawal is the Indian uniqueness. How was it possible?

Brahmanism responded with great intelligence to the soteriological challenge represented by Buddhism, by the *Upanishads* and by Jainism. It proved capable of integrating within the bounds of Hinduism – the name given to the neo-Brahmanical religious world that was created in response to these challenges – movements which had started out avowedly critical of the Vedic tradition as a whole. Thus one of the *Upanishads*, the celebrated *Bhagavad Gita*, which was openly hostile to Brahmanism,[20] gave rise to its own gnostic-type sect within the classical Hindu system. The way in which this integration was achieved was remarkable. Neo-Brahmanism put its religious house in order by arranging the gods in some sort of monotheistic system. This monotheism was not *jealous*, as are those of Christianity and Islam. The whole stress of neo-Brahmanism was on inclusion rather than on exclusion, and this was justified on the ground that there are many ways to God, and that nobody should judge between these routes. This spirit of relativism was very neatly caught by François Bernier, the seventeeth-century French traveller to India whose *Voyages* did much to fix the European picture of the subcontinent:

When I told them that in cold countries it would be impossible to observe their law during the winter, which showed that it was nothing but a pure invention of men, they gave me this rather amusing reply: that they were not claiming that their law was universal, but that God had made it for them alone, which was why they could not receive a foreigner into their religion; that moreover, they were not least claiming that our religion was false, but that it might be good for us and that God might have made several different paths to heaven; but they would not agree that ours was general for the whole world, theirs could be but fable and pure invention.[21]

The neo-Brahmanical orthodoxy thus came to find a place for a series of cults, most obviously those concerned with the worship of Siva and Vishnu, but including more esoteric groups such as the worshippers of snakes and the phallus, within the broad purview of Hinduism. The

20 P. Bannerjee, *Early Indian Religions*, Vikas, Bombay, 1971.

21 His comment is cited by Dumont, *Homo Hierarchus*, p. 368. David Gellner drew it to my attention.

secret of this religion lies in its capacity to tolerate differences rather than in any desire or ability to organise or police belief.

One final point about this extraordinary situation is important. A Greek traveller in the Mauryan era, Megasthenes, reported on the characteristic style of life which Brahmans were then adopting. For the first 37 years of his life, the Brahman was supposed to be ascetic, residing first with his teachers and then living as a public preacher. After this it was considered normal to take wives and have children, and to provide services for the local community. At the end of his life, the Brahman was supposed to renounce the world in order to free himself for the next life. It is this latter stage which is of particular interest. This final renunciation was often not made, but its presence in Brahmanical theory shows the brilliant inventiveness of neo-Brahmanism when faced with attitudes of renunciation. As such attitudes were doctrinal rather than organisational, they could easily be accommodated by the theory of classical Hinduism.

The greatest achievement of neo-Brahmanism lay, however, in its capacity to organise social relationships. The Brahmans extended and regularised the services they performed on every occasion of the life cycle and their presence became firmly anchored in the locality. Increasingly, Brahmans made good their claim to knowledge by pioneering work in mathematics and astronomy, and the mark they left in this respect is the legacy of 'Arabic' numerals that they pioneered. The *Laws of Manu*, finally codified in the early Christian era, demonstrate that the Brahmans provided *law*, perhaps the most crucial of all social services. These laws sought to organise every aspect of social life; distinctions were drawn at every point between different caste obligations and privileges, whilst the very minutiae of social life, including, as the *Kama Sutra* demonstrates, the sexual act itself, became the subject of regulation. The Brahman was sometimes the last resort in terms of conflict between and within castes. However, the great effectiveness of the system lay ultimately in the fact that coercion was managed by the castes themselves. The multiplication of castes prevented the emergence of many situations otherwise likely to have led to serious, but perhaps potentially energising, disagreements. The outcome of this ability to organise society is clear:

This was an easy society to rule. All that a conqueror had to do was to establish his rule in the capital city and go on ruling as those before him had done. No new governmental machinery needed to be set up in such a society. This society had brought to near perfection a mode of self-government which needed the least supervision from a central power. The caste had a cell-like structure.[22]

One development that helps us to understand the situation more thoroughly is that of land grants to Brahmans. R.S. Sharma's *Indian*

22 Karve, *Hindu Society*, p. 106.

Feudalism: c. 300–1200 lists 'grants' of extraordinary size. The seventh-century ruler of the North, Harsa, gave to Brahmans as much land as could be ploughed by 1,000 ploughs (roughly 10,000 acres) on the eve of setting out on a military expedition, and on one occasion a ruler gave a thousand villages in a single grant.[23] Furthermore, such 'grants' often included the permanent transfer of juridical and administrative responsibilities. Perhaps Sharma takes the documents he cites too much at face value. Rulers probably never truly controlled much of the land they supposedly 'granted'; they may merely have been recognising the situation already achieved on the ground.[24] But what sort of 'return' did rulers feel they were getting for their 'gifts'? In those cases where virgin land was granted, Brahmans were able to operate a policy of economic development. They taught the use of the deep plough, and imparted knowledge about the appropriate seasons in which to plant various crops. Further, they brought with them the caste system, and their ability to create new sub-castes proved capable of integrating new peoples into a single social order. More generally, however, the Brahman-dominated social order did the work of an empire not just in opening up new lands but in *the* most fundamental way of all: it brought peace and social order. Its achievements were real and significant, and it is not surprising that the place of the Brahman in Indian civilisation came to stand so high.

The character of the argument being made can be highlighted by means of a short comment upon traditional approaches to understanding ideology in history. Idealist views tend to stress the autonomous impact of ideas, and thereby interest themselves in Weberist questions as to the unfolding logic of a particular doctrinal code. This position is brilliantly upheld in Indology by Louis Dumont. We need to be very suspicious of this approach. The mere presence of a particular Brahmanical view of the world in the Vedic period did not in itself guarantee Brahmanical power and social control. What matters is the ability to organise social relationships, and this was something that the Brahmans only achieved as the result of an historical process by means of which they overcame Buddhism, their great rival. Their triumph was justified. They provided not just soteriological subtleties, but concrete social services without which social relationships could not have continued.

It is important to highlight once more how this was possible, and we can do this by criticising the standard notion, enshrined as wisdom by both Marx and Gandhi, according to which Indian civilisation is but a collection of villages. That this is not true can be instantly appreciated once we realise that architectural, ritual and musical styles are shared

23 Calcutta University Press, Calcutta, 1965, p. 43.

24 B. Stein, 'The state and the agrarian order', in his (ed.) *Essays on South India*, Vikas, New Delhi, 1976, p. 88.

throughout the subcontinent. This society was essentially a cultural phenomenon made possible by the ability of Brahmans to communicate with each other over space. Common training was received in the great centres of learning. The key consideration attested to by modern social anthropology[25] is that the Brahman has geographical mobility; in contrast most Indians are stuck inside a particular locality. It is true of course that rulers and warriors shared a translocal identity and some means of social organisation as well, but they were not able to hold the larger society together, as will be stressed again in a moment. The whole point at issue can be made in a different form by recalling the work of Emile Durkheim. My general approach has been to stress, in the spirit of the French sociologist, the services provided to a community by its intellectuals, and this has placed me at some distance from Weberist approaches. But Durkheim held a passive view of belief in society, seeing it, as did Marx, as a reflection of more basic social processes. This is wrong. When intellectuals can organise a geographical area, they can create a sense of society. In China the largest area of integration was that achieved by military means, but in India (and in Islam and in Latin Christendom) ideological power reached further than any other power source, and provided a sense of identity. The Brahmans staked a claim to the leadership of society early on, perhaps because of their ability to capture the ethnic heritage of the Aryans, and they cemented this claim through the historical processes described.[26]

It should be clear, but it is perhaps worth emphasising, that the position being endorsed is a type of organisational materialism. This is *not* a crude materialism, present at crucial moments in Max Weber's *Religion of India*, in which caste is seen merely as a particularly effective means to create 'false consciousness', and thereby to legitimate the exploitation by the upper castes of a dependent population. The central reason such crude materialism fails is that it does not pay sufficient attention to the services and achievements of the Brahmans, to the fact that they were an historic success -- even if, as will be argued, there was a considerable price tag to the social order they created. More importantly, this form of the social order matters, as it did in China, especially because it affected economic relationships. The Brahman did not simply legitimise exploitation by the rich and powerful. To the contrary, the form of organisation distanced itself from both wealth and power. This withdrawal affected political life very markedly, and it is to this question that we can now turn.

25 E.J. Miller, 'Caste and territory in Malabar', *American Anthropologist*, vol. 56, 1954.
26 Michael Mann first drew my attention to the importance of Durkheim in understanding belief systems. The notion of belief as 'creating' a society, used in later chapters, is his. For a full discussion, see Mann, *Sources of Social Power*, vol. 1, ch. 1.

Kings are recognised as important actors in neo-Brahmanical theory, and this is not essentially out of line with the Vedic tradition. However, they are recognised as individuals rather than as representatives of longer-lasting states, and few expectations are held of them. In particular, they are seen warring with each other, and this is taken to be natural, and is indeed expected. There is no conception of kings as providers of services for the society. Their duty in life is simply to fight, and they have no other secular duty than that of protecting the social order. This is a *custodial* state.

The result of the king having rather little to organise meant that politics had very shallow roots in society. Kings could not gain regular taxation. Instead they were offered tribute on an irregular basis, and the amounts of this varied in large part according to the degree of charisma with which the Brahmans endowed them.[27] Clifford Geertz's recent study of the Balinese state captures something of the character of the Indian custodial state in general. The state organised virtually nothing, certainly not irrigation or communal matters, and was merely a place where court rituals were endlessly performed.

The state cult was not a cult of the state. It was an agreement, made over and over again in the insistent vocabulary of ritual, that worldly status has a cosmic base, that hierarchy is the governing principle of the universe, and that the arrangements of human life are but approximations, more close or less, to those of the divine . . . Court ceremonialism was the driving force of court politics; and mass ritual was not a device to shore up the state, but rather the state, even in its final gasp, was a device for the enactment of mass ritual. Power served pomp, not pomp power.[28]

The irrelevance of political power is neatly caught in those accounts of kingly wars which picture peasants continuing to plough in the sight of the battlefield! The same point is conveyed much more strongly by the constant instability of political rule in traditional India, a situation which makes that account of politics hard for those educated in Western history to follow. In fact, India did not have a political *history* in the Western sense. There was much sound and fury but it really did signify nothing. It led to no long-term developments, no real social evolution.

To this point my argument has been that social identity was provided by a religiously sanctioned order, and that politics, bereft of much opportunity to organise social life, had such shallow roots that it was fundamentally unstable. Perhaps there is more to it than this. On some occasions Brahmans did not withdraw from political power but may have rather actively opposed its attempts to create a new form of society.

27 Stein, 'The state and the agrarian order', passim.
28 C. Geertz, *Negara*, Princeton University Press, Princeton, 1980, pp. 102 and 13.

Something like this was true of Brahmanical hostility to the Mauryan imperial drive, and it may also explain why a multipolar system, that is a set of stable states in constant competition with each other, did not develop in the Indian sphere.

The functioning of the international system, and the degree of solidarity within it, thus depended to a considerable degree upon the Brahmans. But we must note this: within the caste system the Brahmans had a position superior to the warriors from whom most of the kings were recruited. A consolidation of kingly power, possible through international contacts and collaboration – a process that occurred in other international systems – would have tended to reduce the standing of the highest caste. It may well be that it is because of the Brahmans' functions in the field of diplomacy, culture and communications that the international solidarity of the Hindu world remained at a low level.[29]

This argument results from a consideration of the *Arthashastra* of Kautilya, but the argument may well have larger validity. Given the poor state of Indian historiography, it is quite likely that we will never be in a position to be entirely sure.

All that has been said about the relationship of religious to political power can be summarised by saying that the Brahman blocked the emergence of powerful polities, by withdrawal from political power. But the argument cannot be left here. It gives the impression that the Brahman was capable of controlling everything that happened, and tends to play down the very considerable degree of co-operation between ruler and priest which often characterised Hindu civilisation. There are, however systematic reasons why even the strictest co-operation between the two forces was unlikely to lead to a new social system.

... if one seeks to understand Hinduism in relationship to the political system, that is, as an aspect of ideology, then it must be recognised that it often provided for considerable instability. The power of political legitimation was vested with local Brahmans responsible to no superiors, and the religion was characterised by a basic discontinuity between relatively high caste (Brahman and non-Brahman) participants in Vedic sect activities and the mass of Hindus involved in highly localised, non-Vedic, folk religious affiliations. This discontinuity in Hinduism considered as a morally binding force – the gulf between the high and the low – is a factor which historians have neglected. The other side of the coin of ritual exclusiveness is a discontinuous moral order.[30]

The price of the relativism of Hindu religion was, in other words, that a single community of equal individuals was not even aimed at; this made the social material of Indian civilisation that much less pliable for the construction of powerful states. This is the result of the *weakness* rather

29 G. Modelski, 'Kautilya', *American Political Science Review*, vol. 58, 1964, p. 557.
30 Stein, 'The state and the agrarian order', p. 86.

than the strength of classical Hinduism. There is, as was demonstrated in the discussion of China, no general contradiction between strong arbitrary powers and weak infrastructural ones; the two tend to go together. For all the services that the Brahmans provided, they were not 'powerful' enough to react to Buddhism by organising society in terms of any jealous monotheism of their own. Their power was negative, being based on endorsement of what was already in place rather than creation of something altogether new. Nevertheless this form of triumph was not without consequences for economic relationships.

Economic Stagnation

Travellers to India were very impressed with its riches. This should not make us conclude that this civilisation was thereby more advanced than that of Latin Christendom, despite the poverty of the latter during its early mediaeval period. What matters in comparative perspective is whether a civilisation has or does not have a set of blockages that prevent movement to some higher level. The Chinese empire certainly suffered from internal blockages, and the argument now to be made is that Hindu civilisation suffered similarly and as much from such blockages. Two of these are distinguished; each results from the caste system. But one warning must be reiterated: the relative absence of documents in India means that the account offered must necessarily be uncertain.

In the first place, caste proved debilitating to economic life because of its hierarchical conception of social life. Trade expanded during the Gupta period, but so too did caste regulations, and these made its salience more limited.

There appears to have been a lively interest in navigation and trade at this time in India. Yet the law-makers were declaring it a great sin for a Hindu to travel by sea, to cross the black waters, and this may have reduced Indian participation in maritime trade. Ritual purity was becoming an obsession with both brahmans and the upper castes. They objected to travelling to distant lands because it meant contamination with the *mlechchha* (impure) and non-caste people. It was also difficult to observe caste rules when abroad. The ban had the additional indirect advantage for the brahman that it curbed the economic power of the trading community.[31]

This sort of ban nearly prevented the young Gandhi, whose family *came from* a merchant caste, from coming to England at all! A further disadvantage was that the caste organisation of economic life did not allow for a flexible division of labour:

31 Thapar, *A History of India*, p. 150.

It is a possible further disadvantage of the caste system economically that it probably discourages organisation from above by the entrepreneur, no less than it forestalls ambition on the part of the workman. Durkheim has suggested that the function of the division of labour is to give the individual more freedom by substituting an organic for a rigidly mechanical economy, but the organic structure created by the caste system would seem to have provided for the division of labour on a plan ingeniously calculated to avoid giving just that freedom; for occupation is determined by status instead of contract . . . A system of this kind must operate to stifle progress in economic life, giving it an almost paralysing stability.[32]

This divisiveness of caste played a deleterious role as far as the advance of knowledge was concerned. The great advances made by the Brahmans in mathematics and astronomy were treated as their secret knowledge; obstacles were placed in the way of the diffusion of knowledge. The land grants given to Brahmans, furthermore, witness a restriction of the activities of guilds, which never regained the position of eminence they had enjoyed in pre-Mauryan times, to their immediate localities; this blocked freedom of competition.[33] Only the Brahman had horizontal powers of communication, and in this capacity to outflank the rest of society lay his power. In summary, it is worth recording the comments of an economic historian contemplating the various rigidities of caste:

Consider the individual and social consequences of such prohibitions as that an untouchable might not build himself a brick house. There were endless, rigid restrictions of that sort, applying caste by caste and not simply to the worst-off at the untouchable bottom of the heap. The result of this immensely complicated anthropological pattern was to push the living-standards of the lowest caste to a level that presumably reduced the capacity to work; allocate functions on a basis of heredity, not aptitude; instil ritualistic attitudes to work; restrict the market through caste-defined sumptuary rules; and divide the community and reduce the chances of mutual evasion or resistance to exploitation by affording the Brahmans a privileged position within each village. The caste system might be said to have provided job security and a form of insurance, but the price was high. Tensions in society may be reduced by labelling whole categories of people, in the view of other categories, unpersons. Maybe this is even adaptive in the short run. But accepted for ever, this inserting of an artificial 'individual distance' between persons suppressed social interaction and competition that in the European case, at any rate, has proved energising.[34]

The view contained in the last sentence deserves systematic consideration.

32 Hutton, *Caste in India*, pp. 123-4.
33 Sharma, *Indian Feudalism: c. 300–1200*, p. 71.
34 E.L. Jones, *The European Miracle*, Cambridge University Press, Cambridge, 1981, p. 193.

Islam, Buddhism and Christianity are alike in creating societies and in holding them together without the benefit of state regulation over long and crucial periods. In each civilisation culture has been stronger than politics. In addition, all three religions share some ability to penetrate into their society. Hinduism organised more social relationships by withdrawing from power than could Islam and Christianity, despite their greater monotheistic drive, since they were irremediably involved in politics. There is, however a great difference between Hinduism and these other two world religions. The very notion of society that we possess implicitly contains conceptions of universality and reciprocity. The sense of community created by Islam and Christianity was one in which all human beings could participate. A fundamental equality was written into the society by the promise of salvation held out to everyone. Indian society was not universalist in this sense. It had no sense of brotherhood. Its society in our eyes is a sort of anti-society, a community based on division rather than the possibility of shared experience. It seems very likely that this division must have had adverse effects upon economic relationships in Indian life. Individuals at the bottom of society could not have been encouraged by a world view which scarcely took them seriously. More importantly, it seems likely that social interaction was curtailed by this peculiar form. In Islam and Christianity, the sharing of a single set of norms over space made market contact intensive and general. In contrast, an Indian travelling overseas would not be able to recognise and co-operate with everyone who owed some cultural allegiance to the subcontinent. Co-operation must have been affected by caste.

It is important not to overgeneralise this first aspect of caste. There *was* more flexibility to the system than is often allowed. Whole sub-castes could rise within the caste hierarchy, and so too could individuals, although that was probably rather more difficult. Similarly, there was much more co-operation between the castes, albeit not with the untouchables, than any simple model would suggest. All this means that the lack of universalism was by no means a complete blockage, although a considerable amount of time and energy was certainly wasted by these hierarchical aspects of caste. However, this partial blockage combined with the second impediment to economic life for which caste must be held responsible.

Brahmanical organisation of social life by means of caste created a form of politics that proved inimical to economic life in Indian civilisation. Polities were extremely unstable. They could sink no roots into society because the obvious tasks of social organisation were undertaken by Brahmans. Loyalty was given to kings as individuals, and not to the state as a continuing unit seen as functionally necessary for the running of society. Instability made for predatory rule. The hoarding of money, of course disastrous from the point of view of growth in economic relationships, became in consequence a characteristic of Indian civilisation. The most striking aspect of the great wealth of Hindu civilisation is the extreme splendour of its temples. There seems to be a simple explanation for the concentration of wealth in this particular form. Kings had power for such a short period that they simply took what they could: as the state was not long lasting, there could be no conception of nurturing merchant activities with a view to long-term tax revenue. Grants to temples could not be touched by kings, and they got some protection, necessarily limited to entrepreneurial activities.[35] It is relevant to note here that land grants, if they were indeed such, were made at times to merchants as well as to Brahmans. This was perhaps occasioned by the desire to keep money out of the hands of the state. It proved an obstacle to capitalist advance. 'But since they were entrusted with the management of villages they could not give sole attention to their trade and commerce. These charters therefore show the feudalisation of merchants by turning them into some kind of landed intermediaries.'[36] And what was true of merchants came to be true of landlords as well. Even when states paid for services in land rather than money this did not mean that any security of tenure had been achieved. When states changed hands, so too could land ownership. The same was of course true of tax-farming rights. This discouraged investment in the land which was to be exploited as much as possible whilst it was possessed. Certainly the peasants had no reason to invest, nor did they have the chance of escaping to the city, as did their European counterparts.[37]

All these points have concerned the arbitrariness of unstable polities. Predatory rule resulted from the state being merely the custodian of the social order, and this meant interference with economic relationships. The economy, in other words, had no autonomy of its own. This end result is similar to that of China, although interference there was bureaucratic in character and from a capstone state co-existent with the whole culture, rather than being predatory in type and from transient polities within a larger Hindu culture. The mechanism was different but the result was rather similar. Furthermore, there is complete similarity in

35 B. Stein, 'The economic function of a medieval south Indian temple', *Journal of Asian Studies*, vol. 19, 1960.

36 Sharma, *Indian Feudalism: c. 300–1200*, p. 71.

37 This picture of Indian landholding and patterns after the arrival of Islam is suggested by T. Raychaudhuri and I. Habib (eds), *The Cambridge Economic History of India*, vol. I, *c. 1200–c. 1750*, Cambridge University Press, Cambridge, 1982, *passim*, but especially chs 3,4 and 7. Too little is known about landholding patterns before 1200, as about most matters economic and otherwise, to offer any firm generalisations.

the second way in which politics proved an obstacle to economic advance. We have seen that it is no contradiction to say that an arbitrary polity is based on a weak capacity to penetrate and to provide infrastructural services for a society. This weakness was even more striking in India than in China. The mandarin dispensed certain knowledge and occasionally encouraged agricultural advance. These functions in India were not performed by state servants, but by Brahmans. The state floated above society, and provided none of those services – law, peace, universalism – that might have encouraged the creation of economic advance. This point can be highlighted in a most dramatic way. It proved impossible to protect the North-West Frontier, even though a Great Wall there would have been extremely effective; India suffered in consequence a whole series of invasions, some of them hugely destructive. The invaders *were* absorbed by the sponge-like character of the social order, but the cost of unstable politics remained very high. The Muslim invasions did not disturb the power of the Brahmans. Somewhat to the contrary, these invasions decimated Buddhist monasteries, and thereby finally destroyed the power of the great rival to Brahmanical hegemony.

The invaders eventually *united* India in the Muhgal empire, but failed to destroy caste; they reinforced it. The state continued as a result to have very weak roots in society. This is one reason (another is noted in the next chapter) why it was not long lasting; it was not, in the last analysis, a significant exception to the transitory nature of political rule in Indian civilisation. The interference of the state with the economy remained predatory rather than becoming akin to the bureaucratic variety of imperial China.

Unbridled oppression impoverished the peasants and led to financial ruin for the state . . . according to the evidence of travellers and merchants of many nationalities, the Mughal empire of the seventeenth century was on about the level of Persia or Japan, though well above the appalling straits to which Turkish rule had brought the Ottoman dominions or the situation in some poverty-stricken parts of south-east Asia . . . at its peak, income *per capita* was equivalent to that in Elizabethan England. By the mid-eighteenth century India's *per capita* income had fallen and may have been only two-thirds that of England. Life expectancy was lower than in Europe and health was poorer, because of a worse diet, debilitating climate, and a disease environment of tropical as well as temperate zone pestilences. Educational provision was not good and the content resembled that of medieval rather than post-Renaissance Europe.[38]

There was one unique way in which the state interfered with the economy. Muslim traders were taxed at only 2½ per cent whilst their Hindu rivals were taxed at 5 per cent.[39] And even the temporary peace

38 Jones, *The European Miracle*, p. 198.
39 T. Raychaudhuri, 'The state and the economy', *The Cambridge Economic History of India*, vol. I, p. 188.

that empire brought did not encourage secure tenure and thereby investment in land.[40] For the Mughals took very seriously the threat of feudalistic tendencies, and managed to make land revert to the state on the death of any particular landlord. This encouraged the bizarre extravagance of the aristocracy of the time. Consumption rather than production was encouraged. Political security came before economic advancement.

Conclusions

Indian civilisation was held together by Hindu culture, the strength of which derived from the Brahmans' capacity, achieved through historical struggle, to organise much of social life. Each world civilisation has its uniqueness, but this particular civilisation cannot help but seem peculiar to Western eyes. The reason for this is obvious and well known. The 'community' created by the Brahmans was based on division and hierarchy. Such a system did not allow for the autonomous emergence of any economic dynamism of a capitalist kind. It is likely that the hierarchical effect of caste was to diminish the social participation ratio, and thereby to block economic interchanges. Equally important, however, was the instability of political rule that resulted from Brahman withdrawal from power. This encouraged predatory interference with, and prevented the provision of services for, economic life.

40 Jones, *The European Miracle*, p. 198, and T. Raychaudhuri, 'The state and the economy,' *passim*.

4

Islam and Pastoralism

Islam was the last of the world religions to appear, and in certain senses it may be described as the most advanced of them all.

It is a total and unified way of life, both religious and secular; it is a set of beliefs and a way of worship; it is a vast and integrated system of law; it is a culture and a civilisation; it is an economic system and a way of doing business; it is a *polity* and a method of *governance*; it is a special sort of society and a way of running a family; it prescribes for inheritance and divorce, dress and etiquette, food and personal hygiene. It is a spiritual and human totality, *this*-worldly and *other*-worldly.[1]

Islam is scripturalist, egalitarian and very strictly monotheist. It is also very simple. It stresses the conscience of the individual before God; observation of the Five Pillars (acknowledgement of Allah, daily prayers, pilgrimage, fasting at Ramadan, and alms-giving) makes one a full member of the faith. There are no mysteries needing to be interpreted by a formal ecclesiastical organisation.

Put so simply, qualifications are necessary. The Islamic stress on obedience to God via the Koran did allow for the emergence of specialists in doctrine, the ulama, and this group played a role in politics, law and administration. Moreover, the austerity of the classical Islamic vision came to be softened by the emergence of Sufi mystics who offered both group organisation and the ritualistic aids characteristic of other world religions. Nevertheless, the austerity of the Islamic vision is striking. Importantly, the bearers of that vision in classical Islam were city-based ulama who were themselves generally supportive of economic activity, and whose ideology certainly did not impede such activity. Weber himself did not understand the puritanical character of Islam, and no 'Weberist' view that doctrinal attitudes towards economic activity prevented

1 G.H. Jansen, *Militant Islam*, Pan Books, London, 1979, p. 17.

economic advance in Islam holds water.[2] However, this chapter *does* argue that there is something to the 'Weberist' approach, although it does so by paying attention to the political, rather than to the economic, ethic of this world religion.

In Islam, unlike Christianity, there is no distinction between canon law, and any other type of law, since the spiritual doctrine is its own theory. This political theory is very unlike the statist doctrine of Confucianism. It stands opposed in principle to the mundane practice of politics; it certainly does not lend states support by providing any Caesaropapist doctrine. There is a difference here, however, with classical Hinduism: Islam stands opposed to the mundane exercise of power, but cannot do without it. It opposes the political realm, but cannot withdraw from it and organise society on religious lines as did Hinduism.

The form and character of the argument may now be outlined. The first two sections of the chapter present a model of classical Islam. One crucial element of this model is the Weberist notion that the actual form of doctrine mattered at crucial moments; some of the power of ideology here *does* derive from doctrinal terms, although we must also note the practical social services rendered to the larger society. However, two points of a more structural character limit the range of this 'Weberist' position. Firstly, it will prove possible to explain why the doctrine took the form that it did in the first place. Secondly, it must be firmly stressed that the full model of classical Islam depends upon a combination of an attitude towards politics with a particular productive system, namely that of pastoral nomadism. Once the model is established, we can then explain why classical Islam 'blocked' the emergence of an economic dynamic, broadly capitalist in nature. In a final section, attention is turned to certain Islamic polities, some of which appear to – and one of which does – differ from the model presented.

Monotheism with a Tribal Face

The points already made about the total, political quality of Islam are instantly reinforced by considering the speed with which this was achieved. Muhammad died in the early 630s, having united Arabia during his own lifetime, and tribal conquest continued to spread the civilisation, with campaigns beginning in 630 (Syria), 637 (Iraq), 641

2 This is not to say that Weber did not have interesting things to say about Islamic social structures. For an account of his general position, see B. Turner, *Weber and Islam*, Routledge and Kegan Paul, London, 1974. See also M. Rodinson, *Islam and Capitalism*, Penguin, London, 1974.

(Mesopotamia), 642 (Egypt), 650 (Iran), 698 (Carthage), and 711 (the Indus valley and Spain). We do not need to go to very great lengths to explain such conquests. A religious vision asserting that warfare, the Jihad, was a duty combined with obvious material interests and military capacity to allow for these staggering successes. The allegiance of most Arabian tribes to this vision is equally scarcely surprising considering that its capacity to unite them in a single community, the umma, proved to be so efficacious. Nevertheless problems behind this picture do need to be confronted.

Why was the message of a prophet capable of uniting Arabian tribes at this particular time? The traditional answer to this question has been that of Montgomery Watt, who argued that Arabia suffered from particular problems that Muhammad was able to resolve.[3] His argument runs like this. In Mecca, where Muhammad himself was born, perhaps in 570, the growth of the caravan trade had led to an undermining of the traditions of society. Cohesion had previously been assured on a tribal basis which stressed the obligation of the strong to the weak, but increasing wealth led to greater individual assertiveness and a consequent increase in social stratification. Nevertheless, the weak were not the only source of support for Muhammad; younger sons of well-established families were also among his supporters. However, Muhammad was by no means completely successful in Mecca. His prophecy stressed the obligations of the rich to the poor, even though this was combined with genuine respect for individualism. Further, his insistent monotheism encouraged attacks on the local shrine and this made him unpopular with those who profited from pilgrimages. Hence Muhammad was forced to make his famous journey to Medina where he was confronted with a different set of problems. This tribal oasis was experiencing overpopulation; this exacerbated the blood-feuds between different tribal groups that had followed settled agrarian advance. Naturally Muhammad served as mediator, and was able to turn this role into something more by emphasising the role of the umma, the larger Islamic community, obeisance to which allowed for the resolution of smaller local conflicts. This newfound community then embarked on conquest.

There are considerable difficulties with Watt's position.[4] Meccan trade was not large enough to destabilise traditional kinship relationships (Muhammad was, after all, protected by his family), nor is there any evidence that it was *growing* in the early seventh century. Similarly, the presence of factions in Medina was *normal* and did not represent some

3 M. Watt, *Muhammad: prophet and statesman*, Oxford University Press, Oxford, 1961.

4 For an alternative view, see M. Cook, *Muhammad*, Oxford University Press, Oxford, 1983, and a forthcoming study of Meccan trade by Patricia Crone.

sudden breakdown of kinship ties consequent on the development of agriculture. *Other* developments of the early seventh century are more important. The intrusions of the two empires that surrounded Arabia – Byzantium and Persia – had recently increased: these were exceedingly irritating to the Arabs who were united by strong ties of ethnic identity. These two empires were possessed of monotheistic religions, and it is quite possible that some Arabs felt inferior in the presence of stricter and more respectable belief systems. Certainly Muhammad's message from the start was monotheistic and universal; it stressed the community of all Arabs, probably seen as descendants from Hagar, the son of Abraham's early concubine. This message was poorly received in Mecca, quite probably because its universalism would have seriously disrupted the pilgrimage trade. Muhammad proved capable of uniting different tribes in Medina and turned them into a potent military weapon. Although it is impossible to tell exactly what sort of processes were at work, anthropological sense would suggest that the loyalty of tribes to Islam owed much more to its capacity to create a society than it did to any particular observance of Islamic norms, the details of which were still very fluid.

Nomad conquest does not often prove long lasting. Usually tribal unity collapses, allowing imperial rule to re-emerge, whilst the nomads themselves are absorbed through intermarriage. The nomads who sometimes conquered China and the barbarians who conquered the Roman empire felt inferior before civilisation, especially when that civilisation possessed a universal monotheistic creed, a fact which accounts for the speed of barbarian conversion in the West. These barbarians, in other words, submerged themselves within civilisations. The Islamic conquerors were unable to do so themselves since they brought with them their own monotheistic creed. They possessed force *and* value.[5]

But what were the Arabs to do with their conquered lands? How were they to be held together and ruled? The death of Muhammad left a problem of succession which was to plague Islam. In the first fitnah or civil war, ended by the death of Ali, the cousin of Muhammad, in 661, it is possible to distinguish two sides in an ever-recurring debate. Ali himself claimed leadership on the basis of inherited charisma, and he had on his side soldiers who had become discontented by the inegalitarian manner in which the profits of conquest had been distributed. This Shi'ite party was defeated by those in command of military might who then established the Umayyad caliphate that ruled Syria until 750. The fact that their supporters did not care overmuch about the means of access to political power, thus earning the designation Sunni Muslims,

5 This formula is brilliantly propounded in M. Cook and P. Crone, *Hagarism*, Cambridge University Press, Cambridge, 1977.

did not much help the legitimacy of the Umayyads. The dynasty was able to rule for some time on the basis of traditional kinship cohesion, and when this faded, the Umayyads invented a system of military factions to which the converted, the mawali, attached themselves.

It is very important to stress that such politics were far removed from original Islamic purposes. The Arabs did not 'feel at home' in their conquered lands. They were unable to integrate with the settled population because they were the carriers of their own religious vision. This feeling combined with reasons of military security to account for the fact that the conquerors built their own cities at the edge of the desert; they did not wish to be absorbed by 'civilisation'. Furthermore, the Arabs felt very ill-at-ease with the peasants of the countryside of the Near East who probably remained non-Muslim for two centuries. Their relationship with such people was purely fiscal. Crucially, the tribesmen did not feel very comfortable with the emergence of state structures. They had not bargained for, nor were prepared to accede to, taxation, and they hankered for the simplicity and egalitarianism that had marked the earliest period of Islamic history. It is in these Umayyad years that the experts in the word, the ulama, 'codified' Islam. What was involved in this? Islam had always had a certain austerity to its vision since Muhammad was held to be the seal of the Prophets – that is revelation was held to have come to an end. Flexibility remained in the system, however, as long as the sayings of the Prophet and Islamic law had not been systemised. This was done in these years, and the austerity of the vision was much enhanced by the insistence that the 'gates of interpretation' were now closed, once and forever. It is crucial to remember that the ulama were not integrated into the first caliphate, as might have happened had that caliphate been centred in Iraq: the presence of the old imperial bureaucratic traditions might there have bound the masters of literacy to the political elite. As it was, the codification which they made harked back to a simpler tribal past, a past in which there was little room for the necessities of power.

By the 750s, however, Islam had already acquired its classical shape as an all-embracing holy law characterised by a profound hostility to settled states. The *Shari'a* was created by men who had exchanged a tribal past for a commercial present in the demilitarised cities of Iraq, *outside* imperial Iran and in *opposition* to caliphal Syria. Its political ideal can be seen as the intellectual counterpart to the military faction, that is as the price which the Muslims paid for the continuance of the Umayyad state beyond the point where the tribal ties had disappeared. The *ulamā* . . . found that power had lost its . . . meaning, and . . . tried to rediscover it in the Arabian past . . . they were deeply alienated from the existing regime; and their alienation went into the *Shari'a* they elaborated. Where the generals merely exploited the tribal language of their faction, the *ulamā* defined God's law as *haqq al-'arab*, the law of the Arabs, just as they identified his language as the *lisān al-'arab*, the normative language of the bedouin, the consensus being that where God had not explicitly modified tribal law, he had endorsed it. The result was a tribal vision of sacred politics. The simple state of the prophet and the *shaykhayn*, the first two caliphs in Medina, was held up as the ideal from which the Umayyads had deviated, the accumulation of secular and religious power alike being condemned as a presumptuous encroachment upon the omnipotence of God. Kings were rejected as Pharoahs and priests as golden calfs, while God's community was envisaged as an egalitarian one unencumbered by profane or religious structures of power below the caliph, who himself assigned the duty of minimal government.[6]

Mainstream Islam, in other words, came to have a distrust of the exercise of political power. This distrust of day-to-day power was held in common with Shi'ism, despite the difference between the two traditions as to the right form of accession to power. Certainly, the Shari'a law was neither a Caesaropapist doctrine supporting imperial power nor one, as in Christianity, which said that the purpose of religion was purely spiritual, and that accordingly power relations did not matter and could be left to proceed on their own course. Government thus has very slim roots in society, and stability came to depend upon such solidarity as the rulers of society could themselves achieve, as is true of most conquest societies. As such social solidarity tends to be evanescent, government in classical Islam tended to be highly unstable.

All this can be put in a different form. The content of the codification of Islam, its monotheism with a tribal face, is explained by the ability of the ulama rather than the politicians to capture and to speak for the community. Politics could not be ignored, but the ulama were able to gain a monopoly over the sacred norms of society. And what *was* society? It was a large cultural area within which polities of various sizes came and went, or, more theoretically, it was an area held together by an ideology. Islam, in other words, had considerable extensive powers. Ideology did not 'reflect' more basic social processes, as Durkheim and Marx believed: it *was* society.

Flesh can be put on these generalisations about the instability of politics by considering the fate of the first two caliphates. The Umayyads were increasingly plagued by revolts, and these reflected dilemmas of legitimacy. There was a series of religious revolts, the most significant being a semi-Shi'ite one that considered Abbas had a good charismatic claim to the caliphate. These revolts gained much support from the mawalis whose position remained precarious and marginal. Equally important was the support of Khorasani troops, and their very presence

6 P. Crone, *Slaves on Horses*, Cambridge University Press, Cambridge, 1980, pp. 62-3.

deserves comment. The questionable legitimacy of the Umayyads led them to rely on foreign troops wholly indebted to them. On this occasion, however, the loyalty of the troops to the dynasty proved questionable.

Perhaps the single most impressive modern attempt to understand Islam has been that of Marshall Hodgson's large *The Venture of Islam*,[7] and one hesitates to disagree with this source. However, the basic historical theory of that book, namely that Islam entered a classical imperial phase under the Abbasids followed by a more or less degenerate middle period lacking imperial integration, cannot be allowed to stand. The Abbasid caliphate established in Baghdad in 750 lasted really effectively for only 70 years. In 822 the fourth civil war broke out, and following this different provinces of the empire were virtually auctioned off to local emirs. Sometimes this was merely a recognition of what had already occurred. Spain, for instance, had become politically auto-nomous as early as 757. Thereafter, various parts of the arid zone made attempts at establishing empire – the Fatimads and Mamluks in Egypt, the Buyids and Seljuks in the Iranian heartlands, the Almohads and Almoravids in the Maghreb, the Omayyads in Spain – but none lasted long enough to be called 'imperial'. Politically, classical Islam had a *series* of political centres, some larger than others but all, until the Ottomans, relatively evanescent. Yet even in these circumstances the greater cultu-ral uniformity of Islam was *maintained*, and the reason for this will be noted in the next section.

It is as well to highlight the argument. The key observation has been that classical Islamic doctrine has been suspicious of political power. The vision was certainly crucial, in the traditional Weberist sense, in defin-ing the fate of the Abbasids. This caliphate, and particularly Caliph Al-Mamun in the ninth century, realised that the integration of the elite, the binding of the literate to the political order, would help their cause. They tried to execute this policy with boldness and thoroughness. The ulama turned their backs on the offer. Marshall Hodgson, despite his historical theory, sums up the situation well: 'Whenever a crisis occurred in the courtly order, and new ideas were needed to maintain the absolutism under the particular current conditions, the very right of absolutism to exist was put in question by the presence of the more highly sanctioned alternative tradition of norms.'[8] In this instance, doctrine simply did not allow a thoroughgoing convergence of political and ideological power. The ulama turned down the profitable opportunity of becoming a full-blooded bureaucratic clerkly class because their doctrinal code had set. The codification that had taken place insisted that no further revelation

7 Chicago University Press, Chicago, 1974.
8 *The Venture of Islam*, vol. I, p. 348.

or doctrinal change was possible, and this finality was very hard to escape. Doctrine had an important autonomous social impact. Had the Umayyad dynasty been established in Iraq at the start, at the great price of a probable loss of identity, the intransigence of that doctrine might have been reduced, since the ulama would have been much less independent. We should not forget, however, that the Abbasids certainly suffered as well from material problems – in particular, the loss of the irrigated areas of traditional Mesopotamia due to salinisation, and loss of state revenue consequent on the workings of the iqta landholding system. All the same, the actual content of doctrine played a key role in the fate of the Abbasids.

Thus Hodgson's vision of an early period of Islamic imperial splendour is much exaggerated. And there is no doubt, as Hodgson himself admits, that this ideological legacy played a crucial role in the 'middle periods' of Islam. It will be my contention later in this chapter that even in the period of the gunpowder empires from the fifteenth century, this ideological heritage played a vital, distinctive role in every case but that of the Ottomans.

The Sociology of Ibn Khaldun

The invading Arabs were as scared of losing their ethnic (and religious) identity as in all probability the Aryans had been in early Vedic India. Nevertheless, a caste-type situation did not develop by means of which this identity could be protected. The whole drive of the Islamic conquests ruled out such a solution. These conquests were based on egalitarian military technique and in the name of a doctrine which was similarly egalitarian and deeply opposed to ritual observance. Moreover, the Arabs did not bring any equivalent to the deep plough. The crucial difference however is that the ecology of the Islamic world did not allow religious intellectuals to provide the key services which had cemented Brahmanical power. The ulama could not create peace. For the arid zone is that of pastoral nomads, and their addiction to warfare made it impossible to withdraw from political/military power altogether. One could be suspicious of power but its necessity was beyond question.

There is a long tradition inside modern Islamic studies concerned with the character of the pastoral nomadism of the hills and mountains flanking the Mediterranean. The great sociologist of this world remains the fourteenth-century Muslim Ibn Khaldun, whose *Muqaddimah* is one of the greatest works of philosophic history ever to have been penned.[9]

9 Routledge & Kegan Paul, London, 1978.

Recent scholars indebted to this general vision, and amplifying it at various points, including Robert Montagne and Ernest Gellner.[10] The model they offer us of the society of the arid zone is simple and elegant, but it is not naïve, and it will be shown how Ibn Khaldun himself recognised various special factors that effected its workings. The general argument can be highlighted now: political instability in classical Islam is not just due to the distrust of government already described, but to the *combination* of this attitude with the presence of dissident pastoralists.

The Ibn Khaldunian view of Islamic society describes a *system* in the fullest sense, that is an order with mechanisms capable of leading in a circular manner to full self-regulation. We must break into this circle at some point, however, and perhaps the most apposite place to do so is by considering the character of tribal life amongst the pastoralists, whether they keep sheep or camels.

Life among pastoral nomads has typically taken place without benefit of state regulation, and there are a number of points involved in this fact that need to be untangled. The focus here is not on the typical inability of nomads to create states themselves, nor on such spectacular instances, as in conquest Islam itself and with the Mongols, when they do create states. The point being addressed is that pastoral nomads are not habitually controlled by the states of other people. Why is this? Nomads, unlike peasants tied to the land by irrigation in China or olives in Greece, are mobile and thus supremely difficult to exploit. Further, nomads are, despite differences in the size of their flocks and even the possession of an occasional slave, egalitarian; they are deeply suspicious that power might bring in its tail permanent social stratification. All this is a cause of difficulty for Marxist philosophic historians. Nomads, being property-owners, should possess classes, but somehow they seem not to! Finally, nomads are not 'state material' for an entirely different reason. The absence of state protection encourages a high military participation ratio, and this is added to the already considerable military advantage of great geographical mobility.

Given that tribes are militarily active, surely we should expect continual anarchy and blood-letting? Tribal society invented its own means of providing order even in its stateless condition, and the key to such order lies in *segmentation*. Each tribe has a stucture akin to a family tree, thus allowing for co-operation at very different levels. A whole tribe can unite when it is threatened by a rival tribe, but more usually a particular segment can unite when the threat it faces is merely from a segment of a

10 R. Montagne, *The Berbers*, Cass, London, 1973; E. Gellner, *Muslim Society*, Cambridge University Press, Cambridge, 1981.

similar size. The prevalence of collective oath-swearing serves to remind would-be marauders of the backing that an individual can rely upon, and to that extent acts as a deterrent. If one had to name a single human quality upon which segmentary tribal politics depends it would be that of solidarity. This is apparently well understood by the tribesmen themselves, and from it follows a particular attitude to civilised society.

Nomads are not completely independent. Ibn Khaldun tells us quite specifically that cereals and fruit, together with craft products, are necessary for the existence – or anyway the *comfortable* existence – of nomads. Much of this can be obtained from villages, but it tends to entail city life. For it is in an urban market that these goods can best be exchanged for sheep, and this has the additional benefit of bringing in wealth. However, cities require a government so that market transactions can be reliable and regular, although the control of government is limited to the cities themselves and to their immediate surroundings. The essential contrast, to use a Moroccan expression, is then between the Bled el Makhzen, the area of order, and the Bled el Siba, the area of tribal dissidence. It is important to note that the third party, the peasantry, thin on the ground in North Africa but of great historical importance in Egypt, Iran, Iraq, Syria and Anatolia, plays no active role in this picture. Tribes rather than peasants possess military force.

The most celebrated component of the socioligy of Ibn Khaldun concerns the dynamics rather than the statics of Muslim society. His model describes a social system whose exact boundaries were not static, and which exhibited much noise on the surface, but very little *directional* social change below it. These dynamics of Ibn Khaldunian sociology result from the inability of cities to govern themselves. In European society urban self-government depended upon the ability of cities to raise their own troops or to provide mercenaries who were able to defeat other *organised armies operating within a relatively pacified terrain*. Muslim society in the arid zone was not at all like this. Urban citizens faced a land of dissidence capable of great military surges. Not unnaturally, those who could not protect themselves looked for a professional defender and they found him in *one* tribe, capable both of fighting off tribal incursions and of providing an orderly sphere with which the market could function. In this connection that is an interesting contrast between the mentality of Islamic and Christian urban citizens. Only the latter proved to be friends to liberty:

... an 'enthusiastic' (monistic, puritan, scripturalistic) bourgeoisie may indeed be an enemy of liberty and a friend to the state, when caught between the state and tribesmen; while it may become a friend of liberty when it is weak enough to abandon hopes of imposing its forcible views on others, and yet has nothing other than the state monopoly of religion to fear, when the state has tamed or eliminated both baron and tribesmen.[11]

Government had been in the first place the gift of the Arab tribes and it is provided from the outside – by slaves, Berbers or tribesmen – thereafter. But those who needed government remained deeply ambivalent about it. There are two related reasons for this. Most important for Ibn Khaldun himself was the fact that once a tribe became a ruler of a city it automatically began to suffer moral degeneracy. *The* quality that had allowed the tribe to come to prominence in the first place was social solidarity. The ease and luxury of city life undermines this. The local ruler is forced in consequence to rely increasingly on paid soldiers, often of slave origin. However, this merely exacerbates the situation, as Ibn Khaldun makes very clear. It is essentially correct to argue that Ibn Khaldun observes rather than moralises, but there is one moment when he is tempted to the latter role.[12] A ruling house makes its problems much worse by hiring troops as this requires heavy taxation, and the necessary arbitrariness thereby involved breeds rebellion. This leads to the drying up of trade and other sources of taxation, which in turn exacerbates the situation. Moralistically, Ibn Khaldun seems to call for a ruling house to remain puritanical and simple, to avoid the perils of Turkish delight and the harem. However, the logic of the situation is too powerful and the essential message of his sociology is that no ruling house has ever managed to learn this message. This situation seems as inevitable as the generational decline from entrepreneur to anti-industrial aesthete described by Thomas Mann in *Buddenbrooks*.

Ibn Khaldun is slightly deficient here. What is probably more important than any libidinous excess is simply that tribal organisation, once out of its customary water, withers and dies. Segmentary organisation depends upon a similarity of occupation that is undermined by professional rule. Whatever the case, one general point is clear. Ibn Khaldun sees power as tribal and not settled in character. Only tribal life breeds the crucial human virtue of solidarity. This contrasts strikingly with the situation in China:

Tribal conquest belonged at the rock bottom of the cycle, and of tribal decay the Chinese had no real notion: being barbarians, the tribesmen possessed no virtue that could be corrupted. That barbarians could not govern China as such was taken as axiomatic. But were the tribesmen to lose their ancestral rudeness, the Chinese would construe the loss, which the barbarians themselves usually lamented, as acquisition of the very virtues which Chinese government repre-

11 Gellner, *Muslim Society*, p. 15.
12 *Muqaddimah*, ch. 1.

sented: the transition from tribal to settled rule could not fail to be a transition to better, stronger and more enduring government. Ibn Khaldun, by contrast, was fascinated by the inevitable decline of *tribal* dynasties, and where the Chinese tried to define the properties of virtue, Ibn Khaldun laboured to identify the nature of tribal solidarity. In his scheme tribal conquest marks the high point of the cycle, and the loss of tribal ties is seen as a proof not that settled government will win out, but that tribal conquest must of necessity recur. The idea that the transition to settled rule could be a transition to better, stronger and more enduring government never suggested itself to him ... He saw, in other words, that the medieval polity was in the nature of a conquest society, and if the idea of applauding the transition to settled rule did not suggest itself to him, it was for the simple reason that Islam, in such contrast to China, lacked a form of settled government to which the transition could have been made. Politics in Islam had remained the domain of the barbarians: it was precisely the non-political nature of settled society that gave Ibn Khaldun so strong a feeling that civilisation was effeminate.[13]

It was not merely that the 'codification' of Islam enshrined memories of tribal virtues, but the suspicion of the virtues of civilisation did not come from that source alone. The *continuing presence* of tribesmen endlessly renewed the fear of settled and bureaucratic political life.

The second general ambivalence to be noted about government in Muslim society is that of the austerity of Islam already discussed, and it is the element still needed to explain the full cyclical dynamics at work. The situation is simple. Although the urban citizens support the tribal rulers at first, they become increasingly restive, typically about the third generation of the ruling dynasty. We have seen how such rule may adversely affect the economy, and this heightens the hostility of the ulama to the ruling dynasty. Although they habitually support the ruling house and serve it as administrators and as judges, they remain in possession of the sacred norms of Islam which, because of their precise codification, are not nearly as much at the mercy of secular power as was the relatively spiritual doctrine of Christianity. These ulama, or at least some among their number, became increasingly discontented with the ruling house as its purposes more and more clearly became self-interested and corrupt. It is very important to realise that the ulama do not therefore establish an opposition party; arbitrariness of conquest type rule disallows this. However, the ulama, backed on occasion by traders badly done by, do have another card that can be played. They can declare the ruling house to be impious, and invite in one of the tribes of the area of dissidence. Such an invitation is likely to be successful when the ruling house really *is* corrupt, and when the religious call is capable of uniting more than one

13 Crone, *Slaves on Horses*, pp. 90–1.

tribe against the ruling house. It is at this latter point that the presence of an ideology shared with the tribesmen really mattered. One must not exaggerate here. Islam does have some penetrative power, and this is seen in the spreading of a set of norms throughout society. However, it is only in exceptional circumstances that tribesmen will abandon the ritual-addicted, custom-laden version of Islam to which they adhere, and participate in high cultural norms designed to restore Islamic purity.

The general model of classical Islam can be portrayed by a further variation on the initial model. We need a name for the polities of this world, and this is not hard to find. *Cyclical* politics characterise classical Islam. We shall see in a moment how such politics affected economic life.

Two final points must be added to complete the model. Firstly, Robert Montagne has drawn our attention to the fact that the corruption of the ruling house involves more than just effeminacy and spiritual softness. He stresses the occasionalistic quality of real tribal cohesion in the first place, and adds to his picture these comments:

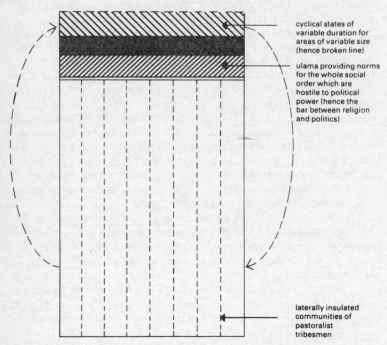

cyclical states of variable duration for areas of variable size (hence broken line)

ulama providing norms for the whole social order which are hostile to political power (hence the bar between religion and politics)

laterally insulated communities of pastoralist tribesmen

Model 4: The dynamics of classical Islam

Sometimes this erosion [of strength] is brought about by the dispersal of those loyal troops throughout a vast empire, as happened with the Almohads; sometimes by their mingling with numerous foreign elements – a sort of dilution – such as probably occurred in the case of the Merinid tribes, surrounded as they were by Zeneta and Arabs. In yet other cases, it is brought about by a military defeat, as we saw . . . in the case of the little Riffian state forged by 'Abd el Krim. A simpler cause is the existence of cleavages between members of the leader's own family . . . at the same time as revolt is brewing amongst the subject groups.[14]

The second point to be highlighted concerns the maintenance of the culture of Islam beyond the boundaries of any single state. At least part of the answer for such maintenance in the case of medieval Latin Christendom is the presence of a rich and bureaucratic church apparatus. This was absent in the Islamic world. The explanation for the maintenance of the Islamic cultural area has to do with the instability of politics. A ruling house very often came to power as the result of a religious spasm, and was correspondingly unlikely to turn against it, and never had the time to do so in any case.

Objections have been made to the view of the character and dynamics of Muslim society offered, and a consideration of such criticisms can further flesh out the bare bones of the model presented here. A general point, however, should preface such comments. The very purpose of any model is to abstract from reality in order that local, historical variations may then come clearly into focus. Such model building only really deserves criticism if it systematically mistakes the character of a whole civilisation. This seems not to be the case here.

The best-known argument made against this model is that it is based far too much on the tribal experience of the Maghreb, and that it does not fully apply to the central Islamic lands. A brilliant restatement of this point had been made by Perry Anderson. He adds to this a two-stage theory of Muslim civilisation according to which early Islam sees tribal instability but slave rulers are increasingly able to hold later Muslim society together.[15] There is a little truth in some of these observations, but not enough, with one exception, to disqualify the model presented. (The exception in question is that of the Ottoman empire, examined later, in which rulers with slave armies *did* create a 'real' empire.) Anderson is right to stress that slave soldiers are unique to Islam, and no attempt to deny this is implicit in the model. Very much to the contrary, the presence of slave rulers is explained by and strikingly illustrates a principal thesis advanced – that political power was distrusted. This distrust

14 *The Berbers*, p. 82.

15 P. Anderson, *Lineages of the Absolutist State*, New Left Books, London, 1974, appendix 2.

was so great that it was preferable to take rulers who were not just geographically but socially outside the society! Ibn Khaldun was well aware of the use of such soldiers throughout the arid zone, and he explicitly argued that the use of such troops signalled the exhaustion of solidarity in the ruling house. From this follows the key point. Slave soldiers did not counteract the political instability of Muslim society; rather, as Ibn Khaldun stressed, the expense of their employment meant that any temporary lease of life they brought was followed all the more inevitably by collapse. There is, however, a weakness in Ibn Khaldunian sociology. Some dynasties do not turn to slave soldiers *in extremis*, being rather founded by them at the start. Government, so necessary because of the threat of dissidence and so distrusted because of Islamic norms, can be given *either* by slave soldiers *or* by tribes.

In general, Ibn Kaldun's three-generational model of the change from virtuous solidarity to corrupt ease works remarkably well in the arid zone. There is nothing in his sociology to rule out those circumstances, such as the use of slave soldiers, which can lengthen the life of a tribally founded dynasty. Egypt typically had a longer cycle because its larger tax base, derived from a significant peasantry, old cadasters and an historical state structure, allowed for a more powerful state. Secondly, Ibn Khaldun maintains that the absence of dissident tribes in Spain means that the dynasty there had no particular need for solidarity, and thus could live beyond its allotted span. Thirdly, he notes:

The real reason why (large dynasties last longer) is that when collapse comes it begins in the outlying regions, and the large dynasty has many such provinces far from its centre. Each defection that occurs necessarily requires a certain time. The time required (for collapse) will be long in such cases, because there are many provinces, each of which collapses in its own good time. The duration of a large dynasty, therefore, is long.[16]

But Ibn Khaldun has a word of caution about seemingly long-lasting dynasties. Often some *éminence grise* uses the traditional figurehead but rules merely on account of the solidarity of its own supporters.

One final point should be made. To say that traditional Muslim society repeats itself is not to deny it some genuinely *historical* moments. Thus there were several attempts to establish Shi'ite states, most notably those of the Fatimids in North Africa from 909 and in Egypt from 969, and the Safavis in Persia from 1517. None of these were able in the long run to solve the dilemma of political power. In consequence, the invasion of the Mongols could not be beaten back. Iraq, already gravely internally weakened, was thereby dealt its death blow.

16 *Muqaddimah*, p. 130.

The Economy in Classical Islam

Classical Islam included within its borders significant and ancient civilisations based on rich alluvial, double-cropping soils, and it further benefitted from its position across trade routes. It was thus ecologically possible that Islam could have created autonomous economic development. There were certain limitations in comparison with Europe. The agricultural strip between the Mediterranean and the mountains is small, and certainly not made up of anything like northern European clay soils. Equally important was simple lack of numbers. The Ottoman empire at its peak only comprised 28 million people, and the market was correspondingly small.[17] Furthermore, the 'ghost acres' that Europe discovered both in the East and in the New World were not available. But the Muslim world had advantages as well; Islam was more 'advanced', it has been argued, than Christianity. Paradoxically, the full-blooded universalism and scripturalism of the Islamic vision, so effective in the modern world, was a disadvantage for Muslim society in world historical perspective. Islam was so advanced as to disallow some of the social institutions involved in the European dynamic.

The first area which requires analysis if the economy is to be explained is that of landholding. Naturally, there was great variety throughout the Muslim world, both geographically and historically, but two basic types of landholding deserve special attention, the iqta and waqf. The former of these were land-grants given to the supporters of the ruling dynasty. Crucially, as dynasties changed, so did the landholders. This partly explains the character of the waqf, formally a religious endowment and therefore typically not touched by a new ruling house, but often in fact a means whereby a family could draw a certain income from the land in covert form by serving as directors of the foundation and so on. The situation is reminiscent of Indian temple economies.

This dual type of landholding proved inimical to agricultural advance. Consider first the position of the landlord. The insecurity of tenure encouraged a predatory use of land. There was little genuine investment in the land.

Those who did invest in land tended to limit themselves, in intention, to receiving whatever revenue resulted from cultivation already going on; that is, the 'investment' was simply a purchase of rights to revenue, and not an actual use of accumulated funds on the land to make it more productive.[18]

17 E.L. Jones, *The European Miracle*, Cambridge University Press, Cambridge, 1981, p. 176.

18 Hodgson, *The Venture of Islam*, vol. II, p. 136.

This made life even more difficult for peasants:

Time and again, a peasant's initiative in cultivating crops that required more investment of time and risk but would yield more return was ruined by thoughtlessly heavy demands for immediate revenue by those who could exact it. A military ruling group that could be sure about their own tenure had little reason not to kill the goose that laid the golden eggs, as they were likely soon to lose the goose anyway.[19]

Finally, the mere presence of a certain security of tenure in the case of the waqf did not result in intensive agricultural improvement. 'The collective character of the right to the income, and the control which the quadi [i.e. the local judge] of the district consequently maintained over the management of the estate, impeded any individual initiative in the exploitation of the land . . .[20] This mattered. In sixteenth-century Syria very large quantities of land were commited in waqf and in later Ottoman times fully three-quarters of agricultural land was so held.[21]

Muslim society did not allow for the autonomous city, and this is the second factor to be emphasised. The burgher was not the most important figure in the city for the obvious reason that the city was the seat of military government. This had significant ramifications on the economy as a series of obstacles to the market principle were thereby set up. The local emir used military power openly in order to gain profit. 'To supplement monopoly profits, Barsbay also had recourse to forced purchases in which merchants or the public in general were obliged to buy fixed quantities of goods at given prices from the Sultan or his agents.'[22] Such interference was epitomised when the Mamluks destroyed the profitable spice trade in order to gain revenue to resist early Mongol incursions. The political power of the empire meant that a premium was placed upon political favour rather than upon the neutral mechanism of the market:

Every property owner, merchant, or artisan had personally to come to terms with the governors, emirs, and officials. Not the office but the man himself became the power to be reckoned with for there could be no appeal to justice, but only to money and countervailing influences and to protection no less costly than previous exactions.[23]

19 Ibid., p. 105.
20 C. Cahen, 'Economy, society, institutions', in *The Cambridge History of Islam*, Vol. 2., *The Farther Islamic Lands. Islam, Society and Civilisation* (eds) P.M. Holt, A.S. Lambton and B. Lewis, Cambridge University Press, Cambridge, 1970, p. 519.
21 I. Watson, *Agricultural Innovation in the Early Islamic World*, Cambridge University Press, Cambridge, 1983, p. 142.
22 I.M. Lapidus, *Muslim Cities in the Later Middle Ages*, Harvard University Press, Cambridge, 1967, p. 36.
23 Ibid., p. 56.

This passage reminds us that Max Weber regarded rational law as a precondition for the emergence of capitalism. In Muslim society, the very perfection of the Shari'a code necessitated a different daily justice, and this was administered by qadis, that is ulama appointed by the government to run the local courts. Such qadi justice was essentially personalistic; here too the political will of the ruler left its mark.[24]

Political power affected society in other ways:

... the prevailing religious and social attitudes of Mamluk society were opposed to independent associations of artisans and workmen, and strongly inclined to suppress any tendencies if any existed. Social leadership and political affairs were so closely integrated that any association, whatever its original purpose, was parapolitical, capable of being turned to political action and resistance in the interests of its members. It was a natural tendency of empires to inhibit the development of foci of resistance ...[25]

This of course reminds us of the traditional fears of the capstone state. Such fears were justified here since the absence of a greedy church meant that no attempt was made to undermine kinship loyalties amongst the lower orders.[26] Thus Islamic cities could quickly become the scene of great, neo-tribal conflicts.

One final point should be made about the city. The absence of autonomy for the city had some impact on eventual limitations for Muslim science. There was less demand for the sort of applied science that proved so important in Europe. It is possible that in this important and little-understood area the actual tenets of Islam also mattered. Natural law was downplayed because happenings could be explained by the will of an all-poweful God who *interfered* with the world.[27]

The argument made so far about the economy can usefully be summarised. The cyclical state in Islam was unstable, and this affected the economy in two ways. Firstly, it was arbitrary and predatory enough to directly interfere in the market, with the workings of justice and the autonomy of cities. The economy never gained real autonomy. On the other hand, secondly, the government was weak. Instability and arbitrariness of government resulted in land going out of circulation in waqf with a corresponding loss of tax revenue and a limitation upon the number of state servants it was possible to recruit. Hence few services could be provided by the state. The situation is reminiscent of that in Indian states, although the mechanisms at work were different in each case. But in both civilisations there was no unitary empire covering the whole

24 Turner, *Weber and Islam*, ch. 7.
25 Lapidus, *Muslim Cities*, p. 103.
26 The impact of kinship is more fully discussed in the next chapter.
27 Cook and Crone, *Hagarism, passim*.

culture, and some of the bureaucratic effects of the capstone state of China were thus ruled out. Such differences are important when we seek to capture the specificity of each civilisation. However, these states will seem very similar when they are compared to the organic state of Europe. All were weak, and the form of their arbitrariness, either predatory or bureaucratic, does not matter from this perspective. All blocked, albeit in different ways, the emergence of capitalism.

Two points in the discussion of Latin Christendom may usefully be mentioned here so as to allow a full characterisation of the economy of classical Islam. In the West, the absence of an empire removed the crucial bureaucratic block on the development of market forces; merchants persecuted in one place could always go with their capital elsewhere. Both Islam and Christianity held together a large area in which equal citizens could recognise each other; each civilisation centred itself on a sense of community. Why then did not Islam similarly help capitalism? In Europe this ability to move was allied to the presence of a more organic state, a *stronger* state, in place over long periods of time, and forced to provide infrastructural services for society, both because of the pre-existence of a civil society and because of the need to raise revenue to compete in war with other similarly stable states. In Islam such organic states did not exist. The fear of tribesmen meant that urban strata could not rule themselves, and a premium was accordingly placed upon military power. The states that resulted were transient and predatory. Governments elsewhere were unlikely to be very much different, so that the mere moving of one's capital did not make much of a difference in the long run. Ibn Khaldun occasionally moralised that governments which did treat traders well would benefit in tax revenue, but his advice was never taken, and so one naturally considers whether something structural was at work below the surface. A part of the explanation lies in the circulation of elites already described, but there is something more. In Europe the emergence of states forced the aristrocracy to gain profits from land rather than from warfare, and the reasonably settled character of the core of Europe meant that monarchs *had* to turn to the provision of infrastructural services in order to gain revenue. In Muslim society, wars always remained the greatest potential source of profit, and the solidarity of a tribe the greatest military asset.

... it was with difficulty that [the barons of Europe] could combine really massive armies under one chief for general indiscriminate slaughter; to concentrate power in one hand, the chances of fixed succession, modulated by dynastic marriages or even by purchase of succession rights, were as important as outright political and military skill. No ruler extended his sway far beyond his hereditary lands ...

... [in Muslim society] the military men were city men and little bound by parochial prescriptions. Nowhere was mobility more drastic than among the soldiery, whose members could rise to the highest social peaks, and could campaign for distances incredible in the Occident.[28]

This whole point can be put in an alternative, simpler manner. Muslim society did *not* in fact have a multipolar state system equivalent to that of Europe in which rationalisation by states of their societies occurred under pressure of war. This difference is probably explicable in terms of the types of warfare in Islam and the West. The slave soldiers of Islam were *so* professional and removed from society that they did not require social reorganisation. Very much to the contrary, states came and went, and were of larger or smaller size at various periods, but were never long lasting enough ever to be rationalised at all.

One final contrast remains to be drawn between Muslim society and the Occident, and it concerns the way in which Islam was too advanced for its own good. Perhaps the key characteristic of European society was its pluralism, the presence of particular associations, church, state, baron, town, manor, and so on. The situation in Islam was really quite different.[29] The corporate quality of European civilisation contrasts with the extreme contractualism characteristic of Islam, in which no organisation (at least in theory, for in fact the tribe clearly does) stands between man and God. The very austerity of the Islamic vision did, in fact, come to be toned down by the growth of Sufi sects, but the point retains validity. The corporations of Europe were able to organise themselves so as to be able systematically to curtail political power, and make it serve their ends. The very openness of Muslim society made this difficult, perhaps impossible. This is not to say that the 'advanced' character of Islam is a permanent disability, and we shall see later the advantages it brings in the contemporary world.

The Gunpowder Empires

The argument of the chapter to this point has been that the merging of pastoralism with a closed scripturalist vision created a politically unstable yet culturally cohesive world unable to indigenously 'invent' capitalist economic development. To insist on the weakness of the Abbasids went against the periodisation of Islamic history suggested by Hodgson, and it is now time to consider the final period in his interpretation of Islam. Is it true that the gunpowder empires of India, Persia and the Near East

28 Hodgson, *The Venture of Islam*, vol. II, pp. 355–6.
29 Ibid., ch. 7.

represent a qualitative change (or to be precise about Hodgson's view, a *return* to the virtues of the early, 'classical', imperial period)? This is certainly the view of Perry Anderson who insists that Islamic society became increasingly more militarised. It is fairly easy to see the consider-ations that are at work in this general interpretation. Hodgson makes much of the importance of gunpowder in undermining the traditional pastoralism of Muslim society:

The effects of these conditions were presumably partially counteracted, by the time gunpowder weapons became militarily decisive, in at least two ways: through the technical demands of gunpowder weaponry itself, and through limitations, to which gunpowder contributed, upon long-distance nomadism. Hence part of the basis for the decentralised, contractualistic, cosmopolitan Islamicate society was undermined.[30]

In a sense, this changing military situation, that is the reduction in the size of the area of tribal dissidence, *proves* the Ibn Khaldunian model so far discussed! But I choose not to emphasise this overmuch, since it is very easy to exaggerate the impact of gunpowder. It made some impact but probably did not change the situation totally. The three empires must be examined in their own terms.

We can best discuss the extent to which these empires opened a new age, and thus disprove the view of later Islam offered by Anderson and Hodgson, by considering three points. Firstly, the empires in India and in Persia do not fundamentally escape from the dictates of the model hitherto described. Furthermore, it is as well to remember at this point that the non-imperial part of the Islamic world *certainly* continued to run along the lines noted. Secondly, however, it will be admitted that the Ottoman empire *is* an exception to the model, and an explanation of the longevity of that empire is required. This longevity introduces a third consideration. The 'stagnation' of Islam has been explained in terms of political instability. The Ottoman empire *was* stable and a different explanation for economic stagnation is required. It will be found in the capstone style of imperial government with which we are already familiar.

Safavid dominance in Persia was not in fact very long lasting. The conventional dates run from 1517 to 1722, and the extent of imperial control at the end of that period is quite doubtful. However before spelling this out it is as well to establish something of the distinctiveness of the regime. The Safavids were an Iranian family, originating in Anatolia and Azerbajan, which had strong links with urban groups. The empire had slave troops and recruited Turkish tribes in Matobia and Azerbajan. It adopted traditional policies in regard to taxation from land.

Legitimacy was gained, unusually and interestingly, by adopting the Shi'ite cause, that is by stressing that the Sadr was the direct descendant of the prophet himself. The Shi'ite ulama gave the regime its legitimacy and encouraged it to attempt the conversion of all to Shi'ite Islam, but they themselves insisted on keeping some distance from power; they preferred for example *not* to be exempt from tax.[31] This lack of integration accords well with the 'Weberist' part of the model presented, and it played a key role in unsettling the empire. By the mid-seventeenth century, it had become quite clear that the population was not converting to Shi'ism, and the ulama correspondingly began to withdraw their support:

The basis of an integrative legitimation of the Safavî state had been a revolutionary principle. It necessarily faded with the restoration of agrarianate normalcy. In particular, the 'ulamâ' had been integrated under the sadr on a basis of a chiliastic mood of dubious orthodoxy – even though the extremer teachings of tarîqah Shî'ism had been avoided in the cities; now they freed themselves from such uncongenial ties. From this point on, the legitimacy of the imperial government was again thrown into question, despite its acknowledged identification with the Shî'î cause . . . By the time of Shâh Sultân-Husayn (1694–1722) . . . the state ceased to be independent of the ulamâ. Some of them tried to retrieve the claims to legitimacy of the Shî'î empire by way of a rigorist dominance by the ulamâ themselves. Under an incompetent monarch they were allowed not only to eliminate the last traces of the dynasty's original religious support . . . but to accentuate antagonisms within the bureaucracy, deprived of a firm hand on the part of the monarch . . . the latent vulnerability of the system emerged . . . rebellion and invasion loomed on many frontiers; the state seemed powerless to respond to the challenge.[32]

Doubtless, gunpowder did disrupt the three-generational model of Ibn Khaldun, as did the presence of genuine agrarian resources and the presence of Shi'ism. Nevertheless the picture of collapse seems broadly in line with the model propounded.

Much the same picture can be drawn of the Muslim empire in India, although the character of that state is rather different. The imperial drive was begun by Timur Lane, who captured Delhi in 1368. The Delhi Sultanate established an agrarian-based empire in which considerable central power was initially gained via tight control over the government central officers, the mansabdars. But there were notable differences from the Safavid state. Most obviously, no compunction was shown about employing Hindus in the service of the state, and they made particularly effective use of the Rajputs as their elite soldiers. This policy came to something of a peak under the Mughals, especially under Akbar in the

31 Ibid., p. 325.
32 Ibid., pp. 53, 57–8.

late sixteenth century. This dynasty paid obeisance to Sunni Islam, but Akbar's position of strength encouraged him to claim rights of jurisdiction over the ulama. This probably had something to do with the key revolt of 1580. After this Akbar increasingly turned to a universalist policy favouring toleration of all religions, and created something of a cult around his own person.

However, in the long run, the ulama could not be so ignored:

In India, the ulamâ were brought under control by Akbar and their role was limited by the cultivation of universalist standards of culture so that the full implementation of the Sharî'ah should not undermine the Muslim-Hindu association on which the empire thrived; in the end, the more intransigent section of the ulamâ was able to shift the balance sufficiently to cause the system to break down . . .[33]

In the late seventeenth century the emperor Aurangzeb reversed the universalist policy of his predecessor Akbar, and tried to create a Muslim empire after the ulama's hearts. Perhaps he was encouraged to do so by the failure of his empire to penetrate the caste system locally.[34] However, the particular alun Aurangzeb followed was not prepared to provide any sort of caesaropapist doctrine. 'In this way [Sheikh Ahmad Sirhindi] provided for the Indian Muslim an alternative sheet anchor with which to face the coming storm. When the Commander of the Faithful in India (the emperor) failed to command and the temporal power collapsed, he could fall back on the sovereignty of God and the congregation of the faithful.'[35] The ulama remained constrained by their ideological inheritance. This had disastrous effects when the empire was under stress. Muslim men of power did not rally to the empire, but instead looked after their own interests:

The Muslims had no sense of purpose and valued the empire only as a stepping-stone to personal power. The so called 'reformers' were elders like the Nizam who stood for the 'good old days' and the stricter ways of Aurangzeb. They had no vision for the future; nothing is ever saved by looking backwards. So the ablest men, instead of cooperating for the common good, carved out kingdoms for themselves to the general confusion. And the most thoughtful theologians like Shah Wali-ullah, instead of calling on Muslims to rally round the throne, took refuge in the concept of the community of the faithful looking only to God.[36]

Not surprisingly, the empire fell to invasions by Persian and Marathans long before the appearance of the British in any significant force.

33 Ibid., p. 105.
34 P. Spear, *A History of India*, vol. II, Penguin, London, 1975, p. 44.
35 Ibid., p. 57.
36 Ibid., p. 72.

But the Ottoman state *was* different in being longer lasting. The strength of the empire rested in part upon factors common to the Safavid and Timurid empires. A strong peasant base provided revenue for the state. Interestingly, the decision not to seek to convert those who owed allegiance to other scriptural religions played some some in slowing down the mechanics of Ibn Khaldun's model. The reforming ulama had fewer troops to call on given that many of them, being confined to their own separate millets, would not heed his call. More important, perhaps, was the height of sophistication to which the institution of slavery developed. The Ottomans instituted the devshirme, a toll of Christian children who were then turned into both soldiers and bureaucrats.

But a fuller explanation of the longevity of the empire is needed. The empire itself had been created by ghazi frontier warriors whose fight to extend the land of Islam was holy. Furthermore, the legitimacy of the early empire was assured by it representing an alliance between the military and the Shari'a-minded ulama. This legitimacy remained automatic, so long as the Ottoman state was continuing to extend its borders – something crucial to its stability anyway since newly conquered land was needed to reward troops. How did the ulama react, after about 1600, to a state which no longer expanded, and in which the sultan became increasingly remote, in traditional imperial style? This is the point at which a modification is necessary to the general model of this chapter. Although the closed nature of Islamic doctrine made it difficult to marry religion and mundane politics, something like this *was* achieved by the Ottomans. They succeeded where the Abbasids had failed in successfully integrating the ulama into the power structure. In this matter it is possible to counterpose to Anderson's thesis of the militarisation of Islam an alternative suggested by Bernard Lewis. The Islamic world *improves* its organisation in Lewis's view from the time when the Turkish political tradition is grafted onto Islam by the Mongols, and this is seen in the fact that the Mamluk sultanate lasted for 300 years without the aid of gunpowder.[37] In the Ottoman empire there was some give and take at the most general level. The state agreed to continue to define itself in Islamic terms, and the ulama accepted the tight organisational control of their educational system created by the Sultan. However, the crucial factor responsible for integrating the ulama was altogether more basic.

The ulama benefited in their pockets, on the other hand, by being exempt from all taxation, and had this advantage over the members of the ruling institution, that their property was safe from confiscation. These circumstances were to

37 B. Lewis, 'The Mongols, the Turks and the Muslim polity' in his *Islam in History*, Alcove Press, London, 1973, ch. 14.

prove of prime importance in guiding the future development of the profession.[38]

Bluntly, the ulama became the richest element in the Ottoman empire, and for this reason continued to lend it their support. They became correspondingly conservative; when Mustafa III, for instance, wished to lead his armies into battle, the ulama would have none of it.[39] The commanding heights of their ideology were abandoned in favour of wealth.

The principal argument made in this chapter concerning the 'stagnation' of Islam has concerned political instability. So, finally, a different account must be offered of the failure to escape stagnation in the Ottoman case, since here stability was proved. The argument to be made resembles that made about the Chinese capstone imperial state, namely that the imperial form was responsible for placing limits upon economic growth. There is one crucial difference between the two empires, however. The Ottoman empire had only one mode of existence, that of expansion, and some of the blocks placed upon the economy result less from bureaucratic interferences and more from the disarray caused by the end of this expansion.

While the Shari'a–military alliance led to an expansion of the state, the Ottoman system functioned efficiently. In particular, expansion provided fresh supplies of land to be given as timar grants, additional manpower for the devshirme, booty and an increasing number of jobs in an ever-expanding state. When the limits of the empire were reached *c*.1600, a series of attendant problems resulted. The power of the central state was not sufficient in the long run to control the timariot system properly, and military obligations ceased to be met. Worse still, the fact that confiscation of land did quite regularly occur made it imperative for landowners and tax-farmers to secure their profits quickly, and the consequence of this for the peasantry, the state treasury and local order was disastrous. A second set of problems concerned the expansion of offices, particularly amongst the janissaries whose numbers swelled from 8,000 in 1527 to 38,000 in 1609. Increasingly the elite corps used its political power in its own self-interest, and this had predictably unfortunate consequences for the economy. Power rather than rational calculation ruled in the market-place, and the exercise of power from the seventeenth century onwards itself became more and more arbitrary. A third general feature of Ottoman decline must be noted. Such power as the state possessed in its classical period rested upon the relative auton-

38 H.A.R. Gibb and H. Bowen, *Islamic Society and the West*, Oxford University Press, Oxford, 1957, vol. II, p. 105.
39 Ibid., p. 108.

omy of the sultan. From about 1600, the sultan became the prisoner of his palace, no longer able to exercise sway between contending factors. The Ottoman empire degenerated into a system serving the extraction interests of ulama, court officials and janissaries.

There were, of course, accidental factors involved in Ottoman decline. Court politics left a strong and disastrous impact in the most direct way. 'The run of thirteen incompetent sultans who reigned from 1566 to 1703 included lechers like Murad III, who fathered 103 children (though he was outclassed by Moulay Ismail, an eighteenth-century emperor of Morocco who produced 888), drunkards like Selim the Sot, and mental defectives, like Mustapha, twice deposed for idiocy.'[40] Further, the expansion of Europe meant a very sudden ending to the spice trade upon whose revenues much of the prosperity of the early empire had rested. Similarly, the quantum leap, especially in military matters, taken by European states and eventually by Russia led to great pressures being placed on the empire – although it was probably arguments as to who exactly among the surrounding states should benefit from the dismemberment of the empire that led to its having an artificially drawn-out senescence.

Nevertheless, these accidents should not hide the point that empire made it always *likely* that centralised bureaucratic policies would be adopted capable of undermining any gains in economic development. Three such general factors about imperial rule are worth recalling. Firstly, the superimposition of religious and military power in the fully developed Ottoman system led to such stifling of innovation in thought that many key European discoveries were not adapted to Ottoman usage. Secondly, and linked to this, the cities of the Ottoman empire never gained any autonomy with the result that power dominated the market; the market never gained autonomy, and 'the economy' did not really exist. Finally, the supposed strength of the empire hid a very weak penetration of society. The Ottoman state provided few of the infrastructural services that increasingly characterised European states, and this was symbolised by the recurrent outbreaks of disease in Constantinople itself. The Ottoman empire had clearly come to the end of its active life span *before* it was dismembered by its neighbours, as had China.

Conclusions

Islamic culture was larger than any single state, and this reflected the fact that the principal element in the elite was the ulama. This intellectual

40 Jones, *The European Miracle*, p. 186.

grouping could not control society in the way that the Brahmans managed to since the presence of dissident tribesmen made overtures to politcal power essential. The principal argument made, however, is that tribalsim combined with a powerful and virtually unchangeable doctrine to make political rule alien, transitory and predatory. This curious antagonism of political and religious power fundamentally ruined any chance which the economy might have had to develop autonomously. Different elements of the elite stood against each other to produce a society which in total sum remained weak, at least in contrast to that of the West, to which we can now, at last, turn.

5

The Rise of Christian Europe

The title of this chapter is that given to an interesting lecture series which argued that European 'dynamism' was in place rather earlier than was once recognised.[1] Thus much is made of the renaissance of the twelfth century (and more could have been made of that of the ninth) in comparison to the better known quattrocento, and the Crusades figure as a precursor to the voyages of discovery. This sort of picture of the European Middle Ages represents something of a hidden consensus among recent medieval historians, and I have drawn upon this in trying to supply the one element that the lecture series did not possess: an *explanation* for this European dynamism. The explanation to be offered is in no way monocausal, indeed it rather stresses that the curious concate-nation of circumstances was miraculous. However, most attention is paid to the role of Christianity since without it the other factors – the market, the organic state and the state system – would not have had such salience.

One final preliminary comment must be made. There is a series of ecological points that was unique to north-western Europe and which provides a background to the medieval dynamic. This is a divided area with several small cores, the majority of which have deep and productive clay soils fed by rainfall. There was no need for irrigation. It is quite likely that this encouraged, or at least allowed for, a decentred agricultu-ral civilisation based on individual initiative. Perhaps more important is the contrast between the ecological squeeze put on the barbarians at the eastern end of the roof of the world, resulting in state formation, and the more favourable conditions at the western end of that continuum which militated against any sort of barbarian state.[2] The consequence of this

1 H. Trevor Roper, *The Rise of Christian Europe*, Thames & Hudson, London, 1966.
2 P. Crone, *Slaves on Horses*, Cambridge University Press, Cambridge, 1980, ch. 2. Certain implications concerning the character of European kinship follow from this, and it is to be hoped that the author will further investigate them; they are discussed below.

was that the barbarians came to Europe less often, and as settlers rather than as conquerors. Moreover, Europe was much better protected. Throughout the classical Middle Ages Russia and Islamic Persia drew off the barbarians, and in any case the forests of central Europe proved an unfriendly but not an impassable obstacle to nomads. When Europe first emerged from its fastnesses it was not fully superior militarily. But in time it *was* able to prove its superiority by the use of gunpowder.

The City of God

The Christian world drew on that of Rome, just as Rome itself followed and incorporated previous civilisations, and it is necessary to say something about this inheritance. This can best be done by noting certain similarities, together with crucial differences, between the great empires of Rome and China.

Rome owed her empire to the strength of her militarism. This militarism characterised elite culture. Even more important, however, was the sheer number of citizens involved in fighting, especially during the Republic. And Roman soldiers were responsible not just for fighting; they also served as civil engineers whose monument is the system of Roman roads. Perhaps the key achievement was straightforward. Rome, unlike China, systematically brought civilisation to outlying barbarian areas. A Mediterranean empire brought northern Europe within the pale of civilisation. This achievement is to be laid at the door of the legions. All this refutes the thesis of the 'slave mode of production'. For even if it is the case that slaves were important for the surplus of the landlords, the legions were necessary for there to be slaves at all.

As we have seen, military success was also imporant in Chinese history. Furthermore, it is possible to identify rather similar sorts of mechanisms in both empires with regard to their economies. There was no exact equivalent to the mandarin suspicion of traders and businessmen, although such activities were scorned, but the centralisation of decisions proved equally debilitating for the Roman economy. Thus the narrow prosperity that the empire had brought was undermined by the doubling of the army under Diocletian. In particular, the market was adversely affected by state production of weapons and clothes and by the resort to taxation in kind. Of course the ambiguity noted when discussing China (as well as India and Islam) applies here too: the very arbitrariness of government that so deleteriously affected the economy resulted in part from the weakness of the state, in particular its inability to break the power stand-off between landlord and state even though the later empire 'tied' the peasants to the land. Nevertheless, only in an empire *could* centralised decisions have had such an impact.

There remain great differences between Rome and China. Rome took within its borders not only marcher areas such as the Maghreb and the frontier along the Rhine and the Danube, but also the old civilised areas of Egypt, Greece and Syria. It was far more cosmopolitan and had a plurality of traditions from the start, unlike monolithic China whose historic parallel is perhaps ancient Egypt. With its culture borrowed from Greece, and in the presence of literacy and the widespread and tradition- al use of coinage, Rome's imperial control was always likely to be that much harder to achieve. There is still more. Rome had been built by a citizen army. The division of the spoils of empire under the late Republic led to the bypassing of popular control,[3] but that control left its mark, at least at the aristocratic level. There was something of a tradition of resistance to imperial misrule, although much rebellion was fired by personal ambition. This republican inheritance was seen in the respect shown for law, property law being an invention of the Romans without parallel in other pre-industrial empires. Indeed the lawyer, an increas- ingly important figure in occidental history, was virtually absent in China. The extent to which the presence of property law in fact affected the style of government is difficult to assess. However, the Roman empire was harder to control because of its pluralistic nature. It had nothing like the morpheme, for instance, to bind the elite firmly together. It was constantly in fear of the many different traditions on which opposition could draw – think for a moment of the vast number of myths, sects and religions, from Manicheanism to the worship of Isis, which the oriental provinces of the late empire fostered! This fear was completely justified. Whereas Chinese capstone government could suppress Buddhism, Christianity proved its independent staying power. In the eastern half of the empire co-optation did occur, but a full-blooded *trahison des clercs* took place in the West. To this strange and fascinating story we can now turn.

In the pre-Christian Roman world religious belief proceeded in a haphazard but entirely comprehensible way. A generalised loyalty was owed to the gods of Rome, but this required little actual religious practice. An extraordinary eclecticism characterised Roman society with cults being imported from various parts of the empire, particularly from the Orient. Roman tolerance is best seen, however, in the acceptance of the Jews *despite* their refusal to pay the most cursory obeisance to Rome's own gods. There were probably three reasons for such tolerance. Firstly, it would have been very difficult, probably impossible, to police religious

3 K. Hopkins, *Conquerors and Slaves*, Cambridge University Press, Cambridge, 1978, ch. 1.

beliefs. Secondly, the absence of an organised paid clergy in the Greek world meant that there was no specialised status group with a particular interest in social control. Thirdly, the elite, somewhat like the mandarins, was not religious in any sense we would recognise today. They simply did not care, especially since their empire had not been founded in the name of religion, as had been the case in China.

By the early Empire this sort of religious eclecticism was beginning to prove unsatisfactory. Judaism was becoming widely admired for the intellectual coherence of its beliefs. More importantly, Greek philosophy was undergoing a Neoplatonic revival which sought to similarly modify and organise belief. If one had to name a single characteristic of this Neoplatonism it would be that it sought to order the universe in such a way as to allow that a *single* religious spirit of some sort controlled the phenomenal world. Much the same underlying current was present in Manicheanism and in Mithraism, so popular with the Roman army. Christianity was in line with a general monotheist trend, but it had much extra force, of course, as the result of being a human rather than an impersonal story.

Before saying more about the doctrinal tenets of Christianity it is as well to comment a little on its social base. One thing is immediately clear: Christianity did not appeal to the upper classes. The characteristic education of the elite involved long training in classics and rhetoric. Much snobbery was attached to this education, and this can be seen in the hostility with which Petronius painted the *nouveau riche* Trimalchio in his *Satyricon*. Only through expensive education was enlightenment held to be possible. Christianity stands in contrast to this in being essentially *vulgar*. This can be seen in the nature of Emperor Julian's distaste for Christianity, and even more clearly in novel Christian ideas of conversion and revelation. Peter Brown's comment on the latter is worth recording:

Between them, the two ideas opened a breach in the high wall of classical culture for the average man. By 'conversion' he gained a moral excellence which had previously been reserved for the classical Greek and Roman gentleman because of his careful grooming and punctilious conformity to ancient models. By 'revelation' the uneducated might get to the heart of vital issues, without exposing himself to the high costs, to the professional rancours and to the heavy traditionalism of a second-century education in philosophy. Pagan philosophers, who might share many aspects of the 'new mood', were bitterly opposed to Christians . . . 'Revelation', for a philosopher such as Plotinus, was not merely irrational: it led to second-rate counterfeits of traditional academic philosophical culture. It was as if the inhabitants of an underdeveloped country were to seek to catch up with western technology by claiming to have learnt nuclear physics through dreams and oracles.[4]

4 P. Brown, *The World of Late Antiquity*, Thames & Hudson, London, 1971, p. 53.

But this is only one side of the question and it should not be exaggerated. Christianity spread for at least its first three centuries in cities. We know this from all our sources, and we know it equally from their very character. They are epistles written from one city congregation to another, from Antioch to Jerusalem or from Rome to Alexandria. Such epistles were read aloud to the local congregation. These bare facts tell us a great deal. To be part of the 10 per cent or so who inhabited cities meant that one was, compared with the peasantry, privileged. This is strikingly reinforced by the presence of literacy, a skill in a pre-industrial society necessarily rare. Moreover, early Christians tended to be craftsmen, recently proselytized Jews, Greeks, freedmen and traders; these were the middling, not the poorest, elements of Roman society. These groups were politically and educationally disenfranchised and Christianity gave them a sense of community. All this is worth characterising afresh in terms of *the* model of the agro-literate polity. The Chinese state was eventually cemented under a single elite with the capacity to monopolise horizontal communication. Non-official horizontal communication could not be suppressed in Rome. This mattered since non-official channels eventually provided a form for a non-imperial social organisation.

What of Christian doctrine? It is immediately apparent that it is very hard to say much that is precise since scholarly debates of the utmost intransigence continue, and are likely to continue, unabated. For example, one only has to open a recent aseptic biography of Jesus to see that there is no agreement as to whether 'Son of Man' – presuming Jesus in fact used the expression – meant a special claim to be God's son, or whether it was a generic expression asserting that Jesus was but one of God's children.[5] But some things do seem clear. Jesus did not follow John the Baptist into the Zealot sect, the Essenes, which represented a nativist reaction against Roman rule. This is most clearly seen in Jesus's insistence to 'render unto Caesar what is Caesar's, and unto God what is God's', a lapidary pronouncement asserting that Christianity's core did not lie in the possession of a political theory of its own. It sought to organise the spirit, and not to control every type of social relationship. Equally he did not respect those who co-operated with Rome, the Sadducees, nor those rather legalistic doctrinal reformers familiar to us as the Pharisees. Somehow the message of Jesus was a middling one, but nobody is really certain whether it was a message only for the Jews or, as sometimes seems likely (but quite possible only as a result of the form the canon later took), for every man. However, we do know that the crucifixion was a very great shock to the disciples, although they were initially

5 H. Carpenter, *Jesus*, Oxford University Press, Oxford, 1980.

able to explain it away. Yet in the years that followed it seemed more than likely that the disciples of Christ would produce a sectarian version of Judaism. Indeed there was an Ebionite sect in Judaism which had exactly this character.

Nevertheless, Christianity did develop out of its Palestinian chrysalis. A crucial historical accident in this process was the destruction of the Temple of Jerusalem in AD 70 by the Romans as punishment for the nativist Jewish revolts against their rule. More importantly St Paul, the citizen of Rome, can be seen throughout the New Testament arguing that Jesus's message was universal and fit for Gentiles who had no need to be circumcised. He turned a tribal religion into a world religion. Further, he gave the religion its essential theological content, namely that individual salvation was open to every man because of the death of Jesus.

Research into the newly discovered gnostic gospels has shown that it took some time before Christianity changed from a sect to a church.[6] These gnostic gospels are those ruled out from the canon created in the second century, but they tell us a great deal about the social world of early Christianity. *Gnosis* means inner enlightenment, and the social consequence of this was that early Christianity had no room for any authority structure. These gospels show early Christianity to have been egalitarian in its view of relationships between men and women. Thus Mary Magdalen is shown as the equal of Peter and Paul in terms of the confidences and messages she receives from Jesus, and the position of Mary was similarly elevated. Here was a religion without central organisation and without an agreed canon. Sects proliferated, most famously the 'gospel of love' preached by Marcion and his followers.

In the long term this situation, however attractive in retrospect, was not stable. Roman satirists made much of the gullibility of early Christians whose monies were repeatedly stolen by rather calculating charismatics of one sort or another. More important probably was a growing dissatisfaction with Gnosticism itself, perhaps especially among non-intellectual groups. Earliest Christianity had confidently expected Jesus to return soon so as to establish the Kingdom of Heaven on earth. When he failed to reappear generation after generation, pressure mounted for the creation of doctrine and rules by which to live one's life in the *continuing* world. If there was to be canonical law and agreed doctrine, authority was implied. But to whom? Obviously to the church. But who constituted the church? In order to answer this tricky problem it is time to say something about the convoluted relations of the Christian church with the Roman state.[7]

6 E. Pagels, *The Gnostic Gospels*, Penguin, London, 1982.
7 P. Johnson, *A History of Christianity*, Penguin, London, 1980, ch. 2.

These relations began on a very bad footing; the early Christians were persecuted. The explanation of the persecutions is an historically complex one. Habitually the Roman state was tolerant, and it in fact treated the earliest Christians reasonably well. Many of the early persecutions resulted not from the state but from private actions by citizens irritated by the 'godlessness' of Christians. All this changed with the famous persecution drives launched by Decian, Valerian and Diocletian. During these years the state adopted the mental attitudes of its citizens, and blamed the Christians for the great disasters that were then befalling the empire. Something further was important to the state. One characteristic of empire is deep suspicion of secondary organisations, and it is quite likely that persecution is finally best explained in terms of the state's fear of a movement which ran on its own lines, entirely free from official control. Whatever the case may be, there is no doubt that the persecutions eventually failed. There were many apostates – particularly among the gnostics who argued that an oath meant little, real religion being an inner spiritual matter – and these left very deep scars. But as a whole the extraordinary courage of the early martyrs improved the public image of the organised church.

Persecution was but the first act in the drama. In 313 the Emperor Constantine, then struggling with his rivals, apparently saw a vision before the battle of the Milvian Bridge. He was victorious and ascribed his success to Christianity. Nevertheless, to the fact of personal conversion must be added *raison d'état*. Christianity was the most vital force in the empire. Hence it is best to see the Constantinian revolution as a deliberate attempt on the part of the state to take over the church. This was a bold initiative, and it was forcibly carried through. Constantine was exceedingly generous to the church; he showered it with land grants, and allowed priests exemption from public service. We must examine the relationship between church and state carefully. How well did each side do from detente?

The church did very well indeed. It became extremely rich. More importantly, its very form of organisation – the hierarchy of bishop, deacon and presbyter – was modelled on that of the state. Further, the church increasingly called upon the state to help it in its battles. Throughout the fourth century the church pushed the state towards a position increasingly hostile to traditional paganism, even though such paganism was especially strong among the traditional landed and Roman aristocracy. St Ambrose succeeded in having paganism outlawed in 380, while one of his pupils, Augustine, had no compunction whatever in using the secular arm to hunt out those he considered to be heretics. In order to establish a single church organisation persecution by Christians rapidly took the place of the earlier persecution of Christians.

But what of the state? How well did it do from the bargain? The hugely interesting answer to this is that it did very poorly out of the deal. It is proper, moreover, to talk only of an *attempted* takeover of the church, since that attempt in fact failed. One imagines that Constantine might have had second thoughts himself. For in the course of the two decades after the adoption of Christianity he found himself in a hornet's nest of controversy. Two controversies stand out. Firstly, Donatism in North Africa, perhaps in part a rallying cry for disaffected provincials, asserted that those who had apostatised during the persecutions should not be accepted as leaders of the church. This might seem a trivial point, but a very great deal was involved in it. The Donatists wished to emphasise the purity of the church community, that is they wished to remain a sect opposed to a world which would sully their purity. This lack of interest in society makes it reminiscent at first glance of Theravada Buddhism. But this analogy cannot be pushed too far since Christians did not seek to escape life, but sought instead to provide rules for daily conduct. Secondly, Constantine found himself deeply involved in the long-running squabble between Arius and Athanasius as to whether Christianity was to be rigidly monotheist or not. Constantine's attempt to compromise at the Council of Nicaea between those who believed God had made Jesus (and was thus the *only* true God himself) and the trinitarians, by saying that Jesus, God, and the Holy Spirit were 'essentially of the same substance', was not successful.

In order to extend the argument, objections to what had been said so far must be noted. Are these matters not theological in another sense entirely? Were they not trivial and unimportant to most Christians? Even more important, was not the empire beginning to gain loyalty from the church? Certainly Eusebius of Caesarea positively welcomed his role as a political adviser, and he created a sort of Caesaropapist doctrine centred on Constantine. It might seem that some Western bishops were also rallying to the empire. Augustine after all fiercely attacked the Donatists, and did so with some success. Yet we must note the arguments he used against the Donatists. He accused them of lacking imagination in wishing to be a sect, an anti-society. He was quite as puritanical as they were, but insisted that a much greater historical opportunity lay in front of them. The church could *become* society rather than merely constituting an oppsition to it. So if the church integrated people into society and (unlike Buddhism) provided them with rules for daily social conduct, the society in question was Christian and not Roman society. In this matter there is a distinctive difference between East and West, caused perhaps by the fact that the empire *did* survive in the East. A complete explanation for the rank ingratitude shown to the empire in the West is hard to find, but it is not difficult to provide evidence showing that this was present. Consider, first, the message of Christian doctrine as it evolved during the last years of the Roman empire:

The church long maintained the suspicious attitude . . . to all forms of government service. An early papal letter declares: 'It is manifest that those who have required secular power and administered secular justice cannot be free from sin . . .'. Pope Siricius and his successors debarred from holy orders all who after baptism had held administrative posts, or served in the army or the civil service, or had even practised as barristers. In the same spirit those who had performed penance and received absolution were forbidden to return to their posts . . . Paulinus of Nola writes . . . urging his correspondents to resign from their posts or abandon the official careers which they contemplated in order to take up a Christian life. 'Ye cannot serve two masters,' he quotes, 'that is the one God and Mammon, in other words Christ and Caesar'.[8]

This stands in marked contrast with the virtual requirement of paganism to devote oneself to politics. Not all Christian writers agreed with Paulinus of Nola and amongst them must be numbered Augustine. Yet Augustine does not really stand opposed to the generalisation I am making. He was one of the socially mobile provincials who came first to Rome and then to Milan where he was elevated to a professorship of rhetoric. The influence of St Ambrose upon him in Milan led to his abandoning the service of the empire and retreating to private study, first at Cassiacum and then in North Africa, before becoming a servant of the church. His *City of God*, perhaps the most single important theological work in medieval Christendom, famously argued that God's kingdom could not be associated with the destiny of Rome. God's timetable was his own and should not be conflated with the destiny of any historical order. This was a remarkable, indeed foolhardy, judgement given that at the time the basic infrastructure of the church, that is literacy, was not yet provided by the church but was the general product of Roman civilisation. Secondly, there are more obvious considerations showing that the church spurned the state. The church became fabulously rich and no emperor, although Valentinian and Julian tried, was able to reverse this; perhaps by the later third century the empire was past such drastic measures. By the fifth century the salary bill of the church was more than that of the empire itself. This was a very novel phenomenon since pagan rituals had in the past been conducted by part-time priests and unpaid attendants.

Edward Gibbon famously argued that the spread of Christianity was associated with the fall of Rome. This is not strictly true. The sudden cost of the church cannot have helped the survival of the state, but this cannot by itself provide the explanation for the fall of Rome since only

8 A.H.M. Jones, *The Later Roman Empire*, Basil Blackwell, Oxford, 1973, p. 984.

the western part of the empire did fall. Christianity proved perfectly capable, moreover, of providing a Casesaropapist doctrine for Byzantium – a demonstration of the flexibility of a belief-system which runs counter to the Weberist ethic as a whole! Perhaps it did more. It has been argued that the feelings of quite large sections of the population were engaged. To fight against the barbarians was not only a necessary act, but also a holy one since they were heretical, being convinced of the Arian version of Christianity.

In the West the church played a different card. It moved from ingratitude to and scorn of the state to a realisation that it could not do without it. It was the church which negotiated with the barbarians at the walls of most cities, and arranged for them to be saved rather than destroyed. There are striking contrasts with the situation in other world civilisations. The barbarians did not bring their own rigorous and advanced religion with them, as did the Islamic conquerors who thus became impervious to the world they came to occupy. Nor were they like the Mongols in possessing strong organisational structures, and this too accounts for their openness to the Christian/civilised world. There could be no doubting the intellectual power of Christianity in comparison with the eclectic mumbo-jumbo of their own pagan gods: all barbarians converted very quickly after arriving. We have seen the Aryans in India differed from both of these instances in being at once unable to dominate while disinclined to let themselves be submerged. Nevertheless, the crucial contrast is with the situation in China, and this is worth re-emphasising. The intellectuals of that civilisation refused to serve barbarians until they accepted the imperial form. In Western Christendom, exactly the opposite was the case. The elite broke ranks. The intellectuals went out to the barbarians and provided services for them as well as the promise of universal salvation. For tribal chiefs the church, as the bearer of literacy, proved invaluable in allowing legal codification. Thus Gregory the Great's mission to England landed in 597, and by 616 more than 90 laws had been written down; much the same story could be told of the codification provided for the Lombards and the Franks. Underlying all this is something much simpler. The church wore the mantle of Rome. It *was* civilisation and the hope of a better life.[9]

This is the manner in which the city of God came to be disassociated from the imperial structure. It is a story pregnant with consequences, and these can be best approached by remembering the difficulty involved in applying the concept of 'society' outside a very narrow historical range. Rome was held together by military means, and China by the curious

9 P. Anderson, *Passages from Antiquity to Feudalism*, New Left Books, London, 1974, pp. 128–44.

character of its polity. But India, Islam and Christendom were cemented by ideological power. Thus if we ask what society was between 800 and 1050, the answer, all mediaevalists agree, is that it was Latin Christendom. The Christian church was, in Thomas Hobbes's phrase, the ghost of the Holy Roman Empire. Ideological power cemented the extensive space previously integrated by the legions.

This must affect our periodisation of history. That Christianity was the religion of the later empire *and* medieval Europe presents, as Engels realised, a terrible problem for Marxist stage theory; superstructures ought to behave better, and vary with changes in modes of production. However, if we do not adopt this stage theory, then we are returned to the traditional division between ancient and modern history. This division is justified for, as we shall now see, the Middle Ages did allow for the establishment of the dynamism that made Europe modern.

The Early Growth of the European Market Economy

Before describing the exact ways in which the Christian church served as an aid to the European economy, it is as well to substantiate the earlier claim that the European economy was taking on an intensive form early in its history. This is another occasion on which it is difficult to be certain of details, given the paucity of source material, but the general picture does seem clear. We can do no better than begin with technological breakthroughs.[10]

The watermill was known to the Romans, but it was not widely adopted by them. Why should it have been when the late empire handed over a legally bound dependent peasantry to the landlord? In early Christian Europe this changed and there was *considerable* investment at the local level. The Domesday Book of 1086 lists about 3,000 villages, and about twice that number of watermills. This itself is a tribute to the engineering capacities of the time and it was but one of several applications of those principles, fulling-mills and windmills becoming important in the thirteenth century. There is another invention that the Romans knew but again did not fully utilise. This is the carruca, the heavy plough, with a heavy iron share that dug deep into the soil, a metal coulter to direct the cut, and a mouldboard to turn the earth over and establish a furrow. The adoption of this plough was fundamental. Settlement need no longer be restricted to light and sandy hilltop soils with natural drainage, but could instead move down to the better, heavier clay soils of

10 Two accessible general accounts are: C. Cipolla, *Before the Industrial Revolution*, Methuen, London, 1976, and M.M. Postan, *Mediaeval Economy and Society*, Penguin, London, 1975.

the valleys. And the invention was itself improved with time. A new harness was invented which made it possible for horses rather than oxen to pull the plough. No single peasant was likely to have sufficient capital to own as many as the eight horses used to pull the heavy plough, so this invention had a reinforcing effect on the communitarian style of village agriculture. There were constant ramifications on land-use as well. Pasture was called for to feed horses of all types, that is for military use as well as for ploughing. This seems to have taken place very early on, and the Domesday Book again provides good evidence. Most place-names prior to nineteenth-century industrial capitalism were enshrined in William's cadastral report on his new kingdom, and that report also makes clear that the cultivation of the great majority of low-lying lands had begun long since.[11] Some note too should be made of the changes in land use, the most important of which is the change from a two-field to a three-field system. The two-field system allowed for one field to lie fallow while the other was planted with spring grain. The three-field system diminished the risk of failure by a single grain crop by allowing winter sowing in one field, spring sowing in another, while only the third lay fallow. Economic historians credit this change as having a considerable impact on productivity, as well as on diminishing the risk of crop failure. Certainly one thing is clear. The image of the peasant as uncultured and conservative is wide of the mark in so far as it is applied to the European peasantry. Time and again adaptability and intelligence are seen. Legumes were adopted since the nourishing power of their roots was well known, manure was spread whenever the local lord did not keep it all for his own land, and specialised crops were used for particular tasks – oats, for example, being grown extensively on recently reclaimed land.

These agrarian technological breakthroughs were fundamental. However many small, piecemeal technological improvements played a vital part in medieval and early modern Europe. This society showed considerable skill at invention, notably the boxed compass, and perhaps even more at adopting and adapting inventions which it borrowed from Islam and China, above all paper and gunpowder. As early as the thirteenth century Roger Bacon was creating dreams akin to Wellsian science fiction, and he went so far as to foresee some sort of submersible.[12]

None of this was immediately dramatic, but two crucial indicators nevertheless show that the change was definite. Firstly, population shows a long-term rise, albeit one which has a temporary setback as the result of the Black Death in the fourteenth century. It is very hard indeed to be

11 Postan, *Medieval Economy and Society*, ch. 1.

12 L. White, *Medieval Technology and Social Change*, Oxford University Press, Oxford, 1962.

precise about the figures involved. The most sustained attempt at producing such figures rests on questionable assumptions. Different assumptions about the size of the family unit in the Domesday Book, and about the number of people who evaded the poll tax of 1377, would create different pictures. The pre-plague population of England in the fourteenth century may perhaps have been just four million, but was probably nearer six to eight million.[13] But this does not really concern us; what does matter is the long-term improvement. The same is true of the situation as far as crop yields are concerned. Here too it is hard to get a long run of reliable figures from representative areas. Nevertheless the work of Slicher van Bath suggests, with increasing confidence after about 1200, that yields improved slowly but surely, although there was some fall-off from the late thirteenth century when newly reclaimed land lost fertility.[14] However, it is extremely important to bear in mind that yield ratios do not give the whole picture. European rainfall agriculture allowed each individual to farm a considerable number of acres. Obviously this became a vital factor in the agrarian revolution that preceded its more celebrated industrial partner. For it must not be forgotten that between approximately 1740 and 1800 British population trebled, and the land, without major technological improvement, proved capable of feeding these extra mouths. Secondly, Europeans always valued pasture. This is not just to say that there was grazing for horses, but that Europeans, with some regularity, ate meat. The diet of the medieval peasant may seem terrible to our eyes, but is was significantly better than that of the other pre-agrarian civilisations. Certainly, the presence of large numbers of livestock represented a type of capital that was missing in China.

It is time to turn from description to analysis and explanation. How was all this possible? Five points seem to have especial prominence.

Normative consensus

The first question we must address is why Europe did not turn into a doggedly local culture. We have seen that pre-industrial empires failed to integrate local communities which were effectively separated from each other; such civilisations only have some measure of elite integration. The fall of Rome could have removed even the latter. Yet this did not happen. The explanation has already been suggested, and it represents the greatest contribution of Christianity to the medieval economy. *Christianity kept Europe together*, and kept localities continuously aware of greater

13 Postan, *Mediaeval Economy and Society*, ch. 3.

14 S. van Bath, 'Yield ratios, 810–1820', *Afdeling Agrarische Geschiedenis Bijdragen*, vol. 10, 1963.

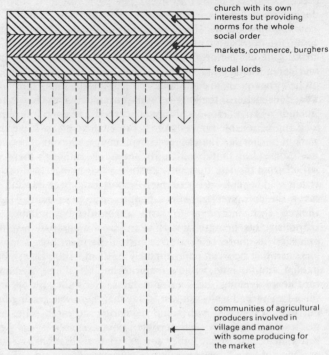

church with its own
interests but providing
norms for the whole
social order

markets, commerce, burghers

feudal lords

communities of agricultural
producers involved in
village and manor
with some producing for
the market

Model 5: Christian Society, 800–1050

horizons. This can be emphasised by means of another model. We must spend some time explaining what is involved and implied here.

Trade began quite early in the Dark Ages, and there is a link between that trade and Christianity.

Paganism may have deterred the primary state from engaging consistently in long-distance trade with the north. This was changed by the end of the eighth century, when most of the Frisian coastline had been brought within the Christian orbit, and in any case the Baltic wealth must have been a vital element in the economic goal of Charlemagne's Carolingia. It was perhaps no coincidence that Carolingian missionaries went with merchants to the great emporia ... thus giving some countenance to the mercantile operation.[15]

The period 600–1000 saw trade in more than luxury articles. The Vikings carried as basic a material as wood, and this meant that the market principle in the European context bit deeper, and was thus more

15 R. Hodges, *Dark Age Economics*, Duckworth, London, 1982, p. 193.

powerful than it had been in Sung China. The general point is clear. The market was made possible because people felt themselves part of a single community. Carlo Cipolla stresses the uncertainties involved in medieval trading networks and suggests that high degrees of trust were needed to make them work over great space and large periods of time. 'It was the widespread sense of honesty, strengthened by the sense of belonging to an integrated community, quite apart from definite legal provisions, which made possible the participation of all kinds of people with their savings in the productive process.[16]

Economists are often prone to forget that the rules of the market must be maintained for individual exchanges to proceed; consensus, to use the lapidary Durkheimian formation, must precede contract. In this early period there is a sense in which the church *was* the government, in that it made people feel part of a single community, and, as was probably not the case with Hinduism, equal members of that community. It is important to contrast this with the situation in Islam. These two great monotheistic religions helped the market principle by making human contacts possible within a large geographical space, but beyond this similarity lies a considerable difference. Islamic polities inside that larger culture, from the beginning and throughout history, proved to be predatory, and enemies of market principles. In contrast Christianity managed for a long period without any significant polity at all. In so doing it gave civil society such strength that it was able to create states that were not predatory in character, and competition between them also limited arbitrary rule.

The church's extensive ability to integrate the community deserves further documentation. It can be seen in its laying down the rules that should apply to warfare; one set of rules applied to Christians but a very different set to the infidel. Rules were also devised by the church to control blood feuds. After an earlier period in which the church placed high hopes on the state as an agency of peace and control, it began to try and create peace by itself. Thus in the tenth century began the important movement calling for peaces and truces of God, and regulating fighting so that it should occur away from markets, should not touch churchmen, and was permissible only on certain days of the week. Such rules were no doubt poorly observed, and even more poorly enforced; but it is nonetheless significant to see which organisation – and the matter, let it be stressed, is organisational rather than doctrinal! – is providing crucial services for society.

Further, the Latin Christian church was ambitious. It was rich, powerful and possessed of a monotheistic consicience. In the ninth century it

16 Cipolla, *Before the Industrial Revolution*, p. 199.

lay down a full-blooded ideological programme designed to bring every-one within the religious fold. The bishops around Charlemagne clearly wished Christianity to be more than a set of pagan rites rewritten in Christian terms, and to that end they codified rites and sought to establish a certain minimal level of exposure to reasonably trained parish priests. Of course, this ideological programme was not fully carried out. Nevertheless it *did* represent a firm assault on popular religiosity. It was an attempt to make the values of the elite, so thinly spread at the top in Rome, those of the whole society. The church *did* organise spiritual life, but it could not organise all social and political life. Only the Brahmans managed this. They accepted much magical and sectarian belief, and organised society accordingly by systematically withdrawing from power. In contrast, there was a long history of attempts to purify the church and establish real Christianity, a history that culminated in the Reformation, and which had a signal success in the taming of magic. In a nutshell, Christian Europe tried to integrate more than the elite, and to penetrate society much more generally. The extraordinary flexibility and adaptabil-ity of the Christian church meant that in the Middle Ages it allied itself with the other two orders in a neat division of labour in which some fought, others worked, and the priests prayed. Peasants often did not believe in this particular theory and regarded their local bishop as nothing more than a feudal lord who exploited them and who was far removed from the poverty, the proper poverty, which ought to have characterised such a man. So there was considerable knowledge about Christianity throughout society, and to that extent the spreading of shared Christian norms was a success, even though there clearly re-mained high and low interpretations of that tradition.

Landlords

Why, however, was there investment in the land via the technological changes described? This question can be given an answer in this section *and* the next, concentrating in turn on the landlord and peasant.

It is as well to begin by recalling that the landlords of the Roman empire were far less technologically imaginative. The fundamental reason for the change is surely that of the presence of the market, for this opened up opportunities that had simply, perhaps curiously, not been seen before. But there are two other factors worth stressing.

Firstly, property was secure. In fourteenth-century China, to take but one example, the Ming accession led to 100,000 deaths, and the arbitrar-iness of court politics, while not always affecting great numbers, always caused uncertainty which made the presence of a member of the clan in the bureaucracy quite vital. In contrast, European landholding was far more settled, among the few notable general appropriations of feudal land being those that occurred as the result of the Albigensian crusade and the Norman Conquest. This is not to say that early rulers would not have liked to have a much firmer control of the land: the simple fact was that they were much too weak to ensure this. This weakness is symbolised by the famous Capitulary of Charles the Bald in 877 which gave benefice status to land previously held on a conditional basis only. Of course, the military situation played a notable part in this development since the requirements of feudal warfare placed a premium on decentralisation. Equally importantly, the church was not really a *government* of early medieval Europe, and was certainly not able to appropriate land in quite this manner, for reasons to be examined. It is worth highlighting the results of this security of tenure.

Security doubtless had something to do with eventually turning the medieval world into a highly corporatist culture. This point was much stressed by a Calabrian monk of Greek parentage called Barlaam who visited Latin Christendom in the thirteenth-century.

The whole people is ruled by laws. Even the smallest matters are subject to regulation and orderly administration. All ranks of society are taught how to behave towards each other. They know how sins are punished and good deeds rewarded and conduct examined: all these things and everything else that is useful for preserving society in peace is defined and guarded by law.[17]

This is an important point which deserves some amplification. The complete disintegration of the Roman political structure created full, rather than merely prebendal, feudalism, that is not just a temporary right to land or to collection of taxes, but rather permanent and total possession of an area, which usually incorporated control over local justice. Such full feudalism placed landlords so firmly in possession of their lands that thereafter any services or taxes could be extracted only on the basis of shared understanding, that is by a process of co-operation. This is of the greatest import. Landlords were in place before monarchs and they were able to establish rights and liberties, as Magna Carta showed. In this area, Adam Smith's praise of towns is somewhat overdone: a concern with the rule of law *has* some roots in the nobility itself. Furthermore, this security in landholding was a vital background assumption to *some* investment in the land, even if levels of investment remained quite low initially. But over the longer time span there is no doubt that the landlords eventually chose to invest significantly. The result was, at least in the British case, that extraordinary type of commercial and capitalist agriculture (and not industrial capitalism as is naïvely

17 Cited in R.W. Southern, *Western Society and the Church in the Middle Ages*, Penguin, London, 1979, p. 81.

presumed) which was the true subject of Adam Smith's *Wealth of Nations*.

Secondly, over the longer time span there were few other outlets by which landlords *could* make money. The relative failure of the French eighteenth-century landlords to commercialise agriculture has traditionally been explained in these terms. Such landlords were not held back by scorn of money itself; they simply found that money gained via the state was a better option. This had been true in China as well. It was by no means continuously true. Early in the Dark Ages considerable profits were to be made in war, and it may be that a significant section of the English aristocracy did rather well out of the Hundred Years War.[18] But in general terms there was no option but to gain money through the land since the state was simply not rich enough to provide much of an avenue of social mobility. As a result, as model 5 shows, local penetration was encouraged.

This is one of the two ways in which the market principle proved to be so strong in Europe. Bureaucratic politics always interfered with the market in China whilst the instability of polities in Islam and India proved quite as deleterious for economic life. In early Christian Europe interference, whether bureaucratic or predatory, was not possible given the absence of real government. The benefits of civilisation were achieved without some of the costs that distorted market relations. Once the market was in place it proved difficult thereafter for states to alter its hegemony.

Peasants

This discussion of feudal landlords is likely to mislead unless a second element in the rural economy is placed equally centre-stage. This is the village community comprised of freemen, those with some of their own land but dependent in part on the manor, and those entirely dependent on the landlord. Here again sufficient information is lacking, but a hint of the point to be made can be found in the Marxist contention that there are two routes to capitalism – one via commercial landlords and the other via large peasant, yeomen farmers. Obviously, much of the investment in the land, not to mention peasant conquest of virgin land in Eastern Europe, represents the application of the greater energies of the mass of the population. Perhaps the impact of the barbarians invading Rome was not one which simply came to the aid of a feudal aristocracy, but rather encouraged the activities of other elements in the population as well.

18 G. Duby, *The Early Growth of the European Economy*, Weidenfeld & Nicolson, London, 1974.

Perhaps too Christianity proved favourable to economic growth. It stressed that everyone was *equal* in the sight of God. The contrast with classical Hinduism is obvious.

This is the second aspect of depth to the market principle in Europe Medieval Europe was of course a highly inegalitarian society, but the slope of that inequality was nevertheless slightly less steep than in China. The social and economic participation ratio was greater than in other agrarian civilisations. The elite of Europe was itself larger than those of other agrarian civilisations. The point being made is, however, slightly different. Participation in society bit deeply, and went beyond the elite altogether; in so far as it did so, model 5 misleads. The market surrounded all society, and was not just something at the 'top' of European civilisation. It is demand that made the European city, whose characteristic contribution has yet to be examined, so vital – a unit of production rather than one of consumption. Most historians now stress that the industrial revolution was much helped by widespread, generalised demand. Liberties, even though of different weight, were scattered throughout society; they provided the baseline for liberal politics. The whole point can be summed up in the rare but significant occasion in which Edward I was taken to court by peasants on the grounds that his exactions for the Scottish wars were illegal!

The precise manner in which the village and the landlord operated as an ensemble is the subject of very lively scholarly debate. Postan's general account is essentially 'neutral' and Malthusian since it stresses that the condition of the peasantry benefited from demographic decline, with the converse being true of the landlord. Marxist thinkers seeking to stress exploitation naturally wish to bring class relations back into the picture. Thus the thirteenth-century rise in landlord incomes is held to have been caused *merely* by an increase in the landlord share via the much hated banalities, that is the right to a certain take from the use of the local mill and so on. Anderson and Brenner pay most attention to a great problem for Marxist theory. The loss of peasant numbers caused by the Black Death should have encouraged the feudal class to use its military superiority in a burst of landlord reaction designed, as had happened in the later Roman empire, to tie the peasant more firmly to the land. Such a reaction *was* tried all over Europe but, interestingly, in the core areas of Western Europe it did not succeed. Anderson suggests that their reaction was defeated by an alliance between rebellious peasants, based on the powerful resources of the village, and the cities which offered serfs freedom provided they lived there undetected for a year and a day – a theory which certainly does not fit the English case. Brenner seeks to emphasise the former of these alone, believing that the number and size of European cities could not have had the decisive impact which Anderson envisages: the core of his argument is that serfdom could not be re-established in Western Europe because of the entrenched position of the peasantry, whereas in Eastern Europe land-lord dominance led precisely to a second serfdom.[19]

It would be foolish to seek to adjudicate this debate. Probably both sets of factors were at work, and the interpretations on offer are by no means mutually exclusive. One comment is necessary however. Postan's analy-sis of the English case makes him insist that it was the smaller landlords who particularly wished to tie the peasantry down: *the greater landlords realised that there was another way to greater profits.* They broke ranks and, one after another, rented out their land.

But whether the demand for wage curbs did or did not come from the feudal landlords, the curbs themselves proved ineffective. As we know now, the laws of supply and demand proved stronger than the employers' pressure and the legislation it produced; and wages continued to rise until some time in the fifteenth century.[20]

This can be put more bluntly: the market principle defeated landlord reaction. The reason for stressing this is that Brenner has sought to discount the explanatory value of the market principle by arguing that this principle encouraged the landlords of Eastern Europe to institute a second serfdom. But the market principle *was* related to the decline of serfdom in the West. In contrast, an already established market of a core area may allow the production of a single crop or commodity by a peripheral area; in such a situation the link between the market principle and the decline of serfdom is less strong, and may even be reversed.

Family and kinship

In recent years, much attention has been devoted to the peculiarities of the Western European family pattern. Although research is beginning to show that there was considerable variety within Europe, particularly between the Mediterranean and more northern areas, the general prop-osition that the European family has long been small, late marrying, nuclear and notably sensitive in reacting to Malthusian pressure, re-mains. This is an important matter to note here, and it allows us to systematise our comments on kinship in pre-industrial civilisations. The absence of strong kinship links in Europe as compared to their presence in the other agrarian civilisations had economic and political consequ-

19 Postan, *Medieval Economy and Society*; Anderson, *Passages from Antiquity to Feudalism*; R. Brenner, 'The agrarian roots of European capitalism', *Past and Present*, no. 70, 1976, and the ensuing debate in that journal.

20 Postan, *Medieval Economy and Society*, p. 170.

ences. The former are discussed here, and the latter later in this chapter. The expansion of the European economy did not occur *laterally*, as in late traditional China, because improvements in output were not eaten up by a massive growth in population. The ratio between population and acreage in Europe remained favourable ultimately because of the relative continence of the European family, although at crucial moments in the thirteenth-century, and as a result of the discoveries, this ratio was much helped by the 'ghost acreage' suddenly opened up in Eastern Europe and the colonies. The evidence with which to explain this vital matter is not available, but it is so important that it is worth considering.[21]

Firstly, we must take note of a thesis on the relation of the Latin Christian church to kinship and marriage.[22] The documentation of this thesis takes it well beyond an occasional remark of Marc Bloch to demonstrate that the Christian church, as greedy for land as had been Theravada Buddhism, attacked the traditional kinship relations of the barbarians. Those relations had been wont to retain land within the kinship system; there was thus a duty to marry the wife of a brother and, importantly, a duty to provide for all members of the kinship network. By a series of detailed measures – attacks on concubinage, the levirate, marriage between close affines and so on – the church created a situation in which the family became detached from the larger kinship system, nuclearised, and therefore in a position whereby land could be granted to the church in return for prayers for salvation. This service provided by the church was not restricted to the lower levels of society. Although European dynastic politics do often have a curiously domestic flavour to them, not least in the nineteenth-century, one must still note the great change that took place. Though Charlemagne divided his kingdom in traditional style between his sons, by the eleventh century has successors were handing their kingdoms to a single heir.

One point needs to be added to Goody's account. His argument is like most in this book that concern ideology, in that it does not stress doctrine, the crucial point in his view being the self-interested actions of the church. This general position can only be strengthened by noting that the ability of the church to operate in this manner itself resulted from the position in which it found itself. The late empire tried to clamp down on grants of land to the church, but it was too weak to be successful, and thereafter the state was even weaker for several hundred years. The power of the church in this matter resulted, in other words, from the lack of a polity above it capable of controlling it. Goody's thesis

21 E.L. Jones, *The European Miracle*, Cambridge University Press, Cambridge, 1981, ch. 1.

22 J. Goody, *The development of the family and marriage in Europe*, Cambridge University Press, Cambridge, 1983.

is an exciting one. It may not be true. Perhaps the weakness of kinship in Europe resulted from the weakness of the barbarian states of the West.[23] Perhaps it was *then* easy for the church to have this impact. Whatever the case, it is impossible to resist speculations on the basis of the *fact* of weak kinship patterns, although speculations they must remain given the fact that inheritance practices varied quite widely throughout Europe. The family was uniquely isolated as a result of greed for land on the part of the church, and it was unique in keeping a favourable man–land ratio. Surely these factors must be related? Is it not possible that the certainty that one's own land was to remain one's own encouraged small families because they could be certain of passing it on to their heirs? Might not the encouragement of individualism, so notably absent in China, India and Islam, have reinforced the market principle, especially in the sale of land? Certainly the joint family system of Hindu India and the clan system of Confucian China made such sales harder to achieve. All this is possible, as is the political impact of weak kinship, namely the relationship between weak kinship structures and organic states noted below.

A further consideration is important. European society was much less prone to suffer from natural disasters, and felt them much less when they came than did a society with irrigation agriculture. There was correspondingly a lesser need for extended kinship system which were so important for recovery from disaster in China.[24]

The church's economic role

In the Middle Ages the church acquired about a third of all land, partly from bequests, partly from purchase, and partly from new orders such as the Cistercians, which on principle insisted on living in and developing marginal land. The church played a vital part in the European economy because it used much of its land very wisely. If we remember Max Weber's characterisation of rational capitalism, as an insistence on discipline, regularity and orderliness, then we can see that the church, and especially monasticism,[25] was the first this-worldly and ascetic organisation of European history. It is deeply significant that many of our records for early medieval history descend from the church. Churchmen applied their literate skills to book-keeping, and this was of course a necessary background to sustained agricultural improvement. The church, itself of course the greatest multinational organisation in European history, en-

23 This idea was suggested to me by Patricia Crone.

24 Jones, *The European Miracle*, ch. 2.

25 This was most true of course on the case of those orders which chose, in striking contrast to the world-renouncing monasteries of Thervada Buddhism, to live in cities.

couraged economic revival both by the demand it created and by continually sending money and goods of its own all over Europe.

Rational science

Rational science, as we have seen, was to some extent blocked in the other world civilisations. But what of Europe? This is a vast matter, but one directly related to our general theme. Two comments may be made.

Firstly, a highly suggestive argument has been put forward by Cook and Crone, and by Milton.[26] The thesis of these authors centres on the doctrinal inheritance of the Occident. They argue that rational science depends upon combining two elements, namely the Greek conception of natural law and the Judaic conception of divine control. Greek natural law by itself merely encouraged the classification of the surface phenomena without seeking to provide an explanation of their structure, while any conception of divine control can militate against rational science since divine intervention may occur on an occasional basis. Only with a pattern established by a God who did *not* habitually interfere with the rules of nature laid down could rational science flourish.

It is beyond my capacity to decide on the validity of this fascinating 'Weberist' thesis. But there is a second, much more obvious side to the matter. European science benefited from the unique autonomy of the European city, from whence much European science sprang. To the explanation of such autonomy and, indeed, to the political construction of Europe as a whole, we can now turn.

The Organic State in the State System

The origins of Christianity within the Roman empire meant that it lacked the political theory characteristic of Islam. But relations with that empire were too short to turn Latin Christendom in a Caesaropapist direction, as was the case in Byzantium and effectively also in China. How did this curious inheritance affect political structures in European history? What role did the character of these structures have on the rise of the West? The argument to be made has three parts: a counterfactual proposition, a characterisation of the organic state and an appreciation of the role of state competition. All of these parts are mutually supporting, and all centre on the undoubted fact that European society did not, despite the

---

26 M. Cook and P. Crone, *Hagarism*, Cambridge University Press, Cambridge, 1977; J. Milton, 'The origin of the concept "Laws of Nature"', *European Journal of Sociology*, vol. 22, 1982.

attempts of Charlemagne, Frederick Barbarossa, Napoleon and Hitler, develop an imperial structure after the collapse of Rome.

At first sight some of the statements in the preceding paragraph may seem slightly overblown. Surely, it might be objected, the church did develop a political theory, and did seek to establish a real imperial papacy? This is, of course, true and it is a further manifestation of the relative flexibility of much religious doctrine. By the middle of the eleventh century a reforming spirit originating in Cluny swept through the church, and created a drive for power seen most clearly in the lives of Gregory VII, Innocent III and Boniface VIII. In this period, between approximately 1050 and 1300, the papacy had, to over-simplify somewhat, certain doubts as to the wisdom of the crowning of Charlemagne as Holy Roman Emperor in 800, and it sought to qualify its previous stance. Most dramatically, the papacy humiliated the Emperor Henry II at Canossa. The origin of many arguments between popes and emperors was in the disputes over the right to grant clerical appointments. Formally the pope won, and it was such victories which help account for the creation of the papal governmental and juridical machine at this period. The church grew even richer and more powerful. But did it manage to establish a new primacy sufficient to give it something like an imperial status? Was it able to translate its theory into practice? The answer to these questions must be negative. The papacy never possessed its own army, whilst the various kings of Europe very plainly did. It was not a real government. Thus all that Innocent III could do to the rebellious King John was to excommunicate him and his whole kingdom. Apparently this made not a jot of difference to the daily running of the kingdom. A greater sign of papal weakness was seen when French bishops sided with their king against Boniface VIII who had challenged him at the start of the fourteenth century. The attempted imperial papacy inflated its promises of advancement in such a way that advancement finally came when the king put *his* weight behind a client. The facade of Christian control over Europe was maintained until the fifteenth century in large part because the secular powers of society had come to learn how the papal machine could in fact be operated to their best advantage.

It is now time to turn to the other side of the coin. If the drive to an imperial papacy was defeated as much by the presence of diverse states as by anything else, how did those states come into being in the first place? Specifically, what role did the church play in the creation of such states? The fact that *several* sets of barbarians came into Europe at the end of the Roman empire, rather than a single set as was the case with China and Islam, was doubtless an initial condition in favour of a multipolar system. We can add to this that the church played a very notable role in making a secular empire impossible. Most obviously it welcomed the rise of states which were able to give more secure protection to its own property. But there is a more important point to be made: the church refused to serve as second fiddle in an empire equivalent to those of China and Byzantium, and thus did not create a Caesaropapist doctrine in which a single emperor was elevated to semi-divine status. Indeed, very much the opposite is the case. The church's habitual playing of power politics encouraged the formation of separate states whose autonomy eventually led to the failure of its own imperial drive. This whole process was symbolised in 1312 when the Emperor Henry VII asked the pope to send Robert of Sicily, the pope's vassal, to the imperial court at Pisa. Clement V issued the bull *Pastoralis Curia* in which he argued that a king owed no duties to the emperor, and was instead master in his own realm. This was not the only way in which Christianity provided the best shell for the emergence of states. The church provided the numinous aspects of kingship – the coronation and the singing of the *Laudes Regiae* for example – which made a king more than one among equals. More important still was its attack on extended kinship systems. The political dimension to the limited European kinship system can usefully and simply be summarised here. In the other world civilisations, perhaps above all Islam, the lower classes could often rely upon kinship systems as a means of protection and mutual aid. The removal of the weapon of the lower classes made the European peasant that much better material for state formation.

With these background comments in mind, the first argument can be presented. Imagine what European history might have been like had the Roman empire somehow been reconstituted, or had any empire taken its place! Empires are, as noted, too centralised for their logistical capacity, and thus have produced capstone government based on their accurate knowledge that secondary organisations are dangerous. Empires usually sought to encourage the economy, but this form of government has historically never ultimately allowed sufficient leeway to the economy for it to gather self-sustaining momentum. Why should an imperial Europe have been any different? One notable characteristic of the Christian tradition is its adaptability to different types of power – from trying to establish its own empire, to briefly supporting a secular emperor, and eventually to acceding to *cuius regio, eius religio*. If there had been a European empire, it is extemely likely that the Christian church would have provided it with an ethic that distrusted economic gain quite as much as did Confucianism.

This counterfactual can be put in a rather different manner. The contention of this chapter has been that a decentralised market system, based on a sense of belonging to a single civilisation, came into place during those years in which there was no real government which could interfere with its workings. An imperial form would very probably have sought to control such 'natural' processes. The point is perhaps best illustrated by a consideration of the European city. Historians agree that Max Weber *was* correct in the more materialist part of his theory concerning the rise of the West, namely in his contention that only in Europe did the city gain full autonomy. Only here did cities possess their *own* governments and armies rather than being controlled by the arbitrary rule of mandarins. It has been argued that it is the depth of market penetration throughout European society that ensured the ultimate success of the market principle, and that it is this which made cities so important. Nevertheless, it would be a mistake to deny the extraordinary importance of the European city. It invented a new civilisation, that of the Renaissance, whose political theory contributed vitally to the rest of European history. It provided a space in which the merchant was politically powerful, and in which bourgeois values could gell and solidify. We live in the world created by this civilisation. With a matter of such import, it is essential to ask how this autonomy occurred. One part of the answer is that the key North Italian cities wedded their monetary might with new military techniques to provide a powerful combination that gave them protection until the invasion of the French at the end of the fifteenth century. It was precisely this combination of money and military means that the Chinese so wisely sought to undermine. Yet the more satisfying answer is that the North Italian cities were themselves the creation of the absence of a single centre of power in Europe. Specifically, they gained their autonomy as the result of a power vacuum between pope and emperor such that they were able, as in Third World countries today, to get the best for themselves by opportunistically chopping and changing their allegiance.[27] How much they owed to their freedom from interference and freedom to experiment is simply seen: once they became part of the Spanish mini-empire they contributed virtually nothing new to European civilisation. The same point can be made by indulging in a 'thought experiment'. Had Philip II created a long-lasting empire based on his new Spanish possessions, what would have happened to the social experiments taking place in the United Provinces and England? It seems likely that social experiments at the peripheries would have been ruled out.

It might at first sight seem contradictory, after the largely negative comments made ceaselessly about the polities of the other world civilisations, to say that the *organic* state of Europe *helped* in economic development. However, no simple view of 'the state' is of much use in social

27 I owe this point to Peter Burke who informs me that it is derived from Jacob Burckhardt.

theory. There are *different* types of state in different historical and social circumstances. For what it is worth, two general principles about the relations of government to the economy can be maintained. Firstly, the absence of all government is disastrous since it encourages localism and thus prevents trade; the argument made already about the service provided by Christianity in holding Europe together shows that no such anarchist vision is encouraged here. Secondly, however, what I have referred to as capstone imperial government, characteristically distrusting secondary organisations and indeed all uncontrolled participation by its citizens, *was* indeed hostile to endogenous economic development. The Indian custodial state and the Islamic cyclical polity, both unstable and hence predatory, interfered with the market just as much. Such governments were not really strong since they were based on weak infrastructural penetration of the society. Their arbitrariness, albeit different in form, results in each case from that shared weakness. This gives us the clue to the distinctiveness of the European state: a limit to arbitrariness combined with, indeed in part caused, considerable and ever-increasing infrastructural penetration. Two such limits are important.

The first limit is straighforward. The European state evolved slowly and doggedly in the midst of a pre-existent civil society. It is no capstone or predatory organisation in large part because it was not a conquest state. Rather its history is typified by the cautious policy whereby, say, the king of France was slowly able to expand from his own domains in the Ile-de-France to dominate the larger region we know today as France. This process took a very long time, and was only fully completed by the French Revolution. This general point can be made a different way. One other uniqueness of the West is the role that parliaments played in its history; indeed so unique has this role been that German historians have considered the Standestaat, the meetings of the three functional estates, church, noble and burgher, to be a distinctive stage in world history.[28] It is quite clear that the prominence of such assemblies owed a great deal to the church. Since it owned so much land it was as jealous as any noble of the powers of the crown to tax. Hence it popularised two tags of canon law – 'no taxation without representation' and 'what touches all must be approved by all' – and these became crucial to these estates. Civil society, for it deserves to be called nothing less, pre-existed the monarch. His only way of gaining money was to co-operate with his society. European pluralism was, in other words, based upon the strength and autonomy of the groups involved.

28 J.H. Myers, *Parliaments and Estates in Europe to 1789*, Thames & Hudson, 1975; G. Poggi, *The Development of the Modern State*, Hutchinson, London, 1978.

Restraint on government in the end generated a large total sum of power in society. Perhaps the most important mechanism in this process was the king's decision to make money by providing a certain infrastructure to the society. This is clearly seen in the provision of justice. The lawyer has a very central place in European society and it results from the king's desire to gain profits from justice. Fees were charged for every legal transaction, and these came to provide an important part of the revenue of most monarchs after about 1200. This is not of course to say that the law was equally open for all to use, but it was present. Increasingly, European states provided other sorts of infrastructural help. They became good at managing disasters of various sorts. By the eighteenth century, for example, considerable help was available to the victims of earthquakes, while disease was quite rigidly controlled by quarantine laws.[29] This was but one example of their seeking to encourage economic growth. Unconsciously, the internal colonialism whereby Scots, Irish and Welsh were integrated into a single community – a process repeated elsewhere in Europe – created a single market. In the more advanced European states (that is, not France until post–1789) this process went hand-in-hand with the removal of internal tariff barriers, and this was an incentive to trade. The rulers had consciously encouraged such trade for a long time – in Hodges's rather questionable view since the Dark Ages.[30] They did so because a disproportionate bulk of their revenues came from customs and excise. They did all they could to attract traders, and a typical piece of legislation in this matter was Edward I's *Carta Mercatoria* of 1297. It is worth trying to summarise the general spirit at work here. It is not being claimed that 'society' had suddenly come to include everybody, although the degree of literacy and the eventual creation of a national tongue do witness the emergence of what is properly called the *nation* state. What is apparent is that large sections of the powerful in society were prepared in the long run to give quite high taxation revenues to the crown because they realised that their own interests were usualy being served. Conflicts of course occurred, and they make up much of European history. Nevertheless the more important fact remains the organic quality of the state. It can be summed up in the phenomenon that so impressed Tocqueville on his visit to England, the pacemaker in European history so far as the evolution of the organic state is concerned. Where many aristocracies – Chinese, Roman, and until 1789, French – hid their wealth from the state and refused to do its bidding, the English aristocracy and gentry manned local government

29 Jones, *The European Miracle*, ch. 7.
30 Hodges, *Dark Age Economics*.

and taxed itself. There was no fundamental power stand-off between state and society and the level of infrastructural support and penetration was correspondingly high. A Confucian bureaucrat who was moved every three years simply could not know enough about local conditions to serve a particular area well; representation to a central assembly by local aristocrats from the area created a different result. The state in Europe was thereby able to penetrate deeper and deeper into society in the long run.

The second general restraint on arbitrariness is also the third general point to be made about the European polity. Individual states did not exist in a vacuum. They were rather part of a competing state system, and it was that system, particularly the military organisation it engendered, which played a considerable part in determining the character of individual states. Political competition proved beneficial to economic progress. Why was this?

Perhaps the most obvious fact about a state system is that it leads to a high degree of emulation. This can be seen in European history most spectacularly in the history of art. The invasion of Italy by the French in the late fifteenth century spread the styles of the Italian Renaissance around Europe, and thereafter rivalry and status-seeking ensured that what was fashionable elsewhere had to be copied at home. This emulation was not confined to artistic matters, but extended to the establishment of various scientific clubs in eighteenth-century France in conscious imitation of their English rivals. Such emulation is ultimately only possible between states which recognised each other as of more or less similar standing. Empires do not tend to copy the culture of small neighbours whom they judge to be mere barbarians! A multipolar system proved beneficial for economic growth in other ways. A state system always had an inbuilt escape system. This is most obviously true in human matters. The expulsion of the Jews from Spain and the Huguenots from France benefited, and was seen to benefit, other countries and this served in the long run as a limitation on arbitrary government. Very importantly, capital was equally mobile. Thus Philip II's abuse of Antwerp led *within a matter of years* to the rise of Amsterdam. In a brilliant passage making this point, W.H. McNeill has shown that time and again Philip II *wanted* to behave like an autocrat but the mobility of capital defeated him. This was particularly true of his relationship with Liège, the foremost cannon-producer of late sixteenth-century Europe. When Philip pressurised them too hard, artisans and capitalists simply went elsewhere. In this connection it is important to remember that one could go elsewhere to a stable state, that is from a rapacious state to a long-lasting and organic state somewhere in the larger society; this was not possible in Islam and India. A certain measure of decent and regularised behaviour was ensured by these means.[31] However, perhaps the most fundamental mechanism at work was that of military competition. Mann's striking reconstruction of the figures for English state finance show with great clarity that the major expenditure of the British state was on warfare, and that jumps in levels of expenditure were occasioned either by wars or by the need to invest in new military technology, pikemen, gunpowder, Italian-style defences against gunpowder, larger armies, conscription, and so on.[32]

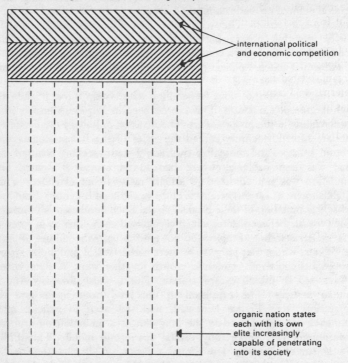

international political
and economic competition

organic nation states
each with its own
elite increasingly
capable of penetrating
into its society

Model 6: European society from 1300

The impact of the slaughter of the First World War on our image of war has been so great that we are all pacifists now in the sense of being opposed to war. Yet we must remember that war was a normal, and

31 W.H. McNeill, *The Pursuit of Power*, Basil Blackwell, Oxford, 1982, ch. 1.

32 M. Mann, 'State and society, 1130–1815: an analysis of English state finances', in M. Zeitlin (ed.) *Political Power and Social Theory*, vol. I, J.A.I. Press, Connecticut, 1980.

usually acceptable, form of behaviour for European states in history. War in European history served as a source of progress. Rome, feeling itself to be the world, never had to dramatically intensify its society since outsiders were felt to be inferior. The situation was very different when states at the same level competed with each other. A revolution in military technology had to be adopted very quickly by neighbouring states on pain of dismemberment – something which famously happened to the Polish state at the end of the eighteenth century and again in 1939.

A final heuristic model is now in order. The model makes clear that the holding role of Christian culture finished by about 1300. But from this a larger framework ensued, comprising the international market and international competition via war. The model is slightly defective in placing these international constraints above states since they rather surrounded them. It is within these international constraints that organic states have had to function. The relations between the two international factors is very complicated. Sometimes the one or the other was in ascendancy; wars were, for example, occasionally fought decidedly for economic gain. But each factor was necessary to the rise of the West, and each possessed its own dynamism.

Conclusions to this Chapter and to Part One

Dugald Stewart recorded that Adam Smith believed that 'Little else is requisite to carry a state to the highest degree of opulence from the lowest barbarism, but peace, easy taxes, and a tolerable administration of justice; all the rest being brought about by the natural course of things.'[33] It is well worth characterising the argument of the first part of this book in the light of Smith's comment. There *are* very considerable similarities. Most obviously, stress here has been placed on the autonomy gained by the European market and an underlying general consideration, justified by historical sociology, is that the first emergence of autonomous economic development was possible *only* in a capitalist form. These sorts of considerations led one critic to say that my argument conceptualised ideology and politics in a negative sense only, that is as blocking forces while the prime mover in the argument remains the economy in the spirit outlined by Dugald Stewart.[34] In other words, the account is recognised

---

33 D. Stewart, 'Account of the life and writings of Adam Smith, Ll.D' in vol. III of *The Glasgow Edition of the Works and Correspondence of Adam Smith*, that is, *Essays on Philosophical Subjects*, Oxford University Press, Oxford, 1980, p. 322.

34 I am grateful to Professor Jürgen Habermas for making this criticism since it has made me highlight the nature of my argument.

not to be naïvely economically determinist, as was Marx's, since it recognises the roles of other factors, but it is held to remain so in a more sophisticated manner in lending motive power to only one of them. What truth is there in this characterisation?

Let me begin by summarising my own argument. The claim being made is that there are two crucial differences between Latin Christendom and the other world civilisations, namely the autonomy and the direction of power sources. In Islam, India and China, it is possible to distinguish social groups, and to note that they exist in some kind of power stand-off situation: the Brahmans withdrew in a particular way from politics, the mandarins limited the autonomy of the empire and the ulama regularly opposed mundane political life. Not all power sources had distinct existences, and this was especially true of the economy. In China, India and Islam the powerful influenced economic relationships, through bureaucratic interference or predatory rule, so much that it is misleading even to talk of a separate 'economic' realm working according to its own principles. In contrast, Christendom allowed for strong and autonomous power sources. Remarkably these power sources did not then block each other but rather went in the same direction. The presence of liberties ensured the creation of organic polities which eventually became translated into liberal systems of rule. We can rationally reconstruct how this occurred, but it is all too easy to imagine things happening otherwise. It was the European miracle.

Smith appreciated much of all this, but there are differences between my argument and his. They can best be approached by critically examining certain key moments in his argument. Stewart's quotation tends to give the impression that market forces are ever present. However, blocking of those forces can occur not just after they exist but in order that they may not gain much freedom in the first place. Both limitations were present in Islam, India and China. Smith did note certain features that lent the market in Europe great depth and salience. The highly idiosyncratic total political breakdown of the Roman empire gave a special prominence to both landlords and peasants. The former were admired and defended by Smith and Hume because they were not parasitical; unlike their Chinese, Islamic and Indian counterparts, they interested themselves in commercial agriculture. Dugald Stewart tells us that Smith accurately noted that:

... it was the general diffusion of wealth among the lower orders of men, which first gave birth to the spirit of independence in modern Europe, and which has produced under some of its governments, and especially under our own, a more equal diffusion of freedom and of happiness than took place under the most celebrated constitutions of antiquity.[35]

35 Stewart, 'Life and writings of Adam Smith', p. 313.

Stewart goes on to suggest that this diffusion of wealth accounted in Smith's eyes for the rapid diffusion of printing and literacy, and we can add to this, as Smith does not in so many words, the Keynesian-inspired wisdom of modern economic historians to the effect that this diffusion created a home market of sufficient size to enable capitalism and, later, capitalist industrialism, to prosper.

The characterisation so far does admit that there is a broadly Smithian quality to the argument. Not much follows from this in terms of modern political recommendations. The subject matter of much of the second part of this book is precisely that this capitalist style of development is *not* historically very prevalent in any other case than the first emergence of modernity. More importantly, there are differences between Smith's account and the one offered here, and they centre on the positive qualities of ideology and politics.

Smith's concern with 'a tolerable administration of justice' is in fact by no means as negative as it might sound, and there is something like a theory of an organic state present in his work. But leaving aside the question of the exact character of Smith's theory, it is clear that politics are often seen here in quite 'positive' terms. The organic state did not merely prevent interference, of one sort or another, with the market; it also provided an infrastructure which helped it in important ways. However, not all political action was caused by economic needs. Many positive developments depended upon a purely political, and not an economic, 'logic'. This is true of the internal colonialism whereby, for example, England absorbed Scotland, Wales and Ireland and in the process created a larger area for market forces. Crucially, it is true of the competition between relatively equal and firmly established states. The rationalisation of society consequent upon war or anticipated war was caused by politics, although its effect was beneficial for the economy. So it is not just the form of politics, often stressed above, in the negative, non-blocking, sense which matters: rather the very goals of politics advanced the economy.

Islam, Christianity and Hinduism created societies. In one sense, Hinduism is 'the most powerful' of the three religions in having organised so very many social relationships. The costs of this process and the debilitating effects of its hierarchical model of social life were so high, however, as to suggest that either Islam or Christianity deserve the accolade at issue. Competition and contractual relationships fare best within an area of agreement and consensus, but one must be already 'equal' to make contract at all. Beyond this, however, Christianity differs from Islam, as well as from Hinduism, since it did not 'block' politics, and so did not encourage a climate of instability which limited the autonomy of market relationships. Smith may well have understood this latter point about stable political rule. But the more general point about the extensive capacity of ideologies is not 'Smithian' in spirit. This was well beyond the understanding of an eighteenth-century philosopher whose hostility to religion led to his ignoring its crucial, and myriad, roles in the rise of commercial yet liberal societies.

Part II

The Modern World

Prologue

A Logic to Industrialism?

The dynamic created in north-west Europe enabled it to dominate the rest of the world. This process began with the voyages of discovery, and it took on a much greater intensity when industrial technology, particularly the steamship and the railroad, allowed for thoroughgoing political control of and economic extraction from large parts of the globe. The sheer increase in human power was brutally seen in the two world wars which Europe began in the twentieth century, and is massively evident in our capacity to send men to the moon, and to destroy ourselves.

In the first half of this book two sets of claims were made, and recalling them can set the scene for the analysis of the modern world. *Conceptually* attention was concentrated on the nature of power, although it also proved possible to make useful comments about other key theoretical matters. As modern world society was created by European expansion throughout the globe, it is no accident that the concepts so far developed are useful in understanding our present social condition. I shall have much to say about the changing nature of ideological, political and economic power, and about the relation between these powers and liberties. A single theoretical example at this point must serve to demonstrate the continuing usefulness of concepts so far developed. Social theory depends upon an historically provincial view of 'society' in that it presumes identity and organisation to occur within nation-states. This view was not even much good for understanding the world in which it was articulated since states inhabited both a larger state system, conflict within which deeply affected their own social evolution, and the larger arena of international competition, to which they had to respond vigorously. We certainly need to handle the notion of 'society' with continuing scepticism. For to which society do we belong? There is no simple answer. Sources of power and identity are multiform and overlapping. We belong to our particular nation-state, perhaps the European Community, NATO, and the Free Trade area whose characteristic institutions are the IMF and GATT.

Substantively the argument of the first half of the book was that competition between rivals within a larger cultural area helped to create human progress. The claim was strong, little qualified and optimistic. This substantive connection between competition and progress *is* still operative in the modernity, but qualifications of various kinds are called for by changed social circumstances.

The central, brutal fact of the modern world has been and remains the unevenness of economic development in the world. Imitation rather than indigenous invention thereby becomes the natural route to modernity, a simple statement which carries in its tail profound political consequences. But what is the social unit which it is trying to imitate? Adam Smith's *Wealth of Nations* basically conceived of competition and emulation between states sharing certain organic characteristics. However, development inside a nation-state such as Denmark or Belgium is one thing. Development within recently liberated colonial territories, scarcely able to boast a state apparatus let alone a strong sense of national social solidarity, is a very different matter. As it happens, forced development involving nation-building does not, as pessimists would have it, seem impossible; on the contrary, it is the stuff of current world politics. Hence there is everything to justify the contention that there are two key elements to the social contract of modernity: affluence and rule by members of one's own society, that is industrialism and nationalism.[1] As with all philosophic arguments, this one gains its power from exclusion: no mention is made here of democratic-constitutional systems. The qualification to the optimism of the first half of the book largely results from noting that forced development does not, as nineteenth-century evolutionary theorists presumed, naturally dovetail with the spread of something like the Westminster model. However, things are by no means so bad that every hope in this direction must be abandoned, although hope will be discovered in strange places. Worries will have to be expressed, alas, about other areas once held confidently to be placed permanently above visceral political conflict. All this can be summarised by saying that much attention will be paid to the polities of modernity, or more precisely, the chances of liberal polities in the modern world.

The questions to be approached can best be generated by a two-step argument. The first task before us must be to try and specify exactly what consequences for social life follow from an industrial productive system. Once this has been done, three paths to the modern world, broadly derived from Barrington Moore's *Social Origins of Democracy and Dicta-*

1 E. Gellner, *Thought and Change*, Weidenfeld & Nicolson, London, 1965, p. 33 and ch. 2, *passim*.

torship,[2] can be outlined. Each of these paths does *not* correspond to the three chapters which follow. Within the developing world, for example, some states favour the Soviet model, but there are others who choose some sort of authoritarian capitalism. Reality is so complex that it would be a mistake, moreover, to encourage the illusion that 'models' are followed without significant variation occasioned by local circumstances.

The notion of an industrial society has a long history behind it which will for the most part be ignored here. It is possible to do this since the social theorists of modernity, and particularly the sociologists whose very subject matter was the origin and characterisation of the industrial age, were in substantial agreement as to the essential signs of their times. This agreement was well founded and judicious for it accurately portrayed the age.[3] Any list of the characteristics of the industrial productive system is bound to be partial but five, necessarily interlinked general criteria can usefully be mentioned.

Sectoral change

The most obvious change involved in the creation of modern industrial societies concerns the sectors of the economy. Most agrarian civilisations require something over 90 per cent to work the land in order to support a small elite. In contrast, most advanced Western societies now have an agricultural labour force of between 5 and 10 per cent of the working population, and this labour force is capable of supporting an urban population which has grown not just relatively but absolutely as well. It is important to know, however, that the secondary sector of the economy involving industrial workers was never much above 35 per cent, and seems now to rest somewhere in the region of 25 per cent, again in the more advanced industrial societies. The tertiary sector involving various types of services is therefore numerically important. Its character has changed so that a typical occupant of this sector will no longer be a domestic worker but a welfare officer or a teacher. It is by no means wise to regard such tertiary activity as unproductive.[4]

It is useful to recall the key concept of Barrington Moore's *Social Origins of Dictatorship and Democracy*. A modern society is likely, Moore argued, to take its character from the way in which it loses, or, in cases such as that of China, disciplines its peasantry. This is the peasant 'problem'. At one extreme stands the English case in which a peasantry

2 Penguin, London, 1969.
3 K. Kumar, *Prophecy and Progress*, Penguin, London, 1978.
4 J. Gershuny, *After Industrial Society?*, Macmillan, London, 1978.

was slowly dispossessed of customary rights and forced to leave the land; at the other, stands Stalin's drives into the countryside and his consequent forced collectivisation. The link between political systems and the style of peasant dispossession is obvious, and will concern us a great deal.

Productivity

Adam Smith's *Wealth of Nations* opens with a paean of praise to the productive potential of the division of labour. A worker without any help forced to undertake every process involved from mining to packing might produce a pin a day; the same man benefitting from the division of labour would be capable of producing 4,800 pins in the same period. The example is jaded, but the point made is correct. When one adds to the division of labour the utilisation of fossil and nuclear fuels, the exponential growth in human technological power is clear and staggering.

Rationalisation

Unquestionably, rationalisation is one of the key concepts of the modern social sciences and it is the master concept of Weber. It is hard to pin down precisely what is meant by the term. Most spectacularly and uncontroversially, the application of Western scientific standards to industry, above all from the late nineteenth century but with an ever increasing tempo, is clearly a major part of the explanation for modern productivity. Secondly, rationalisation also involves characteristic styles of decision-making. Max Weber insisted that a rational-legal modern order would tend to rely upon a bureaucratic style of decision-making. This style depended in his eyes upon meritocratic recruitment via examination and thus entailed the abandonment of clientelist patronage politics.

Auguste Comte, the founder of the French positivist social movement, believed both that science would destroy religious prejudices *and* that it would replace such prejudices with a properly validated metaphysic. To this end he created positivist chapels, some of which are still in operation. Weber's sociology is systematically opposed to this. For Weber, science destroys religious certainty but it does not, and cannot, replace it with any moral equivalent. Our rationalised world is thus held to be 'disenchanted'. This whole matter can be put another way. Behind Max Weber stood the ghost of Nietzsche, and the sociologist is but taking seriously the philosopher's insistence that 'God is dead', and that modern man has to live life without benefit of salvation.

Centralisation and hierarchy

Bureaucracy implies centralisation and hierarchy, and much power in modern society is clearly of this type. This is strikingly true of the modern state. Most Western societies now funnel between 35 per cent and 50 per cent of all GNP through the state. Even when a great deal of this is handed back to various groups in civil society, there can be no doubt about the centrality of the state. This is, by definition, even more true of state socialist societies.

The general picture is reinforced by noting that modern weapons systems require control both by political leaders (which may be possible) as well as by battlefield commanders (which may well be impossible). Finally, one should note that centralisation and hierarchy are not the exclusive property of the state. The modern business corporation, subject to mergers and with enormous international reach, is quite as centralised and hierarchial as the state. The modern state does seek to control in a centralised manner economic life. Some states have dramatic success in this regard, and all have some. Nevertheless, the international market remains bigger than national states. Centralisation of corporations does not necessarily mean centralisation *within* states. Capital remains mobile. The essence of its power lies in it being hard to locate and thereby hard to capture. The corporation may be centralised, but capitalist power remains diffuse.

Communication

The social theorists we traditionally lend credence to were European, and in consequence were socially blind in one respect. They wrote within established national societies with historic shared languages and cultures, and in which the people were soon to take part in the social and political scene. In many underdeveloped countries history has not evolved a single community in this sense at all. Rather, such 'societies' are but straight lines drawn by colonial powers boxing in very diverse groups, languages and cultures. They correspond precisely to Ernest Gellner's model of the agro-literate polity, and it is worth recording a comment he makes about the duties that a state seeking to modernise feels bound to undertake:

By some criteria, it may well be that a fully developed agrarian society actually has the more complex division of labour. The specialisms within it are more distant from each other than are the possibly more numerous specialisms of an industrial society, which tend to have what can only be described as a mutual affinity of style ... the major part of training in industrial society is *generic* training, not specifically connected with the highly specialised professional activity of the person in question, and *preceding* it. Industrial society may by most criteria be the most highly specialised society ever; but its educational system is unquestionably the *least* specialised, the most universally standardised, that has ever existed. The same kind of training or education is given to all or most children and adolescents up to an astonishingly late age.[5]

Industrial society depends upon people being able to communicate, and this explains the generic education provided. If all modern states require this social infrastructure, it is obvious that ex-colonial areas will be forced into nation-building if they are to achieve this. There is something else at work here. The myths of agrarian society tend to stress their static and unchanging quality, whereas the myths of industrial society stress their openness. While there remains a structure of inequality in the advanced societies and while some mobility did occur within agrarian societies, these myths do accurately reflect social reality. Social mobility has been historically very high in industrial societies and the gradient of inequality is markedly less than in agrarian civilisations. Such a rate of social mobility is only possible when members of the same geographical space feel themselves to be citizens of a single society. In a nutshell, perhaps the most single crucial prerequisite of industrial society is a certain cultural egalitarianism.

Two general points need to be made about this ideal type of the industrial system of production. Firstly, the model is internally self-contradictory, although this is the fault of reality rather than of my constructive skills. On the one hand the need for examinations in bureaucracy hints at widespread educational rights, but on the other hand the structural need for hierarchy has also been stressed. In principle, it would be possible to 'reconcile' these two, somewhat in the manner of Confucian China, by envisaging a scholarship meritocracy without any impact on the larger society. However, industrial society requires generic patterns of communication. So modern society sails, as it were, in a ship with two flags at its mast: *democracy* in the sense mentioned, and *productivity* which involves hierarchy. Obviously, much modern politics is going to concern itself with how these incompatible goals can be somehow reconciled. Relations between elites and the people do not lose salience in the modern world.

This contradiction is relevant and leads naturally to the second general point. What social consequences follow from industrialism? At one time, industrial society theorists maintained a very strong thesis claiming that convergence would occur between state socialism and liberal capitalism.

5 *Nations and Nationalism*, Basil Blackwell, Oxford, 1983, pp. 26–7.

It was argued that the industrial productive system would entail for the former more room for the market and for liberal institutions, and for the latter more room for social justice, especially the ending of class privilege. In the interests of clarity, it should be said now that there *are* certain points in the following chapters when hopes are entertained that industrialism, particularly late industrialism, might lead by a logic of its own to a softening of particular polities, although the idea of convergence of political institutions in the USA and the USSR *is* simply fantastical and silly. Furthermore, some concept of industrial society is needed to enable us to understand the experience of those Third World countries seeking routes to modernity (as well as those who have achieved it!) by means of the Soviet model in a manner alternative to capitalism. This latter point can be put in a different and more pointed way. Marxists are wont to dismiss the notion of an industrial society altogether on the ground that capitalism still rules in the West, and these arguments are to be examined in a moment. But it is noticeable that Marxism has been notoriously poor in conceptualising state socialism. This is not surprising since such societies are clearly not capitalist. They cannot be understood without some generic reference to industrialisation and to the autonomous impact of political power. The general position taken here parallels that taken in the first half of the book. Just as the agrarian system of production could be created and run by regimes that differed in their political and ideological relationships, so too can the industrial system be created, supported and run by different political economies, most obviously either by state socialist directives or by the workings, by now of Byzantine complexity, of the capitalist market.

Let us turn our attention to the contention that Western societies are still best understood in Marxist terms. The more naïve of the industrial society theorists suggested that class privilege would disappear, and they were clearly wrong, as is shown in the next chapter. However, to admit the fact of class privilege is not, by any means, to allow that Marxist concepts provide us with a full and proper understanding of the modern Western world. It is possible to gain considerable analytic hold by considering the conflict between labour and capital, but reservations are important here as well. It will be recalled that Geoffrey de Ste Croix's sophisticated Marxist account of the ancient world saw class exploitation of peasants but failed to detect class consciousness capable of creating a different type of society.[6] Despite changed circumstances, and despite the fact that full class consciousness can and does sometimes arise, it will be claimed that this view effectively characterises much current conflict. Working-class action is often an attempt to get more without any pro-

6 *Class Struggle in the Ancient Greek World*, Duckworth, London, 1981.

found hostility to the system as such – indeed sometimes it gives grudging *acceptance* of the system on the grounds that its productivity is so much greater than that of state socialism. This point can be put in a different way. Working-class action may be best seen not as directed against odious and disproportionate profits made by private individuals, although that can occur, but rather as a generic difficulty of industrial society, present in a different guise in Eastern Europe, in reconciling hierarchy with a complex division of labour.

Two final points must be made. Firstly, *class conflict occurs within national societies* just as corporatist arrangements linking classes takes place within national societies. This means that nation, and hence political conflict between nations by means of war, remains as vital an historical motor in modernity as it was in the past. The theorists of industrial society expected their new age to be peaceful and harmonious. This expectation has been refuted. Marx was not much better prepared to deal with the dynamics of war. The working class has not, as Marx expected, become a transnational force, and most of his prophecies thereby lack force. Secondly, the argument has so far been to say 'yes, but'; Marx's concern with capital and labour is helpful and accurate, but it does not thereby give us a full guide to social dynamics. Modern national societies are not simply capitalist and their working classes do not seem to be about to man revolutionary barricades. Nonetheless, it must be stressed again that national societies themselves exist within a larger arena. Certain facets of this international society, that it is based on political as well as economic competition and that it is dominated, in the West, by the United States, will have to be emphasised. But there is no doubt that international economic competition has been pioneered by capitalists who are often *not* as tied to a national society as is the working class. International capitalism remains a vital source of change and (with reservations to be noted) of progress in the modern world. These points can be summarised: historical change results from international political and economic competition rather than from industrial society *per se*.

Qualifications to the optimism of the first half of this book largely result from doubting that competition and development will ally themselves to liberal politics. However, this is but a first approximation, and we need to note characteristic issues at work in the types of society resulting from three routes to the modern world.

The first such political economy is that of the modern liberal state existing within larger capitalist society. The manner in which this liberal system was achieved has been hinted at in the first half of this book, and will be spelt out again soon. It is a miracle which matters, and it is more than a formal facade. One way in which this is so is admirably put by Edward Thompson, in whiggish mood, at the end of his history of the repression of peasant customary rights by means of the law created by the early eighteenth-century English aristocracy:

I have shown . . . a political oligarchy inventing callous and oppressive laws to serve its own interests . . . for many of England's governing elite the rules of law were a nuisance, to be manipulated and bent in what ways they could . . . But I do not conclude from this that the rule of law itself was humbug. On the contrary, the inhibitions upon power imposed by law seem to me a legacy as substantial as any handed down from the struggles of the seventeenth century to the eighteenth, and a true and important cultural achievement of the agrarian and mercantile bourgeoisie, and of their supporting yeomen and artisans.[7]

This system at least allows for the possibility that a poor government can be removed. The reality of these formal freedoms underlies and makes possible the conflict between capital and labour; class conflict is formally accepted and allowed. However, there is a considerable change at work here. International competition requires adaptation. Traditionally this was achieved by *laissez-faire*; the forces of capital and labour were not equal and workers were forced into accepting the disciplines of the market. Modern national societies have seen a change in the balance of power and the state now provides a general social infrastructure of welfare and education. This changed balance of power may, in certain circumstances, make it harder to achieve flexible responses to international competition. Is it *possible* to reverse this balance of power, as those on the radical right hope? If such a reversal took place might it not go against the logic of late industrial society in producing a docile but unskilled workforce? If, to take an alternative view, success for any national society depends upon competing as a unit, assuming that conflict between capital and labour is too expensive in economic terms, *are* there ways in which national social cohesion can be created which will allow for flexibility? Finally, what chances are there for 'socialism' in these circumstances? These are the questions to be addressed in the next chapter.

The autonomous emergence of one part of the world is not repeatable, and societies that industrialised after the emergence of industrial capitalism did so with the knowledge that such economic power was possible. They had increasingly accurate views as to how such power could be achieved, and all development since about 1870 has been *forced* in character. Forced development is likely to require dictatorial means. Nevertheless two sub-types within this category must be distinguished.

The first such sub-type, and the second political economy in question, is based on central planning, the formal suppression of classes and rule by a monopolistic elite legitimised by a total ideology, usually of socialist

7 *Whigs and Hunters*, Penguin, London, 1977, p. 265.

hue. The virtues of this model for forced industrialisation are clear. In Russia it allowed for a forcible solution to the peasant problem, and for massive investment in heavy industry. Consumer preferences would have preferred to do without this investment; it was only made possible by the fact that the Soviet model was a power system. This model has perhaps even greater attractions to, and can prove more necessary for, societies which are seeking to establish a single community for the first time. It is therefore no surprise to find that this model, albeit with striking variations, is quite widely spread around the globe. All these comments reinforce the generalisation that forced ideocratic development entails dictatorship. It is at this point, however, that the questions concerning the industrial system of production, particularly in its more advanced, sophisticated conditions, have great salience. Is it the case that late industrialism's stress on skill, communication and science is the secret to modern productivity? If so, is it possible that the need to encourage these qualities may affect this type of social structure? Is it possible that demands originating from the economy can somehow undermine power even though that has been massively centralised by successful revolution? The future of regimes, in Eastern Europe and elsewhere, which developed under the aegis of a single ideocratic party is one of *the* questions of the age, and it concerns us in chapter 7.

But the second sub-type of forced development, and the third type of political economy in question, was seen before the Russian revolution and is still much in evidence in the developing world today. There is no automatic and easy connection between liberty and capitalism, for revolutions from above can seek to combine authoritarian government with a capitalist market. Germany and Tsarist Russia were the first examples of such states, and many Latin American states approximate this model today. Barrington Moore has argued that such regimes are unstable:

As they proceeded with conservative modernisation, these semiparliamentary governments tried to preserve as much of the original social structure as they could, fitting large sections into the new building wherever possible. The results had some resemblance to present-day Victorian houses with moden electrical kitchens but insufficient bathrooms and leaky pipes hidden decorously behind newly plastered walls. Ultimately the makeshifts collapsed.[8]

This is one question to be addressed. Another question concerns the manner in which such regimes fall. A brilliant article by Raymond Aron, written *de haut en bas* to other members of the educated elite of world politics, argued that there were variations in the manner of collapse of such regimes.[9] This argument chided the German elite for irresponsibil-

8 *Social Origins of Democracy and Dictatorship*, p. 438.
9 R. Aron, 'On liberalisation', *Government and Opposition*, vol. 14.

ity in trying to exclude rather than integrate the people from the political stage. Aron thus endorsed that comparison between the intelligence of the traditional British elite and the short-sightedness of the elites of France and Germany first made by Tocqueville. The great French sociologist was much impressed by the skill with which the Spanish and Greek elites liberalised their regimes in recent years, so much so that he suggested that a decent liberalisation of society was more likely to come from an authoritarian capitalist regime than from one that had suffered, or perhaps enjoyed, a full-scale modern ideocratic revolution. This interesting idea, granting such a positive role to elite behaviour, suggests that there *is* some link between capitalism and liberal politics. Such hopes, slight in the context of the overwhelming attractiveness of the soviet model, are examined in chapter 8.

6

Liberal Polities inside
Capitalist Society

Commerce and Liberty

Adam Smith and David Hume claimed that there was an elective affinity between commerce and liberty, and the argument of the first half of this book has lent considerable support to their position. We can summarise it by recalling the character of pluralism in European history:

Liberties had even deeper roots in the Western world. They emerged amid the final political collapse of the *imperium* of Rome in the West. In those chaotic centuries often the happiest way to deal with higher powers was to buy one's way out of the obligations to them. Those powers – the Germanic tribal successors to Roman authority – had little sense of public office or public ōbligation. They had a strong sense that if they possessed anything – cows, servants, courts, churches, lands, labour dues, rights of way – they could trade it, or sell it, or give it away. Everything they had was up for grabs. The obligations they remitted by sale or gift came to be called franchises, or freedoms, or liberties. The spectrum of liberties was as varied as the rights of rule or authority that the lords of the land had. Liberties, that is to say, were treated as if they were property. Since property was one of the things that all who had it most ardently strove to keep, all through the West communities invested sizeable amounts of thought, energy and armed force in seeing to it that all their property, including their property in their liberties, was secure.[1]

Such a spread of liberties is by no means unusual once an empire collapses. Christianity, however, encouraged those in possession of liberties, and most were, to regard each other as members of a single civilisation and this was a baseline without which a revival of trade would have been impossible. Increasing commercial activity itself helped to strengthen European pluralism. Moreover, the pre-existence of civil society made the European state 'organic' rather than predatory and

1 J.H. Hexter, 'The birth of modern freedom', *Times Literary Supplement*, 21 January 1983, p. 51.

coercive. What causal links can be distinguished in this process? The pattern is complex, but was in part detected by Smith and Hume themselves. The political condition of Europe, bereft of a single centre, helped the emergence of capitalism. The absence of despotism, capable either of bureaucratic or predatory interferences, allowed the economy to gain autonomy. Equally, however, emergent capitalism helped to create and reinforce liberal, organic polities. These states were fundamentally strong because they were able, in large part as capitalists wished, to penetrate and organise social life. Adam Smith argued that the key mechanism at work here was psychological, that the power of aristocracy was broken as the result of it preferring luxuries to retainers. There may be some truth to this, and it certainly reminds us that European capitalists were by no means confined to cities. Nonetheless, far more important was the institutional fact that capitalists would have no truck with despotically inclined rulers, and either helped fight them, as in the English civil war, or moved away from them, as did the capitalists of Antwerp, to more liberal climates. This movement could not be ignored since the wealth they brought increased the political strength of the receiving nation. Those states which respected the autonomy of capitalist groups benefited from their energy. Liberities led to development and both were intimately associated with the absence of arbitrary rule.

This combination of political liberty and capitalist economics is a curious one. It deserves to be further characterised in more abstract sociological terms. The development of a commercial, and eventually an industrial, society did not destroy the pre-existing civil society for the banal reason that this development was not planned. Central planning designed to create an industrial society *could not take place*. Planning only makes sense and becomes a significant factor when an already existing industrial society is being imitated. In European history such planning was not possible since nobody had the slightest conception until the mid-nineteenth century that an industrial society was possible. The general pattern can be neatly seen in the intellectual careers of most nineteenth-century thinkers who struggled hard to try and understand exactly what was the unplanned turmoil in the midst of which they lived. What is at issue is in effect *time*. Industrialism was added to capitalism very late in its career, and the pre-existance of capitalism made it possible that the addition could be made without disrupting the whole society. Consider the peasantry. All roads to modernity require solving the peasant problem. Ways must be found to encourage the peasants to move from the land into industrial employment. Any sudden 'solution' to this problem is going to disrupt the whole society from top to bottom, and is almost only conceivable when done under the aegis of centralised power. In the English case the peasantry was dispossessed via enclosure from the sixteenth century in a process that took over three centuries to complete. It is quite possible that this slow and long drawn out fate involved more human suffering in the long run than the short sharp bursts of collectivisation in certain Eastern European countries in the years after the Second World War. Moreover, the whole process was done under the aegis of something that, at least in peasant eyes, must have felt like a despotic centralised authority, namely the united landlord class working through Parliament. Yet this does not detract from the *fact* that the slowness of the whole process allowed certain liberal inheritances to remain undisturbed.

There is still a puzzle. Why did not the newly rich capitalists choose to buy retainers and power, rather than to continue to be satisfied with wealth creation? Perhaps well-organised states made the 'power-road' to riches more and more risky. Perhaps Weber was right to note that capitalists were encouraged by their puritan beliefs not to spend their money but to reinvest it in order to do the work of God. Certainly Maynard Keynes felt this to be the case in those brilliant pages – perhaps *the* most illuminating ever written on the character of capitalism – in which he described the double bluff of nineteenth-century capitalism whereby owners were free to consume profits but refrained from so doing, and workers to issue excessive demands but again did not do so.[2]

What were the relations between state and society in the Britain that the Scottish moralists knew? Two points must be stressed. Most obviously, the state was one without much real autonomy, except in matters of foreign policy. The state was run in the interests of a united commercial capitalist class. In Britain the gentry and aristocracy taxed themselves at a high rate in the certainty that the state would do their bidding. This can be contrasted with the power stand-off inside French absolutist society where the aristocracy distrusted the state so much that it refused to allow itself to be taxed. These co-operative relationships between society and state in the British case allowed for the generation of a greater total sum of power, and it is accordingly a considerable mistake to think that absolutism made France stronger than Britain. For in the test of war during the eighteenth-century, the more organic of the two systems came out on top four out of five times. No wonder that by the middle of the eighteenth-century French intellectuals were coming to Britain to try and learn the secrets of its rule, apparently with some success. Nevertheless, the crisis of state finances brought on by the combination of war and the social blockages of the aristocracy led to revolutionary ferment. Competition between states had again shown its dynamic effects.[3]

2 *The Economic Consequences of the Peace*, Macmillan, London, 1919, ch. 2.
3 T. Skocpol, *States and Social Revolutions*, Cambridge University Press, Cambridge, 1979.

The French revolution seemed at first likely to affect other European societies in *two* related ways. It seemed that Napoleon's historic import- ance would be his revival of citizen armies prepared to wage total war. The Prussian reformers around Hardenburg, most notably Scharnhorst and Gneisenau and with Clausewitz as their greatest intellectual figure, helped in the abolition of serfdom after Austerlitz precisely because they felt that only free citizens could combat Napoleon's armies. In actual fact those armies were not, after the initial revolutionary years, by any means always composed of French citizens, and nor was it the case that Napoleonic strategy meant that a recourse to total war had suddenly changed the rules of war. Clausewitz himself did originally think that total war was the order of the age, but as he witnessed the combination of states destroy Napoleon he moved, at the end of his life, to insisting once again on the importance of political control of military affairs. 'Had death not prevented Clausewitz from elaborating his thesis on the two types of war . . . perhaps instead of interpreting Frederick II's strategy in the light of Buonaparte's, the German command would have recog- nised Frederick's true greatness in the light of Napoleon's catastrophic defeat.'[4]

There is no doubt however that the French revolution did affect European society in another way. It helped to introduce the people onto the political stage. The second important point about the British thinkers of the late eighteenth-century who noted the connection between com- merce and liberty is that they were not democrats in any sense of the word. 'Liberty' for such thinkers meant only the rule of law, and the right to free speech. Smith and Hume both felt that their social order worked precisely because commerce was combined with respect, as the result of certain natural propensities of the human mind, for the established hierarchical order. Capitalism and hierarchy were allies, albeit allies within a non-despotic order. Neither had to *defend* this hierarchy. Burke, who shared many of their ideas, was forced into this position, and he consequently produced his *Reflections on the Revolution in France and upon the Proceedings in Certain Societies in London Relative to that Event*. As this defence of hierarchy was cognitively low-powered, the question re- mained: how was capitalism to be combined with the entry of the people into politics?

The first industrial nation provided a subtle solution. Demands for democratisation in British life began well before industrialisation, although industrialisation here and elsewhere gave a significant boost to such demands. Pressure from below came from craftsmen, particularly

4 R. Aron, 'Reason, passion and power in the thought of Clausewitz', *Social Research*, vol. 34, 1972, p. 621.

printers, who were able to take full advantage of new communications networks across the country, and from those like the Luddites who suffered from and opposed the introduction of new machinery. The British ruling class sought to control the horizontal linkages of 'the dangerous classes' by Stamp Acts and Combination Acts in those early nineteenth-century years in which, *pace* Smith and Hume, widespread repression was tried. Interestingly, such repression did not last long. The Combination Acts were repealed in 1824 and the franchise extended in 1832. Why was this authoritarian reaction so shortlived? Why, in other words, did liberty survive?

Moore suggests that civil society in commercial – for it was not yet industrial – British society was strong enough to resist the creation of an authoritarian solution.

England's whole previous history, her reliance on a navy instead of on an army, on unpaid justices of the peace instead of royal officials, had put in the hands of the central government a repressive apparatus weaker than that possessed by the strong continental monarchies ... The push towards industrialism had begun much earlier in England and was to render unnecessary for the English bourgeoisie any great dependence on the crown and the landed aristocracy. Finally, the landed upper classes themselves did not need to repress the peasants. Mainly they wanted to get them out of the way in order to go over to commercial farming; by and large, economic measures would be enough to provide the labour force they needed. Succeeding economically in this particular fashion, they had little need to resort to repressive political measures to continue their leadership.[5]

Other crucial explanatory variables at work have been identified by Dick Geary:

... the major determinant of the forms of political action adopted by the different national labour movements was the role of the state and of the social groups it claimed to represent; for at the level of industrial action clear similar- ities existed between similar occupations in different countries. Furthermore, it remains true that certain kinds of governmental interference in industrial rela- tions did transform what began as economic protest into political action.[6]

In the British case this means that the presence of a liberal state encour- aged workers to concentrate their struggles in the workplace. It is in- teresting that in the workplace capitalists did not act in any bunker-like fashion, and it is striking to note the amount of recognition and the relative ease with which it was achieved. Perhaps the relative softness of the British industrial capitalist class has something to do with its position as the leading industrial power of the time. Softness could be afforded.

5 B. Moore, *Social Origins of Dictatorship and Democracy*, Penguin, London, 1969, p. 444.
6 *European Labour Protest 1848–1945*, Methuen, London, 1984, p. 60.

But it is worth commenting on what we might describe as a virtuous and self-reinforcing cycle. Liberal politics bred industrial conflict rather than no-holds-barred political struggle. Yet it was perhaps the absence of political struggle that encouraged the retention of liberal politics in the first place. How can this cycle be broken into? A part of the answer in Britain was the absence of universal suffrage throughout the nineteenth century. This meant that the middle class never felt so threatened as to be forced to make alliances with other groups in order to systematically control labour.[7] Nevertheless, the cycle certainly worked. There was no Labour Party until the beginning of the twentieth century, and this development *was* connected with a move against liberalism, the Taff Vale court decision, which militated against the industrial position and activities of the working class. This was not typical, and the mixture of incorporation into society together with controlled expansion of the suffrage did, as the liberal intellectuals of the time had hoped, create social stability.

The People, War and the Revolutions of the Twentieth Century

British experience provided a model that had remarkable power over the modern imagination until quite recently. This is scarcely surprising for what was being promised was nothing less than a combination of affluence and democracy. Nevertheless the model came to be questioned for two reasons. Firstly, the German experience, the subject of this section, raised again in pertinent form the question as to whether there were natural links between capitalism and liberalism. The German situation is still often presented as 'flawed' or 'problematic', but we must reject this formulation immediately: Britain was exceptional, pathological if you like, whereas the German attempt to force development, entailing the ruling out of liberalism, was normal. The argument to be made is that consideration of the German case, although there are difficulties of evidence, does not force us to rule out hopes that the connection posed by Smith and Hume may yet have some life in it. Secondly, however, it must be stressed that the nineteenth-century Westminster model was but a transitory moment in the history of the relations between capital and labour. These are taken up later, and there they give rise to a measure of pessimism.

Much of historic Germany belongs to Eastern Europe, a geographical

7 Ibid., p. 68.

area which had diverged noticeably from the land to the West of the Rhine since the fifteenth century. Where the market in the West encouraged and depended upon a civil society, the same principle had exactly the opposite effects in the East. Production of corn and rye was for an already established market and landlords could be guaranteed a decent return by concentrating on a single crop. To this end they undermined the position of the towns, and often relied upon Jews to serve as middlemen between aristocrats and peasants. The middling sector of society was small, powerless and keen to gain a safe position in state service. This tradition of state service developed because Brandenburg-Prussia, by outwitting local estates, found a way in which they could survive and prosper by militarising society.

This traditional ruling class received a vitalising shock as the result of defeat at the hands of Napoleon. As a result and in part for reasons of military planning, the Prussian elite sought during the nineteenth century to unite the German people and to modernise German society. Their plans placed them in exact opposition to the British liberal model's stress on retrenchment, reform, free trade and peace. The role of the state here was necessarily greater, involved as it was in nation-building and in a form of industrialisation where state loans and state contracts behind tariff walls proved vital. There was no automatic link between this form of modernisation and peace, indeed probably there was an elective affinity going in the opposite direction. The nobility had retained a feudal ethic and increasingly had the problem of justifying its privileged position. One way of doing so was by means of military adventure for home consumption, and this clearly payed some part in Bismarck's wars. These wars naturally intensified state competition and so in turn made the need for industrialisation all the greater.

What was the role of the middling elements in German development? Roughly speaking, it represented the reverse side of the coin to the British experience. The Eastern European impact upon German political culture meant that these elements were from the start more dependent upon the state than had been their British counterpart. There was a vicious circle at work that neatly contrasts with the one already described. Authoritarian political forms meant that labour was forced into political action since without key political changes it would have no chance of prospering in industrial conflicts. And because extremist politics appealed to the working class, the bourgeoisie chose to ally itself with the authoritarian right. Moreover, its fears were realistic since late nineteenth-century German politics was based upon mass suffrage. The consequences in the workplace were striking:

German employers and especially those in the heavy industrial sector revealed an almost total hostility to independent working-class organisation (although many were prepared to establish dependent company unions, the so-called 'yellow' unions) until the political pressures of government in the course of the First World War and above all in the wake of the revolution of 1918. This is clear if one compares the figures concerning the number of workers covered by collective agreements in Britain and Germany before 1914. In Britain in 1910 no fewer than 900,000 miners, 500,000 railway workers, 460,000 textile workers and 230,000 metalworkers benefited from such agreements, whereas in Germany three years later the equivalent figures related to only 16,000 textile operatives, 1,376 metalworkers, and a miserly 82 miners.[18]

There was then no affinity, let alone an automatic link, between capitalist bourgeoisie and political liberalism in these circumstances.

However, it is necessary to expand our focus if we are to understand the historic fate of this particular social formation. Whilst some of the German ruling elite welcomed war in 1914, the war itself was essentially the result of typical inter-state competition in the European scene. If the German elite had been unwise in failing to realise that greater stability in the long run was achievable only by incorporation of the working class, the elites of all contending powers proved themselves unwise in the conduct of the war. A part of the explanation for this was the technical surprise of industry applied to armaments which led to the creation of war economies with a decided momentum of their own. A greater difficulty was that the war could only be fought with gigantic citizen armies, and it proved necessary in consequence to increase the stakes of the conflict. For the British, the war quickly became a 'war to end all wars', or a 'war for democracy itself' – this was ironic given that in 1914 war had been for Belgium alone, and on the part of society in which the majority of the adult population did not have the right to vote! This made it impossible to bring the war to an end in 1917 when it had become clear that the costs were outweighing all possible gains. The war ceased to be fought according to the Clausewitzian injunction that it should be the continuation of politics by other means. Instead the military took control from the hands of the politicians. This was a turning point in European history as members of the European elite then and since realised.[9] Before saying exactly why this should be so, however, it is worth digressing for a moment to stress again the monumental importance of the fact of war.

Marx and Lenin believed that class was a transnational social force, not only for the capitalist but also for the worker. However, the national representatives attached to the Second International, with the exception

---

8 Geary, *European Labour Protest*, pp. 56–7.

9 I have in mind Maynard Keynes and Raymond Aron. See Robert Skidelsky's biography of the former (vol. I, Macmillan, London, 1983) and Aron's *Clausewitz* (Routledge & Kegan Paul, London, 1983).

of those of Russia and Serbia, voted in 1914 to support the war. The fundamental and unavoidable conclusion to be drawn from this is that *nation therefore represented a factor with greater salience than class*, a crucial admission given that war changed European history. It is perhaps mistaken to take everything here at face value. There is no evidence that workers who fought for their countries shared with their rulers at every point the same understanding of 'the nation'. The German working class fought for a combination of reasons, none of which meant that national loyalty thereby entailed the absence of class loyalty. A calculation was made, probably correctly, that opposition to the war would be deeply unpopular and would lead to the destruction of union and SPD organisations.

Furthermore, much working-class support for Germany's war effort in August 1914 stemmed from the genuine belief that their country was about to be invaded not only by a foreign power but by Russia, by the bulwark of European reaction, the arch-enemy of progressive labour, Tsarist despotism. Thus the SPD's initial declaration of support for the Reich government on 4 August 1914 was conditional upon the defensive nature of Germany's war.[10]

The SPD insisted that participation in war could only be bought by the state if it made concessions to organised labour, and this it duly did, granting for example the right to unionise state servants. This last point is vital. However strong class consciousness was, and it *had* occasionally been strong before and was again to be so after the war, gains were either granted or won via the nation-state. What matters here, as with Imperial China, is the *form* that class conflict took. National rather than international organisations had locatable sources of money and so it was natural that class conflict took place inside their boundaries. As the gains of social justice and citizenship, and especially those achieved by participating in conscription war, were real, loyalty tended to be accorded to the state. There were hopes that further gains could be won, and these were realised, notably at the end of the Second World War. Yet these reservations do not detract from the brute fact of participation in the war.

The war played the fundamental causal role in the two revolutions of twentieth-century European history. It is clearly the case that the Russian state finally came to grief, as it had nearly done in the Crimea and in the war against Japan, as the result of a crisis of state finances brought on by war. The state machinery collapsed as the result of war, and a clear polarisation took place between the landed elite and a mass of impoverished peasants. It was in these circumstances that Lenin's brilliance as an activist proved capable of creating a revolution and driving it towards

10 Geary, *European Labour Protest*, p. 116.

socialism.[11] Defeat in war played an equally vital part in the success of fascism, and it is important to spell out why this should have been so.

The German people had gone to war as had other Europeans over the centuries as members of states whose sovereignty included the right to final resolution by armed might. However, the escalation of war aims consequent on mass conscription led to Germany being found, at the Treaty of Versailles, guilty of aggression. Added to this moral insult were war reparations on which were blamed, probably unfairly (although *that* did not matter), the catastrophic inflation that wreaked havoc on the German economy throughout the 1920s. Thus was born the legend of the stab in the back, as well as much of the social material, notably in ex-soldiers alienated by the failure to redeem promises of social justice made during the struggle, capable of manning fascist organisations. It was precisely the possibility of defeat in war leading to nationalist reactions that Keynes had feared as early as 1917, and it led him to write *The Economic Consequences of the Peace* in 1919. Keynes was often right in his analysis, but there is a most subtle charge against him: that he was wrong to express his fears. Perhaps he helped to create a climate of moral guilt and hence of appeasement among enlightened opinion in France and England. Without this climate more resistance might have been shown to Hitler in 1936 or 1938.

Certain factors internal to German politics also proved crucial in the emergence of fascism. The German military elite was keen to hand over power to the Social Democrats even before the war ended as it did not wish to be lumbered with blame for defeat. The result of this was that the Social Democrats found themselves in a position in which they had to play the role of the party of order, and suppress revolution in various parts of Germany in 1918/19. Much of their motivation for so behaving was meritorious. They wished to save German society from further upheavals, although the fact that they were suppressing Communists meant that their zeal for order was probably excessive. These developments meant that Germany became increasingly polarised, bereft of a strong centre capable of holding society together. The SPD itself might have strengthened the centre had it acted more boldly just after the war, by purging the army and civil service of those who were inherently hostile to the new regime. More importantly, however, the German bourgeoisie did not thank the SPD for providing a modicum of order, perhaps not suprisingly as labour did rather well out of the Weimar years. Here there was certainly no automatic link between the commercially minded and the protection of liberty, rather a dull resentment and witholding of support from the Weimar republic.

11 Skocpol, *States and Social Revolutions*.

Polarisation increasingly occurred between two very different groups. The Communists who had suffered at the hands of the SDP in the post-war years did not wish to join any popular front with them. This was especially comprehensible given that their social roots were, remarkably, among the unemployed whose position the highly respectable SPD largely ignored. The Comintern did not, of course, encourage such an alliance since it had recently been stung by Chiang Kai-shek's attack on his supposed allies the Chinese Communists; little sense was generated by the Marxist view of history which insisted that fascism was just the last gasp of monopoly capitalism. For the second group which squeezed the centre with increasing success was, of course, the Nazi party.

The case made so far has been that the social forces of late imperial and Weimar Germany did not support a liberal political system. One can go slightly further than this. The alliance between Junker and capitalist tried to make reaction popular in the countryside by means of agrarian leagues that were set up from 1894; the areas where these leagues had success later produced support for the Nazis.[12] Nevertheless, despite all this, and the crucial fact that the authoritarian right allowed Hitler into power via backstairs manoeuvre, it is *still* necessary to criticise simple-minded Marxist theories of fascism. The notion that fascism is called into being to serve as an agency of capitalism designed to protect its interests at the moment when it can no longer function peacefully is terribly weak. The two most obvious and outstanding objections to this view concern cases other than those of Germany and Italy. England and America, clearly leading capitalist powers, were not in any serious ways troubled by a fascist threat even though the crisis of capitalism that affected them was quite as serious. For the Marxist theory to have general validity they too should have come under fascist rule. On the other hand, fascism flourished in a series of countries in Eastern Europe which were essentially agrarian in character, most notably Rumania. The economy of these countries was in certain ways capitalist, but it was clearly a nascent capitalism, and thus not subject to those contradictions of late or monopoly capitalism supposedly necessitating fascism. In Germany capitalists did not support the Nazis, with the single exception of Fritz von Thyssen, until 1932 when they had clearly become a good bet. Nor was the war that followed desired by capitalists: the war was Hitler's, and its ideology was racist and imperialist rather than capitalist.

It is possible to say something more general about fascism. The transition to modern society, whether capitalist or socialist in character, involves the creation of a new sort of citizenry. This process is extremely

12 Moore, *Social Origins of Dictatorship and Democracy*, ch. 8.

painful when it occurs at speed. Insofar as the carrot of greater affluence is continually held before those whose lives are being disrupted, the transition can be made without disaster. Fascism results when populations in the middle of the transitional period, armed with memories of a more cohesive and simple pre-industrial world, suddenly have that carrot removed and are left anomic, disrupted and temporarily aimless. In these circumstances the lesser intelligentsia gains credence and power by producing a total ideology which promises at once economic efficiency and a return to older, and warmer, communal values. Fascism is not a simple product of capitalism, but rather a pathology of forced modernisation. It is likely to occur in any country where the transition to the industrial age is disrupted, although the fascist element may be hard to recognise if jumbled up with nationalist, Islamic or even Marxist elements. However, once the period of transition has been passed, as it had been in England and America by the 1930s, the likelihood of a fascist movement on a large scale seems small. This is not to say that other authoritarian movements in modern society are thereby ruled out.

Before trying to draw some general conclusions, something in a comparative vein should be said about the experience of fascism in Spain. There is a fundamental difference between the two cases in that Spanish, as well as Italian, fascism was not totalitarian as was Nazism. The secret of Francoist rule was that of maintaining social passivity rather than of mobilising the people; this reflects on a different role being played in international politics. This is not for a moment to deny the foul atrocities that Franco committed in Spanish society, especially amongst the Basques and Catalans. There is no doubt, moreover, that the early Spanish bourgeoisie proved no more of a support for the republican government under attack from Franco than their German colleagues had proved to be pillars of Weimar. However, Spanish fascism lasted longer, and it is very interesting to observe its evolution when it sought to finally modernise its society. Difficulties for Franco arose when he discovered that modernisation would require educated labour. In particular, the expansion of the universities was related to the growth of political radicalism. Capitalists played, for their own reasons, an important role in the liberalisation of the society:

There is no natural, 'ideal' fit between a given social structure and a political constitution. If anything, we have shown that the bourgeoisie may opt for forms of autocratic and anti-parliamentarian rule as the most adequate solution to its continued hegemony. Yet, it seems clear that at certain stages of economic development it may choose the vast negotiating process entailed by the liberal political framework as the best way for furthering its interests. In this context, it is interesting to note that in Spain, still without having switched their allegiance to a representative, multi-party system, the members of the industrial bourgeoisie were already moving towards unofficial collective bargaining and negotiation with the clandestine unions at a very early stage, bypassing the official channels. This started to happen as soon as wage settlements through peaceful means began to look more attractive than outright repression, from the late fifties onwards..[13]

In comparison with the German bourgeoisie, the Spanish capitalists were not threatened by mass suffrage, and therefore gradually learnt the lesson of their nineteenth-century English peers that accommodation can be cheaper than repression. In this they were much helped by restraint shown throughout society as the result of a collective memory as to exactly how catastrophic repression could be. The power of such collective memories elsewhere will be seen in a moment.

What final conclusions can be drawn from this discussion of the connection between capitalism and authoritarianism? In truth the key conclusion must be that we are not in a position to decide key questions – Are such regimes inevitably unstable? Can capitalism accommodate itself permanently to authoritarian rule? – simply because special circumstances pollute our evidence. We do not know how long lasting a combination of capital and authority could have proved in Germany since the Allied victory in the Second World War ended this experiment. Similarly, it is rather dangerous to read too much into the Spanish case because part of the motivation of the elite desiring liberalisation seems to have been the desire to create a liberal polity in order to participate inside the EEC. It can be clearly said that the relationship between capitalism and liberalism was strong only in the British case where a civil society was already in place. In other societies, capitalists, especially if they are large-scale *early* capitalists, may well link themselves to authoritarian forms and effectively undermine parliamentary democracy in such a way as to give the radical right a chance. There remains the possibility that, as capitalism becomes industrial, it will come to depend more and more upon education being spread throughout society. It may require the presence of something very like a civil society. Capitalists may find, as they did in Spain, that there is something to recommend liberal politics after all. No final closure is possible on this question. But the question will surface again when examining those semi-peripheral countries of the Third World, particularly in Latin America, which face similar problems today.

13　S. Giner and E. Sevilla, 'From despotism to parliamentarianism: class domination and political order in the Spanish state', in R. Scase (ed.), *The State in Western Europe*, Croom Helm, London, 1978, p. 218.

The Rise and Decline of Keynesianism

It is scarcely necessary to point to the dramatic effect of the Second World War. A division inside Europe had occurred as early as 1919/20 when the allies made sure that the Bolshevik infection did not spread, a course of action made much easier by the deliberate self-isolation of the Soviet Union. This division of Europe was only confirmed by the Second World War at the end of which two hostile pacts of states, each dominated by a superpower, came to face each other in the European heartland. Europe had destroyed its primacy in world history as a result of its own Peloponnesian-type conflicts.

How can we understand the political economy of Western countries today? Let us begin in a negative manner by establishing what the characterisitic political economy of the societies in question is *not*. I have in mind here the claim, made by the more naïve, full-blooded industrial society theorists that the relations between capital and labour were, as the result of key social changes, now no longer such as to create large-scale class conflict capable of creating fundamental social change. Ralf Dahrendorf in his striking and influential *Class and Class Conflict in Industrial Society*[14] stressed the importance of four developments in society:

1   Capitalism is held to have decomposed. By this Dahrendorf means that early entrepreneurial and family capitalism has now been replaced by larger corporations in which real power is wielded by managers. Dahrendorf follows a long line of social theory and research, the most well-known representative of which is J.K. Galbraith, in insisting that managers are more concerned with stability and harmony than increasing profits, and that they justify their business activity in terms of social efficiency.

2   Social mobility is held to have increased. This is of vital importance for Dahrendorf's general theory of class conflict since the absence of individual mobility, it is argued, encourages the creation of solidary, and therefore conflicting, social classes.

3   Perhaps the most crucial element explaining the rise in social mobility is the creation of shared citizenship rights. Such rights are held to include not just legal and political but also social contents. Thus they include rights to education such that life chances are no longer held to be dependent upon the possession of privilege. Equality of opportunity is held to have been achieved.

14 Routledge & Kegan Paul, London, 1959.

4   A very important point for Dahrendorf, though perhaps of less salience to our purposes, is the acceptance of conflict. Class conflict is said to be more intense when attempts are made to suppress or ignore it. Western societies, Dahrendorf believes, have learned to live with conflict, and have made it especially beneficial by providing a framework of regulation within which it need not be explosive.

These four points can be summed up by saying that Western societies are now 'post-capitalist'. Social justice is now apparently sufficient to allow modern industry to work within a social democratic framework. This is not to say, however, that post-capitalism is held to be inherently socially peaceful. Dahrendorf made it perfectly clear that modern competitive social democracies will be endlessly restless, but that such restlessness will typically occur via individual rather than collective strivings.[15]

This position has been persuasively and justifiably challenged by thinkers of Marxist persuasion. Studies of the behaviour of managers, of the residual power of shareholders, and of the interlocking of directorships, have all shown that this picture of a socially responsible, non-aggressive form of business community is exaggerated. Shareholders' demands for profit in the market-place weigh on managers; they cannot replace the profit motive with some sort of social service ethic.[16] Recent studies of social mobility have shown, in addition, that the picture of an open society is again exaggerated. The most recent and careful such studies have shown a good deal of gross mobility but explain this in terms of changes in the occupational structure, and in terms of differential fertility rates. In other words, the upper classes have not recently had enough children as to be able to fill all the top positions.[17] Such studies insist that one's life chances remain dictated by parental background, and could become so increasingly if the occupational structure ceases to change, and/or if the upper classes have more children. It remains the case that citizenship changes have not been sufficient to override old-fashioned privileges gained by class advantage.

The conclusion to be drawn from this is that the forces of labour and capital remain in place. Merely to say this, however, tells us little. How in the post-war world was it possible to combine capitalism and democracy? It is necessary to draw a distinction in order to answer this question. For 20 or so years after the war, social peace was achieved by what deserves

15   I have discussed Dahrendorf's work in *Diagnoses of Our Time*, Heinemann, London, 1981.

16   J. Scott, *Corporations, Classes and Capitalism*, Hutchinson, London, 1979.

17   J.H. Goldthorpe (with the assistance of C. Llewelyn and G. Payne), *Social Mobility and Class Structure*, Oxford University Press, Oxford, 1980.

to be named Keynesianism, although the great economist might well not have accepted all that was done in his name. More recently, however, we have become aware of the costs and difficulties of running political economies by Keynesian means. In the last decade, it has *not* proved possible to combine capitalism and democracy with any ease.

The original Keynesian formula can be seen in formal or substantive light. Formally, a bargain was implicitly struck whereby capital accepted certain welfare provisions, while labour accepted the market economy. The idea behind this, more or less clearly formulated, was that cohesive national societies would then be able to compete successfully in the international capitalist market, the workings of which have yet to be examined. I suspect that what really created national cohesion, however, was a shared feeling of national reconstruction in European societies which, with the exception of Britain, had all suffered a catastrophe within living memory. Whatever the exact explanation, there is no doubt as to the result: it was the extraordinary years of economic growth that characterised the whole of the free market world for at least two decades. This growth provided the substantive reason for social peace. Societies in the capitalist world have prospered and remained democratic because of growth. Such societies depend on Danegeld.[18] Discontent from below was removed by the growing size of the national cake. There was little positive adherence to capitalist society, however, and those who believed there was, both on the left (the workers are brainwashed, according to Althusser and Marcuse) and on the right (the system is now accepted as just, according to a myriad of American thinkers), had little empirical evidence to support their case.[19] Capitalism was accepted pragmatically simply because it delivered the goods.

There was always a worm in the bud of Keynesianism, and it can be uncovered by recalling Keynes's own intellectual presuppositions. Keynes endorsed capitalist society for the reasons given by Hume and Smith:

There are valuable human activities which require the motive of money-making and the environment of private wealth-ownership for their full fruition. Moreover, dangerous human proclivities can be canalised into comparatively harmless channels by the existence of opportunities for money-making and private wealth, which, if they cannot be satisfied in this way, may find their outlet in cruelty, the reckless pursuit of personal power and authority, and other forms of self-aggrandisement. It is better that a man should tyrannise over his bank balance than over his fellow-citizens; and whilst the former is sometimes denounced as

18 The metaphor is Ernest Gellner's. See his 'A social contract in search of an idiom: the demise of the Danegeld State', *Political Quarterly*, vol. 49, 1978.

19 S. Hill, N. Abercrombie and B. Turner, *The Dominant Ideology Thesis*, George Allen & Unwin, London, 1981.

being but a means to the latter, sometimes at least it is an alternative. But it is not necessary for the stimulation of these activities and the satisfaction of these proclivities that the game should be played for such high stakes as at present. Much lower stakes will serve the purpose equally well, as soon as the players are accustomed to them. The task of transmuting human nature must not be confused with the task of managing it.[20]

His worst fears were fulfilled when, in the late 1920s and early 1930s, the power systems of fascism and Bolshevism came to the fore, promising solutions to all economic ills. He loathed such power systems since they removed the softness of life characteristic of the liberal society which he appreciated. His purpose in the *General Theory* was to find a way in which the troughs and peaks of capitalism could be removed. As is well known, he argued that deflation was aggravated by the hoarding of money, and that intelligent government action could encourage such funds to be released in depression, thus avoiding political cataclysm while not neglecting to restrain inflationary tendencies during a period of growth.

What presuppositions are at work here? Most importantly, Keynes believed that applied intelligence would help capitalism back on to an even keel. The state would act, in the striking phrase of modern Marxists, as the best capitalist. Capitalists were *stupid*. The clever mandarins of Keynes's world, Oxbridge scholars with experience of Royal Commissions to a man, could simply iron out the irregularities. The hidden presupposition of this was that the mandarin governing class would always behave with a sense of economic responsibility. Like Lord Reith, their sense of public duty would mean their thinking in the long and not the short run. Keynes's second presupposition was that organised labour remained sufficiently deferential to accept the wise councils and economic logic that government would outline to them. The world of Hume and Smith was held to be still extant. Keynes's belief was based upon the reasonable principle that such organic co-operation would lead to social stability, and he was prepared to add to this some measure of redistribution. However, he did not think the time was yet ripe to remove all privileges from the capitalist class, whose 'disgusting proclivity' for money he despised.

Both these presuppositions proved flawed. At the end of his life, Keynes noted that there was no inherent reason why the working class should listen to the economic wisdom handed down from on high by mandarins and governments. One can go somewhat further and say that

20 *The General Theory of Employment, Money and Interest*, Macmillan, London, 1983, p. 374.

Keynesianism perhaps saved liberal society temporarily at the cost of damaging it further in the long run. The enormous expansion of Western economies in the period from 1945 raised expectations in such a way that it was extremely difficult in times of crisis to return to neutral economic logic. Thus the oil shock of 1973 led to massive inflation; a growth in real wages was allowed for political reasons which had disastrous results for the economies involved. Similarly, in the winter of 1978/79 in Britain economic logic showed that a very small percentage increase for wages under the still extant Social Contract would have allowed for some growth in the economy, and this would have ensured that the growth in wages was a real one. Competition between different sectional groups meant that much larger increases were achieved even though they proved self-defeating. Such working-class action was sufficiently powerful to cause the political economy terrible problems. The state no longer had the room, to use another striking Marxist phrase, to steer the system, and this meant that Keynes's other presupposition was increasingly of little use. Deference was no longer shown to the hierarchy which had to act in a market situation where it had to compete for votes. It very rapidly became clear to politicians that the tools of demand management could engineer instant if short-lived growth which would help them win elections. Only one British Chancellor in over two decades stood out against the demand to reflate before an election, and the political fate of Mr Roy Jenkins, at least inside the Labour Party, was sealed there and then. All this deserves summary. Keynes presumed that the establishment would act in the interests of economic rationality: electoral ambition, however, makes for irrationality both in matters of reflation and when dealing with factories and industries that have the political limelight but which are no longer profitable.

The argument made has the conflict between capital and labour to the forefront, but the general scenario does not easily fit in with Marx's expectations. One wonders in retrospect why Dahrendorf felt that the social changes he noted would lead to social peace. It is probably rather the case that they changed people's reference groups, and so perhaps increased rather than lessened demands. Certainly, recent history has seen the growth of widespread worker militancy, and this matters far more to the political economy than did the transient student movements of the late 1960s. Thus the British working class played a considerable role in toppling governments of both parties in 1969/70, 1974 and 1978/79, something that disproves the view that the working class is brainwashed into accepting the necessities of the capitalist system. Nevertheless, such class action ill accords with the Marxist scenario of a working class armed with socialist ideology seeking to achieve a new and more just society. If a single aphorism sums up the character of such action it remains that of Bernard Shaw who spoke bitingly and despairingly of 'the capitalism of the proletariat'. All this can be put in another way. Capitalist morality has been all too successful in spreading throughout society. Whether one calls the doctrine of self-interest a social ethic, or the absence of one, is a matter of choice. There are well-known problems associated with this ethic. As Durkheim insisted long ago, it does not enhance social cohesion. It is in the interest of all individuals to have a society based upon relationships of trust. Nevertheless, it is equally in the interest of each separate individual to ignore such rules, to free-load, albeit hoping that everyone else does not. This seems to be something like the contentious and dissatisfied society of ceaseless demands that now confronts us.

'Liberties' has tended to change its meaning in recent times. Liberties in the West allowed for a high social participation ratio, and this led to a great total sum of energy. Different groups co-operated together; the state *was* very largely a 'capitalist state', notably in eighteenth-century Britain. 'Liberties' is now often used to describe privileges held *against* the public of a particular national society, and something real is being hinted at here. A power stand-off between social groups is coming to characterise national societies in the advanced capitalist world with consequent diminution of total power. Perhaps the inflationary effects of the Danegeld solution were being felt *before* the oil crisis of 1973, so that the collapse of growth is not simply attributable to an external shock. Anyway, any social order is bound to face such shocks at some time or another. Whatever the truth may be in this important matter, entrenched positions now often adopted remove a flexibility in society and the steering room for the state, both of which are needed if growth is to be restored.

One response to this situation has been to diminish the liberties enjoyed by labour. This radical alternative, offered by Mrs Thatcher but not by Helmut Kohl, occasionally presents itself in the guise of the highly abstract economic theory of monetarism. There is every reason to doubt that this technical doctrine will be followed. It requires politicians to abandon tools of manipulating the economy. Politicians are required to behave like Ulysses, who bound himself because the sirens were so tempting. Though prediction is notoriously hard, I do firmly prophesy that modern politicians will not take the Ulysses route. In fact it is already clear that the rigours of this doctrine have been very substantially watered down. One reason for this is that the pressure on governments coming up to elections remains and is not, despite rhetoric consequent upon the whole matter becoming more or less public knowledge, any more likely to be avoided now than hitherto. This right-wing alternative can only be understood in *political* rather than in purely economic terms.

It is designed to restore the stick to capitalism by means of unemployment. As such it is, of course, deeply unpleasant. However it is also possessed of a certain machiavellian wisdom in that it 'takes on' not so much organised labour as those who are helpless. Providing that provision is made for the young, older workers who become unemployed and thus lose their union cards are scarcely in a position to fight back.[21] Nevertheless, one may doubt that this route will succeed. Public expenditure, boosted by unemployment payments, has not fallen, nor has the economy improved. The unions remain in place, and seem likely to come into action in ways already familiar if and when the economy improves. *Crucially*, one may doubt that the creation of a complaisant and cowed workforce nineteenth-century style is the best way in which to run a much more advanced, technologically sophisticated, late industrial society. In this matter Mrs Thatcher does not begin to understand her supposed mentor Adam Smith. The great enlightenment thinker insisted that rich countries *needed* high wages to encourage productivity. Exactly how low would wages in Britain have to sink before it could compete with economies like that of Taiwan? Certainly Japan, Germany and America spend more on education, importantly on *general* rather than vocational education, than Britain did even before recent educational cuts were instituted. Perhaps in this matter Mrs Thatcher, like the French generals, is preparing to do battle in the last economic war. There is no doubt, however, that Mrs Thatcher has given the state some – but only some – steering room, but only at a vast cost. Her aim is permanently to lower expectations. One wonders if national cohesion will result from a policy which clearly benefits some sections of the community at the expense of others. It seems more than likely that the power stand-off characteristic of recent British society will merely be reinforced so as to do more damage in the longer term.

What of the leftist alternative, seeking to create full-blooded democratic socialism? One obvious problem faces this strategy, at least in most Western countries. The forces of labour are not engaged in a Marxist-type class conflict such that they actively wish to create a socialist society. On the contrary much working-class action wishes simply for more of the benefits that capitalism, which it by no means rejects completely, can bring. This leftist strategy has accordingly considerable electoral problems to face, especially if it remains linked to a demand for full-scale central planning without being able to offer a reasonable case in favour of its efficiency. More importantly, the mere presence of a leftist government does not by itself guarantee the removal of the power stand-off noted. Some of President Mitterand's plans were defeated by the anti-

21 A. Gelb and K. Bradley, 'The radical potential of cash nexus breaks', *British Journal of Sociology*, vol. 31, 1980.

socialist attitude of his trade unions, and the same is broadly true of the situation of the British Labour government in the 'winter of discontent'. Were class privileges to be abolished entirely, there is no guarantee that the problems of the political economy would thereby be solved.

There is a more important consideration concerning this leftist strategy. We have already seen that the policy of the radical right may not be economically successful if other national competitors can remove their social blockages and yet retain the services of a well-trained, highly educated workforce. This is to take account of international capitalism. Should it not be held responsible for the destruction of left-wing governments through formal (the intervention of the International Monetary Fund) and informal (capital flight) means? Is it the case that it is in this larger arena that all power resides? Are nations, in other words, dependent upon international forces? Is the international arena a force of total *control* which leaves them no autonomy of their own? No brief is held here for *every* element of international capitalism, and various proposals will later be put forward concerning the role of the United States, terms of trade, and the International Monetary Fund so as to adapt this arena for present circumstances.

In all honesty, however, beyond this I believe good arguments can be made *in favour* of strong international economic competition taking a broadly capitalist form; and these arguments against nationalist chauvinist protectionism are developed openly in the conclusion to this book. Anyway, bluntly, the international capitalist arena is in place. Let us draw distinctions as to its operations. Whilst it is true that this arena would be opposed to any *complete* socialist state in its midst, its workings otherwise are best seen in relatively neutral terms. It provides a context of competition rather than a complete domination of national processes. It *constrains* and does not completely *control*. The notion of control much too easily blames outsiders for internal failings. The impression is sometimes given, for example, that a well-organised, successful and dynamic Labour Party was defeated by forces beyond its control in 1976. Nothing could be further from the truth. The Party had not thought out the implications of having to borrow money, and looked manifestly unlikely to resolve internal social blockages.

Over the last 15 years, great disparities of growth rates have resulted between Western societies at the end of every trade cycle, and it behoves to ask about the general social characteristics of successful societies. The key shared characteristic seems to be some type of corporatism internally which avoids the power stand-off so characteristic of British society. Such corporatism has deep historical roots within various nations, and cannot be invented at will whatever the institutional setting. In Britain, for example, the presence of vast numbers of unions militated against this arrangement for the simple reason that the centralised union movement could not control its own members. Corporatism takes, moreover, vastly different forms in different societies. In Sweden, corporatism is being currently allied with a left-wing strategy which is quite determined not to be thwarted by trade union liberties. A very considerable increase in social rights has been granted in order to achieve national consensus; the aim is thereby to allow greater flexibility in the face of the market. Capital may 'fly' from such a socialistic state, but it looks more likely at present that it will stay. Certainly a high trained labour force together with national cohesion will allow for greater profits than does the alternative policy of Mrs Thatcher in Britain. International capitalism and a large measure of socialistic internal improvements are not necessarily opposed, and there is much greater room for the autonomy of national societies than those insisting on the controlling powers of international capitalism allow. On the other hand, however, Japan and Germany seem likely to have pioneered a type of micro-corporatism binding unionised workers, replete with great privileges, to large corporations but allowing for an open and highly competitive labour market below this level.[22] This combination of carrot and stick seems to be proving equally successful.

Before discussing these matters further, however, something much more systematic must first be said about the international arena, and about the position of America within that arena.

Splendours and Miseries of the Pax Americana

Keynes believed that a decent ordering of the international capitalist arena was as necessary as those changes he proposed in the workings of national political economies. It is sometimes argued, and with much justice, that modern capitalism works well when a leading power disciplines and provides services for the system as a whole, somewhat in the manner, although by now infinitely more technical, in which medieval Catholicism provided a shell with which competition occurred. Britain was the banker of the world in the nineteenth century. It used that position to insist upon an open system of free trade which was very much in the interests of the economically ascendant power. The inability of Germany and Britain in the late nineteenth and early twentieth centuries to share the leadership of the system as a whole encouraged a climate of

---

22 J.H. Goldthorpe, 'The end of convergence: corporatist and dualist tendencies in modern Western societies' in his (ed.) *Order and Conflict in Western European Capitalism*, Oxford University Press, Oxford, 1984. I am grateful for having been able to see this essay prior to publication.

international recrimination leading to protectionism and trade war. This turned international competition into a zero-sum game in which any gains were made at the expense of a competitor since growth in the system as a whole was stymied. Keynes wished to prevent this happening again, and at Bretton Woods in 1944 he proposed a marvellously ingenious set of rules for the international capitalist system as a whole. His proposals centred upon restraining weak *and* excessively powerful economies with an eye to establishing regulated international competition. His plans were defeated by the United States which did not wish to surrender the freedom of action consequent upon being the leading economy. Furthermore, the United States watered down such proposals of Keynes's as were accepted. He had hoped that the International Monetary Fund would be generously financed, and that it would allow a period of adjustment for any nation in trouble. In fact, the Fund was not given large sums of money, and has sought thereafter to impose its own rigidly deflationary rules of behaviour on debtor nations. But a system *did* emerge, and it had economic and military components to it. It was the Pax Americana, and the great achievements and current problems of this system must now be examined.

In 1945 Europe was unable to defend herself and therefore sought the protection of the United States, a situation which was formalised with the creation of NATO. The alliance had several benefits for Europe; it was cheap, did not involve nearly as much political control as other European states suffered under the Soviet umbrella, and it avoided dealing with the German problem. In other words, it did not necessitate the rearming of the power whose ambitions had played a key part in the creation of two world wars. The more sophisticated exponents of Atlanticism pointed out that a positive contribution from Europe was by no means ignored in all this. On the contrary, European pressure would help civilise and restrain the more naïve impulses of the fledgling superpower. The economic benefits of the Pax Americana were even more striking for Europe. World trade was ordered by the dollar serving as an international currency whose value was assured because it could be converted into gold. More importantly, America proved itself incredibly generous. The Marshall Plan was a type of *acte gratuite* in economic terms based on the sound political judgement that greater security would result from having prosperous allies. Moreover, the United States did not prevent, indeed at times encouraged, the emergence of the European Economic Community. The outcome of these institutions and policies was clear and dramatic: Europe benefited from that glorious quarter century of sustained growth already described. This would not have been possible without the contribution made by the United States.

There have *always* been tensions in the relationship between Europe and America. This was not an alliance between equals, because only one element provided monetary and military leadership. This inequality was felt earliest and with the greatest force in matters of defence. During the 1950s American strategic thinking asserted that it would launch massive reprisals from the United States in the case of an attack on Europe. The most loyal Atlanticists could not believe this easily and comfortably. Would an American president *really* consign his society to destruction if West Berlin was invaded? In these circumstances the Europeans were extremely glad of the presence of American troops, who served as hostages guaranteeing American involvement.

There were economic differences as well. In the first years after the war Europe had suffered from a dollar deficit which was only corrected by means of the Marshall Plan. But in the late 1950s the American economy began regularly to run a budget deficit, and to do so without any serious long-term attempt to correct this imbalance. Of course this laxness was entirely contrary to the rigid financial rules which the American-dominated International Monetary Fund imposed on all other debtor countries. America was using her position to break the rules of the system she pretended to uphold. Why was this accepted, and how was it justified? America provided the defence of Europe and its budget deficit was justified in Washington as a backdoor way of insisting on some contributions from increasingly rich Europeans. This view was initially endorsed in Europe, most enthusiastically by West Germany. However, there was a cost to such complaisance. Americans invested hugely abroad, and most of this capital came to Europe. It seemed as if Europe, holding on to dollars created by the deficit, was financing the expansion of American capitalism. Though Europe benefited from such investment, the situation nevertheless was a source of resentment. All this shows that military and economic matters often cannot be considered in isolation, although it will be seen that a certain primacy should be accorded to the former.

These tensions were accepted for a long period because the costs of the Pax Americana were less, on both sides, than the benefits it brought. America was the first to question the relationship as a whole. Its economy suffered increasingly from extensive military commitments abroad, and its budget deficit grew vastly as a result of the Vietnam war. It was impossible to tax at greater rates American citizens used to a higher standard of living. Inflation resulted. By 1968 a two-tier gold system had been created which effectively dishonoured the dollar to gold convertibility pledge. In 1971 Nixon unilaterally took the dollar off gold and imposed import controls. The White House of Nixon, Kissinger and Connally argued again that such action was a justified means of getting the capitalist world, and especially the advanced societies therein, to contribute to the burden of American defence. This attitude is a constant of American polity. But how did this feel to the Europeans? Was endorsement still willingly given to Washington, or was there instead some perception that the rules of the system needed to be changed? Military/political and economic sources of conflict can be distinguished. They are, of course, interlinked because of the latter largely being occasioned by the need to finance the former through the holding of dollars by, or by greater contributions from, Europe.[23]

The most celebrated area of conflict in recent years has been that concerning defence matters. Europeans, most notably Helmut Schmidt, feared the 'uncoupling' of America from its NATO partners, and called for modernisation of military technology, in the face of the perceived threat of Russian SS20 'theatre' nuclear weapons. Ironically, attempts to 'couple' increased the fear of 'uncoupling'. Nuclear weapons in Europe might lead the superpowers to limit war to that area, something once contemplated publicly by President Reagan. Such a scenario could not but terrify Europeans, although it should be noted that it remains a highly unlikely one. It seems that Russia regards cruise missiles in Europe as American, with great justification, and would reply directly to the United States. The uncertainty that it might so behave is enough to prevent any pre-emptive strike by America. Perhaps a more basic European fear was, to be blunt, that democracy would come to rule American military strategy. Nuclear weapons depend upon the rationality of state leaders, and this 'personified intelligence of the state' depends upon the operation of Clausewitzian signalling principles at a very sophisticated level.[24] The elite consequently needs 'steering room'. It certainly has it in the Soviet Union. One *must* hope, too, that it has it in America and that domestic considerations will never prove strong enough to force an American president into anything other than minor wars. It is noticeable that the American elite is far more liberal and enlightened than its public, and Europeans have been truly terrified by the thought that a president might be elected who did not care about the sophistications involved in the nuclear world. This has not happened and Reagan's militarism is very much for home consumption. The fears are, nonetheless, genuine. Such fears have been increased by discussion of laser weapons in space, since these could probably only protect American bases in Europe. Such weapons would require even more centralised decision-making than hitherto, and underline the fact that the superpower has total control

23 My ordering of these conflicts benefits from attending a lecture by Professor David Calleo in November 1984 which asked 'Can the United States afford NATO?'. I am generally indebted to his work, and comment on it below.

24 R. Aron, *Clausewitz*, Routledge & Kegan Paul, London, 1983; also M. Mann, 'The roots of modern militarism', unpublished paper.

over the alliance. Closely related to these defence issues are increasingly different political perceptions as to the state of world politics. Europe clearly wishes to draw closer to the Arab world, and it is not prepared to forego the benefits of detente. Considerable conflict with the United States has ensued. Charges of 'disloyalty' have recently been made by the superpower, and these increasingly generate hostility in Europe, as well as countercharges about 'simple perceptions of the world'.

In the last analysis, against much current opinion, present military/political tensions are best seen as a continuance of a discontent that has *always* been present. The economic conflict with Western Europe (that is, the whole area that had developed on the dollar and not just the members of NATO or the EEC) was also present in embryo from the start, but it seems to be taking on a genuinely novel intensity. It is true that the American-based monetary system had always led to the export of inflation:

... the nature of the world monetary system meant that America's domestic inflation was rapidly exported to the world at large, with powerful reinforcement to all the inflationary tendencies in other countries. American inflation was transmitted through America's soaring balance-of-payments deficits. With the dollar as a reserve currency, US balance-of-payments deficits had no restraining consequences for the domestic American money supply. By a similar process, private banking flows were creating liquidity in Europe without reducing it in America. Even countries strongly resistant to inflation could not keep it out. Under the Bretton Woods arrangements, countries might try to use 'open market operations' to reduce their national money supplies in compensation for the dollar inflows. But the techniques for reducing the money supply almost invariably raised domestic interest rates and thereby attracted still larger flows. Thus, even large countries, unusually determined to resist inflation, found the 'sterilization' of dollars increasingly difficult without exchange controls. Foreign governments therefore found themselves with two options. They could align their monetary conditions with the dollar inflow, that is, inflate. Otherwise, they could revalue their currencies, a step believed harmful for foreign trade and domestic employment.[25]

The era of floating exchange rates that followed Nixon's 1971 move to make the dollar non-convertible to gold has made the whole situation much more precarious. Europeans were placed in a particularly difficult dilemma. If they did not support the dollar by continuing to pay the costs of an ever-increasing American deficit, American industry would then gain a competitive advantage. The costs of a high, perhaps overvalued dollar were equally difficult to bear. This became apparent during President Reagan's first term when the dollar was propped up by high

25 D. Calleo, *The Imperious Economy*, Harvard University Press, London, 1982, pp. 108–9.

interest rates; large amounts of capital were in consequence attracted away from Europe to the American money markets. What was striking about all this was the impact that movements of capital, in large part to speculate upon currency rates, had upon the European economy. The American budget deficit had created in the 1960s a huge pool of Euro-dollars and to this pool was added the new capital of the oil states in the mid-1970s. Speculation grew, as did indebtedness. It is extremely interesting to note that there were movements here to a genuinely *international* capitalism. When President Carter tried to control American inflation in the late 1970s he was largely prevented from doing so by the behaviour of the international banking system. The ability of the system to speculate against currencies significantly added to international economic instability, but more important in this case was the ability to funnel funds in legally questionable manner from the Euromarket to America, in order to undermine the domestic credit squeeze. American international banks and multinational corporations were clearly prepared to act on their own behalf rather than in American interests since they traded as much against the dollar as against other currencies.[26]

The relations between Europe and America, in all their forms, are currently in a state of flux, and recent developments include concentrated raids on the dollar and the development of the European Monetary System based on the Deutschmark. These are discussed in the conclusions to this book. The huge amount of money in the world banking system is of crucial importance to the Third World, and this is discussed in the same place. But some provisional assessment of the state to which the Pax Americana has come can be offered at this point. Nixon and Kissinger responded to increasing American economic weakness by reiterating the traditional insistence that the new economic power of Europe be tapped in order to share the burden of empire. This demand was not matched by any process of agreement, but was instead imposed by force. Thus American leadership, for example, did not create a common plan to deal with increased oil prices but rather sought to minimize them, to America's advantage, by letting the dollar slide so as to obviate them. All such unilateral action ruled out many advantages that could have been realised by intelligent planning, and further exacerbated tension.

One very interesting American argument against this United States policy has been that pursued over many years by David Calleo. He has noted that the manipulation of the rules of the world economy has not been in the long-term interests of the American domestic economy. One suspects that he is right, and that much of the new growth achieved

26 M. Moffitt, *The World's Money*, Michael Joseph, London, 1984.

under Reagan's first term is not 'real'. It is not based on increased productivity in high technology industries, but is something of a speculative paper phenomenon based upon an old-fashioned consumer boom. If this is so, the escalating size of the American budget deficit occasioned by stepping up the arms race will eventually incapacitate the American economy. Perhaps this is already happening. In 1985 America became a net debtor nation. This makes the high interest rate policy of the Reagan years less and less rational for America, and the attractions of a cheaper dollar, probably combined *à la* Nixon with general import controls, are likely to come to the fore. Such a policy would increase American competitiveness to Europe's disadvantage. But Europeans would nevertheless have the right to object to this policy on two grounds. Firstly, its protectionist character would mean that the world economy was still being run on a zero-sum basis. Secondly (and even more importantly) it is unlikely that any new policy would be consistently adhered to by the United States. A cheaper dollar would make it harder to pay for international defence commitments, and a return to high interest rate policies designed to support the dollar cannot be ruled out of court in the long run. Nobody knows exactly what will happen since the situation is volatile. But the most likely outcome seems to be that of continuing oscillation of policy, and this certainly makes life difficult for Europeans. The reason for this is clear: no way has yet been found to deal with the structural problem of the United States being militarily overcommitted throughout the world.

David Calleo does not quite face up to the problem that arises from his analysis as a whole. Why was American policy so blind to these long-term economic consequences? A part of the answer is that manipulating pure rules allowed the expansion of American business abroad. Calleo is right to note that this does not, as Britain has discovered, help in the domestic economy in the long run. That is perhaps an irrelevance. For the state in America has limited steering room, not so much between capital and labour, but rather apart from capital alone. American society may not benefit as a whole, but if large corporations continue to do so this policy may nevertheless be continued. More important still is the indefinable pleasure, or, in an alternative formulation, the freedom of action, that hegemony affords American leaders. To insist upon retaining this freedom of action while asking for contributions from Europe, and a Europe anyway suffering from the self-interested economic actions of America within the world economy as a whole, is a recipe for increased conflict. This is not to say that such contributions should not be asked, merely that some sharing of leadership must result if a stable relationship is to be built.

Specific policy assessments are offered in the conclusions to this book, but theoretical points of great interest can usefully be made now. One crucial question is the extent to which capitalist society is larger even than the United States. Can the United States continue to be the leading power if its economy declines? Nobody knows the answer to this in the longer term, but it seems to me clear that America still has the capacity to manipulate international economic relationships. One reason for this is the sheer size of the American economy. But there is a second reason which concerns the ultimate source of the United States' power over Europe. Given the relative strength of the European economies, and the fact that they could manage (having their own food and being their own greatest market) without America, one must suspect that American power rests ultimately on its military supremacy. Until Europe has her own defence, it is supremely unlikely that the workings of the international economic arena can be changed. European laziness in defence matters gives us, in the last analysis, little right and no capacity to criticise America. We are, after all, only a colony.

Conclusions, Pessimistic in Tone

These can only be interim conclusions. The capitalist world extends to certain Third World countries, and some of the motor for internal change results from the arms race with the Soviet Union. 'Society' today is world society and further attempts to stress this are made in the conclusions of this book. Nevertheless, it is possible to note a certain tone to this chapter and to highlight certain unresolved ambiguities about it.

Let us recall the debate in the Scottish Enlightenment concerning the future of rich countries. Hume's contention was that rich countries would eventually have their international trade taken by poorer rivals blessed with cheaper wages. This need not, in his opinion, lead to poverty since a rich country could withdraw from international trade and survive through expanding its own internal market. Smith, in contrast, argued that a high-wage, ever more productive economy could retain its advantage indefinitely and he insisted that such a policy could expand the world economy to general advantage. When we apply these ideas to modern circumstances, interesting results emerge. Economic competition exists between national societies within a larger capitalist society. It is possible that a group of societies may wish to withdraw from this competitive arena, or that such a group, or even single societies, may seek to protect themselves via tariff walls of one sort or another. In the extent to which they can and do so act, they will accord with Hume's approach – although, as in the inter-war years, probably at the cost of diminishing the total size of the world economy. This crucial matter is discussed again at length in later chapters. But what hope is there of Smith's view triumphing in the advanced countries of the capitalist world? Can they remain sufficiently flexible to cement their unique historical achievement of the combination of liberties, economic development and liberal politics?

The tone of much of this chapter has been pessimistic. The British experience seems to suggest that liberties in modern national society create blockages such that economic development is curtailed. There has not been any *direct* attack on formal democracy to date, but this failure of the economy matters vitally, as unemployment and race riots make clear. Moreover, doubts were expressed as to the capacity of right and left to make a late industrial political economy, which combines inequality with democracy, work efficiently. Interestingly, both left and right often end up calling for the creation of a new communal ideology to legitimate social arrangements. One may understand this point, and thus praise the brilliance of the analysis of a book such as Alasdair MacIntyre's *After Virtue*.[27] Yet that book is representative in *not* telling us what the new ideology is to be, and one wonders if something so important should be kept such a well-guarded secret. I do not see any sign of a new ideology, nor of sufficient social disruption to again give intellectuals their characteristic chance of gaining power. As the last attempt to re-enchant an industrial society was at the Nuremberg rallies, perhaps we should manage without it.[28] Hence other arguments seem more important. Social peace may be better sought by nothing less than uncoupling the traditional linking of reward and status, so as to increase the resources available in society. According to this scenario, those with crucial but miserable jobs could be rewarded in monetary terms, whilst those with inherently interesting jobs would have to be prepared to work for less. It is all too easy to see the difficulties attached to the implementation of this proposal, but the order of imagination nevertheless commands attention.[29]

Is such pessimism *really* justified? The centres of capitalist success have never remained the same. The leading edge of capitalism has thus variously passed from North Italy to Holland, then to Britain, Germany and America, and perhaps now to Japan and the Confucian capitalist states of South-East Asia. The decline of Britain in this context is

27 Duckworth, London, 1981.

28 E. Gellner, 'The absolute in braces' in his *Spectacles and Predicaments*, Cambridge University Press, Cambridge, 1981.

29 This idea was pioneered by the late Fred Hirsch in *Social Limits to Growth*, Routledge & Kegan Paul, London, 1977. For a full discussion, see A. Ellis and K. Kumar (eds), *Dilemmas of Liberal Democracies*, Methuen, London, 1983.

historically normal. Any pessimism should be limited by an awareness of prosperity elsewhere. Two particular areas are worth noting. Firstly, many European economies have prospered in recent years and some, notably those of Germany, France and Sweden, look set to prosper more. But how firmly is *that* course set? It is possible to wobble between two options. On the one hand, one can note that national cohesion was gained by the feeling of national reconstruction generated by historical castastrophe, and argue that such feelings are increasingly less relevant to the younger elements of Western nations. On the other hand, however, one can note that such societies have different institutional patterns, gained through complex historical processes and not easily imitable elsewhere, which may allow for continuing flexibility in the face of international competition. If time proves the pessimistic case, however, and all the advanced societies of the capitalist world come to suffer from power blockages, then secondly, a measure of optimism may be retrieved if it becomes true that such countries as Brazil become new capitalist giants. Economic development in these countries, desirable for its own sake, may in addition, as will be argued below, help them create more liberal polities.

These reservations do not, however, mean that all pessimism should be ruled out. If the mixture of liberties, development and liberal polities cannot somehow be made to work efficiently, it may make liberal politics less attractive to other countries. As classical liberalism was right to argue that the control of unbridled political power is as great a problem for humanity in the long run as the control of unbridled wealth, this possible development *must* occasion regret and concern. Further, the international element of capitalist society is currently in great difficulties. At the least, it seems that conflict is now taking on a zero-sum character, and this certainly makes development in the Third World that much harder to achieve. The situation would be immeasurably worsened were there to be a collapse, as is conceivable, of international banking. All this can be put in different words. Even if the centre of economic power in the world is going to change, hopefully towards some newly industrialising countries, the period of transition may be exceptionally difficult and painful. Humanity cannot stand too much pain.

7

Beyond the Soviet Model?

The main thesis that has run through this book has concerned the manner in which competition, both military and economic, has led to social evolution. To this point the thesis presented has been a strong one: competition led to economic development *and* to the creation of liberal polities. Two qualifications were offered in the previous chapter: firstly the combination of factors characteristic of Western societies may perhaps be coming unstuck; and second an alternative route, that of authoritarian capitalism, as in Japan and imperial Germany, was a serious and decidedly unpleasant possibility, and one with great influence today in the Third World. These qualifications do not detract from the clear statement that the 'world historical' importance of the Soviet Union lies in its refutation of the strong thesis. Military and economic competition certainly led to economic development and this was achieved by self-isolation from the international market in a one-party state cemented by an ideocracy. This ruled out liberal politics. The strong thesis, therefore, has to be replaced by a weaker one: competition leads *only* to economic development.

All this is to stress the state socialist character of the Soviet Union. This is scarcely novel, but it remains a key element if we are to understand a very different world from our own. But two further factors, much less often given their due, are equally crucial, and a consideration of them is central to this chapter. It is sometimes claimed that socialism, unlike capitalism, is inherently peaceful. This is naïve for a myriad of reasons, most obviously that warfare between states in Europe preceded the emergence of industrial capitalism and often runs according to its own logic. What is striking about the Soviet Union is that its state formation and character owe quite as much to military competition – an area in which it has, on occasion, played an active and aggressive part – as it does to socialism.[1] The Soviet Union is the Prussia of the twentieth

1 D. Holloway, *The Soviet Union and the Arms Race*, Yale University Press, New Haven, 1983.

century in that its military power is based upon a poor standard of living. This policy has been successful and the Soviet Union is, of course, together with *only* the United States, a superpower, and this is the second claim of the Soviet Union upon our attention. In order to understand why this militant route was taken it will prove necessary to think ourselves into the general situation facing the Soviet Union, and to be particularly sensitive to its recent historical experience.

The third and final factor to be stressed is that the socialist world, although only 70 years old inside the Soviet Union and less in its satellites, is not the simple monolith its enemies love to hate. It is very important not to equate all state socialism with Stalinism and the classical Soviet model of heavy industrialisation associated with the great Soviet autocrat. The first section of this chapter does describe the origins and character of the classical Soviet model but an attempt is then made to evaluate its significance. An important part of the argument will stress that this model was under question even in Russia in the middle 1950s, as Khruschev's famous speech to the Twentieth Party Congress in 1956 demonstrated. The nature of the difficulties caused by the classical Soviet model are then illustrated by an analysis of the social evolution of three of the Eastern European satellites. These regimes exhibit those strains very clearly indeed, and a discussion of these cases is anyway useful in adding to the general picture of Eastern European complexity. Each of the countries to be discussed, Hungary, Czechoslovakia and Poland, has made rather different attempts to 'liberalise', and informed speculation as to the possible futures of state socialist societies is offered. Probably the future of the satellites depends on the specific evolution of the imperial power, the Soviet Union, but that evolution cannot itself be divorced from world politics. A discussion of this problem concludes the chapter.

Social Origins of the Soviet Model

The old regime in Russia collapsed very slowly. It is impossible to exaggerate the impact which Napoleon's invasion of Russia, and the driving back of his armies to Paris, had upon the Tsarist regime. Within ten years the first of a whole series of Westernising groups, the Decembrists, tried to reform their society so as to enable it to catch up with liberal and advanced Western Europe. This was certain to be a major undertaking since the characteristic social physiognomies of Eastern and Western Europe were different. The former lacked the civil society of the latter. In the East a large and illiterate peasantry faced a landlord class without the presence of an urban sector equivalent to that of the

West; such middle-class trading functions as existed were usually monopolised by distinct ethnic groups, particularly by Jews. The old regime itself was similar to others in having ambitions well beyond its capabilities. Throughout the nineteenth century the state did try to become more autonomous of its landlord support, and in the process it expanded the university sector. In so doing it created the classic conditions for the emergence of an intelligentsia, often overproduced and hence underemployed, but equally clearly cut off from the peasant masses. These ambivalences of the intelligentsia – whether to become Westernisers or to join the people in a 'populist' movement – were famously the subject of the great novels of nineteenth-century Russia, perhaps most strikingly of Dostoevsky's *The Possessed*.

Significant sections of this intelligentsia did eventually adopt and adapt Marxism, and thereby contributed massively to one of the great movements of the modern age of ideology. But nineteenth-century Russian political history involved more than the workings of this single force. The crucial story is that of the state finally unable, as had been the case in France, to shake off the landlord class and emerge completely free of its social moorings.[2] This was most apparent in the way in which serfdom was abolished. The state was not powerful enough to oversee the abolition of serfdom. In consequence landlords created a serflike dependent peasantry, which was certainly not, as the government had hoped, the stuff from which commercial agriculture could be made.

Yet the attempt at a revolution from above, somewhat along the lines of imperial Germany, was beginning to have considerable success by the end of the nineteenth century. Russia began to enjoy a noticeable industrial growth rate with the consequent birth of an industrial working class, especially in St Petersburg. There is no inherent reason why this growth rate, even though it was largely financed by foreign capital, *could* not have led to the full industrialisation of Russia. Such a successful revolution from above required time, and pressure of inter-state activity did not allow this. Russia was beaten in the Crimean War and by Japan in 1904/5. Social reforms followed defeat but even these could not break the fundamental power-stand-off in society between landlord and state, and the latter therefore remained too weak to surmount the crisis of the First World War. Defeat in that war led to the peasants forcibly seizing the land. This was absolutely crucial since the peasantry provided the bedrock of the revolution. Peasants tend, unlike their industrial colleagues, to be a revolutionary class, and this was particularly so in Russia where the relatively egalitarian peasant commune, the *Obshchina*, encouraged mutual co-operation. Such industrial workers as did strike

2 T. Skocpol, *States and Social Revolutions*, Cambridge University Press, Cambridge, 1979.

were much aided by retention of traditional peasant organisational linkages.

The mood of the first month after the collapse of the old regime is brilliantly captured by Boris Pasternak's *Doctor Zhivago*. It was bliss to be alive when one could in the morning join a committee to reform marriage, in the afternoon the economy, and in the evening discuss the future of socialist art! But this bohemian world, so uncannily close to that of Marx's Utopian vision, was scarcely likely to facilitate the running of a modern bureaucratic state engaged in a war for survival. It was in these circumstances that the seemingly absurd Bolshevik claim to be able to take over power suddenly came to be realised. This was surely a triumph of political impulse over theoretical rigour for these were decidedly not the circumstances in which Marx had envisaged a socialist revolution. Nevertheless, at this moment Marxism established, in the form of Lenin, its real major claim to attention, namely its supreme ability at seizing power. In order to do so it was quite prepared to act flexibly. One of its first acts was to legitimise the peasant seizure of the land, thus giving the revolution its essential stability, even though this went against the whole tenet of socialist ideals.

The initial period in the history of the Soviet Union was that of the total drive for 'war communism' in order to hold off the Germans and Austrians, and then to repulse the White armies. This period saw total and massive organisation of society and the creation under Trotsky of the Red Army. This was an heroic age, extremely attractive to the revolutionaries themselves, even if the peasants were far from content with the vigorous actions of the military. It was in this period that the fears that the revolution might be destroyed from outside entered the Soviet mind. Trotsky believed that only a revolution in the rest of the world would cement Soviet achievements. His hopes in this respect were defeated by 1919 when the allies destroyed red movements throughout central Europe (most obviously in Hungary). After this, it was perhaps but a matter of time before a militarist society seeking to establish socialism in one country emerged. And a personal grudge had its origin at some moment in these years. Stalin served under Trotsky in the Red Army and he developed there the chip on his shoulder, the inferiority complex, that so significantly affected his behaviour thereafter.

One might have expected war communism to have introduced permanent changes in society. However, the period from 1920/1 to 1927/8 saw the dismantling of the nationalised economy. This period of the New Economic Policy allowed the profit motive to flourish in agriculture and industry and there was much unhappiness about this. By 1924 it was apparent that the works of Marx and Engels did not themselves give sufficient information as to how a socialist society was to be run. The future of Marxism was to that extent 'up for grabs'. Clearly, the party was *not* a monolith. Marxism did not *automatically* lead to Stalinism, although some elective affinities between the two will be noted later.

The key debate in this period was between some sort of market socialism proposed by Bukharin and supported opportunistically by Stalin, and a system of complete central planning advocated by Trotsky, theorised by Preobrazhenskii, and eventually adopted, although in a spirit all of his own, by Stalin in 1928/9. Yet these were alternatives within certain limits. Both schools believed in the leading role of the party, and both had the same ultimate communist objectives. The dispute was over means rather than ends. Bukharin's hope was that the raising of wheat prices would encourage middling peasants to produce goods for the market. The increased demand generated by their profits would in turn, Keynesian-style, encourage industrialisation via the production of consumer goods. This approach was peaceful, relatively non-coercive, and seemed to have great success until 1927. The critics consistently argued that such success was illusory. They claimed that the improvement in industrial production represented no more than the re-establishment of the pre-war plant, and that the Russian peasantry was inherently inefficient and therefore incapable of responding to market forces. In addition, the critics warned that this policy would lead to the restoration of capitalism. Bukharin responded rather weakly by saying that he too was against Kulak speculations, but that the middle peasantry would, provided that there was an infrastructure of socialist institutions, accept socialism rather than revert to any private acquisitive ethic.[3]

Nevertheless it was the positive proposals of Preobrazhenskii that increasingly set the terms of debate. He argued that 'a law of socialist accumulation' must be obeyed if the Soviet Union was to advance. This law envisaged the collectivisation of agriculture and heavy industrialisation; it explicitly stated that industrialisation must be paid for by peasant sacrifices. In 1926/7 even Bukharin was beginning to admit the necessity for some collectivisation and for much more state investment in industry. The case for the more radical programme became almost overwhelming in 1927. External fears, principally caused by Chiang Kai-shek's sudden and near-complete destruction of the communists in China, increased the need for modernisation.[4] Internally the state's receipts of grain actually began to fall in the same year. An additional pressure for heavy

3 S. Cohen, *Bukharin and the Russian Revolution*, Oxford University Press, Oxford, 1980. Alternative developmental plans are much discussed, and the whole matter is one filled with controversy. Cohen's arguments seem to me high powered and convincing, and I draw upon them in the next paragraphs.

4 Military pressure had encouraged and, in the eyes of key actors, necessitated the speedy industrialisation *from the start*. On this point see Holloway, *The Soviet Union and the Arms Race*, ch. 1.

industrialisation was that it was labour intensive; the NEP was slowly displacing people from the land and depositing them without jobs in the cities. Hence in 1928 Stalin went on the first of many tours of the countryside and began to extract grain from the peasants by force. This led, as Bukharin had predicted, to the alienation of the peasantry, and this was seen dramatically in the wholesale slaughter of cattle and in large-scale famine. Perhaps five million peasants died. Stalin's policies had an enormous impact by 1933, however, and this can be indicated by very obvious means. Twenty-five million private agricultural enterprises of one sort or another had been replaced by a quarter of a million collective farms. The grain harvest of 1933 was five million tons less than in 1928, nevertheless *the state's share of the take had doubled*. It was this doubling that allowed the very rapid industrialisation of the 1930s.

It was in these years that Stalin *did* create a single monolithic party machine. He turned Marxism into a simple doctrine. There is no doubt that he was able to appeal to the socialist instincts of many Bolsheviks in order to do so, for such revolutionaries had always been lukewarm about the rather passive, non-heroic NEP period. There are of course two great ironies involved in this. Firstly, the ideology that Stalin finally systematised was in many ways far removed from original Bolshevik aims. Thus he encoded what had probably become objectively necessary in any case, the doctrine of socialism in one country. More obviously, he attacked full egalitarianism as a petty-bourgeois deviation, and made it quite certain that there was to be no logical link between socialism and equality. The irony of this Stalinist version of Marxism is simple. This 'Diamat' formula stressed very heavily the later and more deterministic writings of Marx. Yet industrialisation and collectivisation in fact saw the full emergence of the Soviet state: Stalinism was the autonomy of that state in dramatic flow. Under the aegis of a deterministic theory a fully fledged voluntarism was at work.

The second irony is altogether more horrible. The period of Stalin's ascendancy as a whole, but especially the late 1930s, saw the full excesses to which the name Stalinism has been given. These were the subject of Solzhenitsyn's great *Gulag Archipelago*. The phenomenon includes the Great Purge of 1936–38, a purge so effective that 70 per cent of the Central Committee elected in 1934 had been arrested or shot by the time the Eighteenth Party Congress was held. Perhaps there was some initial basis for the rabid fear that characterised Stalin's mind. In 1934, for example, there *had* been a move for Kirov to replace him. Furthermore, at a structural level, one can also note that the purges encouraged a sort of social quiescence precisely because they allowed for social mobility. Nevertheless, Stalinism cannot be understood without an appreciation of the character of its mentor. His view of the world was inherently fearful as was seen in his doctrine (his only single original contribution to the Marxist tradition!) that class struggle intensifies the closer one approaches socialism. Added to this was an increasingly pathological mentality, nurtured by the fact that with power, as so often happens, his associates preferred to tell him what he wanted to hear rather than anger him with what was actually happening. The extent of Stalin's depredations in Soviet society will finally remain unknown. It is certain that he killed more people than did Adolf Hitler.

Stalinism and Socialism in One Country

It is important to reflect upon this Soviet experience. In what senses were there systematic links that led from Marxism to Stalinism? The connection was *not* absolute. The party had been endlessly split in exile, was further split by the industrialisation debate and, as we shall see, is often split today. Complete uniformity was possible *only* under Stalin. It would be a mistake to consider the whole matter purely as one of theory for it was military insecurity combined with underdevelopment that made a very complete centralisation of power almost inevitable. This is not to say that centralised power was always well used. Bukharin was probably correct to say that if collectivisation proceeded merely by means of a stick and with no carrot at all, then Russian agriculture would suffer permanently. The feasibility of alternatives inside Soviet Russia is a subject of intense debate. The evidence suggests that Bukharin's own dream of a non-coercive Marxist route forward was in large part illusory given military pressures, and it was coming under pressure *before* the first moves against the peasantry. Even Bukharin's biographer admits that resistance by the peasantry was not simply *the result* of state intervention by Stalin.[5] And Bukharin's route is the only one that deserves to be considered as a serious alternative. Trotsky was, whatever his apologists may say, no libertarian, and would have forced industrialisation in a manner not dissimilar to that of Stalin. And in passing we can dismiss Trotsky's characterisation of Soviet society as state capitalist. This term should be reserved for those societies, such as Wilhelmine Germany, in which private property rights are safeguarded, but in which the state massively helps industrialisation and the running of the economy in general. The first of these conditions does not in any way fit the Soviet experience, nor could it apply at all to any Eastern European country unless very considerable social changes were to take place, notably the

5 Cohen, *Bukharin and the Russian Revolution*, ch. 8.

admission of the right to invest private capital and to take profits in consequence.

But all these qualifications do not detract from three crucial points at which there does appear to be an elective affinity between Marxism and Stalinism. Firstly, we can note that the repressive apparatus of the Soviet state goes back before the period of Stalin's personal power. It was Lenin who established the Cheka, the forerunner of the KGB. His view of the disputes of intellectuals, both in exile and in the early years of Soviet Russia, were always strikingly intolerant. Secondly, activists were alienated by the more libertarian NEP years. Bolshevism's heroic appeal made a centralisation of power designed to create a new society popular among crucial elites. In this connection, it must always be remembered that despite all the barbarities involved, and the creation of long-lasting economic inefficiencies, Stalinist centralisation did *succeed* in turning the Soviet Union into a member of the world polity capable of contending as a superpower with America. Thirdly, we must remember that Marx considered that the sole source of evil in human affairs resulted from economic exploitation by social class. In consequence he had little conception of the need for restraints to be placed upon power. It is at this point that there is surely some link between Marxism and Stalinism. At a personal level Bukharin, for all his alternative economic policy, firmly believed in the power of the party. When acting as Duumvir with Stalin he helped remove Trotsky and Kamenev from public life in 1927. What someone like Bukharin did not realise is simple, and can be put in terms of a negative generalisation. Where no checks are placed upon power it is at least possible that someone occupying the seat of power will choose to abuse his position. There is a task of politics, and it is not that of choosing the best rulers: it remains that of making sure that rulers cannot do too much damage.

A second general reflection is in order. Stalin believed that the pact he had made with Hitler in 1939, an event with powerful ramifications on Marxism internationally, would protect Russia from invasion. Of course it did not, and the Soviet Union as a result lost 20 million men. It is impossible to exaggerate the impact that this had on the thinking of the Soviet leaders. The Soviet Union resembles America in being highly militarised, and any dealings with that society will have to accept its historically based fears of aggression. Something important follows from this. In 1941 some Russians welcomed the invading German armies, just as some peasants had welcomed the barbarian invaders when Rome fell. The war changed this situation. The Russian victory over Hitler made Marxism, once and for all, a piece of the national heritage. This is *not* true in other countries in Eastern Europe: Marxism is seen there as a doctrine imposed by force from the outside. Any dealings with the Soviet

Union must recognise not just that Marxism is not going to wither away, but that it represents the national style of that country. Despite everything, Stalin remains one of the fathers of the Russian people.

State Socialisms

In 1953 Stalin died. Three years later Khruschev formally admitted at the Twentieth Party Congress that mistakes had been made as the result of a 'cult of personality'. The impact of this speech on international Marxism, in combination with the invasion of Hungary, cannot be exaggerated; an internal admission counted for much, much more than all the criticism produced by those hostile to the regime. Marxism has still not come to terms with Stalinism. The very notion of a cult of personality is an affront to historical *materialism*. However, the argument to be made now is that Stalinism was of limited duration, but that nobody yet knows exactly what sort of regime will emerge in the longer run. The strategy adopted here in order both to demonstrate the demise of Stalinism and to provide the information for the discussion of liberalisation which follows is to consider three state socialist societies. This can only be done tentatively given the author's limited knowledge. Greater knowledge – particularly of Sino-Soviet relations, Yugoslav-Soviet relations and the impact that both have had throughout the Soviet Bloc – would surely *increase* the sense of complexity and variety that is at issue.

Before turning to the individual countries, some analytical points can be made about the characteristic strengths and weaknesses of the Soviet model of industrialisation, although this is only one factor which has affected the recent history of Poland, Czechoslovakia and Hungary. The logic behind the Soviet model is obvious. A monopoly of power on the part of an ideocratic regime is necessary so a central plan can be pushed through against the natural preferences of various groups in society; it is for this reason that classes cannot openly be represented. Trade unions are organised through the state, and in every group in civil society a member of the party will have the possibility of control. This is not to say that classes do not exist. Eastern European sociologists themselves recognise class differences between peasants, workers and intellectuals but these are deemed to be non-antagonistic in character. Open class conflict is not allowed. Such genuine class conflict has been avoided in part by the considerable success of state socialist regimes in forcibly recruiting those of peasant background to higher occupational categories. This great social, or perhaps *political*, mobility hides something, and we can consider it the first of three characteristic problems of the Soviet model. High social mobility was mostly caused by changes in the occupational structure consequent on industrialisation, although this went hand-in-hand with the destruction of some part of the traditional elite. Clearly there was a strong upwards pull involved in the creation of an industrial society. What will happen in the longer run? All sociologists know that downward mobility represents a political motor far more potent than upward mobility. If a class *structure* as we understand it, namely the ability of the advantaged to give their children a privileged start in life, is not to emerge in Eastern Europe, then such downward mobility will be necessary. It can be said at once that rates of upward social mobility throughout Eastern Europe are falling, although the social and political consequences of this are not yet obvious. The second general problem concerns central planning. A mechanism that was very powerful in heavy industrialisation was never much use in Czechoslovakia and East Germany, which were industrialised before becoming communist, and it is very inefficient at running a more complex late industrial machine. The slowing growth rates and poor harvests of the Soviet Union demonstrate this beyond question. The consequences to be drawn from this are also as yet unclear. Finally and most importantly, the monopolistic elite justifies its power by reference to Marxism-Leninism, and it tries on this basis to inculcate a new type of socialist morality. However, organised mass enthusiasm palls, and the regime faces the problem of legitimacy in the longer run. If politics returns to normal the claims of the elite are correspondingly weakened unless a more technocratic elite can, Keynesian style, provide goods rather than indoctrination. The dilemma of legitimation via Keynesian-type growth, or via a continuance and enhancement of socialist morality, is central to the rest of this chapter. But let us begin with the three satellite countries.

Hungary

When Hungary gained its independence at Versailles its social structure was typical of that of Eastern Europe, being composed of a mass of illiterate peasants and a highly reactionary aristocracy with only a small middling trading/intelligentsia section which was largely Jewish. This middling section played a big role in the short communist revolution under the leadership of Bela Kun in 1919. This revolution was terminated by international military involvement, although a lack of wisdom shown in trying to collectivise land immediately played its part as well. As a result of the defeat, inter-war Hungary became one of the most repulsive of all Eastern European societies. Reactionary under Count Bethlen to the extent of placing a *numerus clausus* on Jews (which sent such men as Teller and Mannheim to Weimar, and to subsequent intellectual fame), it became fascist under Admiral Horthy. Hungary joined in Hitler's campaign against Russia but was then 'liberated' by the Russians. The Communist Party performed poorly at the polls in 1946, but nevertheless came to power in 1948 under the leadership of Rakosi. His period of rule was Stalinist in character, as the show trial of Rajk and his associates demonstrated. Rakosi succeeded in making the Communist Party the main organ in society. The power of the Catholic church was removed, an easy task in Hungary given the religious mix between Protestants and Catholics. The land was also collectivised, although the manner in which this was achieved differed in crucial details from the collectivisation engineered by Stalin. These details are not even now fully known, but clearly they involved the carrot quite as much as the stick, and for that reason the agriculture of Hungary has since been highly productive.[6]

The death of Stalin had an immediate impact on Hungary, and the reformer Imre Nagy for a short period replaced Rakosi. It was in this short period that the Hungarian liberalisation took root. This flowered in 1956 when Hungary, again under Nagy's leadership, announced that it would pursue its own route to socialism. This did not prove acceptable to the Russians who sent the Warsaw Pact tanks into Budapest. It is surprising and absolutely fascinating to realise that it has been under the leadership of the Russian-imposed leader, Kadar, that Hungarian society has nevertheless achieved many of the reforms it sought in 1956. It was Kadar who famously declared that the legitimacy of the regime had changed its basis from 'he who is not with us is against us' to 'he who is not against us is with us'. This signalled something like a new social contract. Kadar's economic reforms of 1968 introduced a measure of decentralisation, and of market-type principles into the economy, with the clear hope that a more affluent country would allow the party to retain legitimacy by means of growth rather than through ideological indoctrination. This hope seems to foreigners to have been realised, although these impressions may tend to underestimate the complexity of the situation. There is no doubt, however, that the attempt to create a socialist morality has declined; Western pop records, blue jeans and second houses for the middle classes are now the rage. There are dangers to this policy, akin to those that face the national societies of Western Europe. What happens when growth fades? Furthermore, Hungarian social mobility no longer occurs at the high levels of the industrialisation period, and the middle classes are consolidating their power. Without growth, there is cause for eventual conflict here. Significantly Hungary is too small a country to be economically autarchic, as indeed

6 C.M. Hann, *Tázlár: a village in Hungary*, Cambridge University Press, Cambridge, 1980.

are all the Eastern European satellites. Hungary has therefore chosen to trade increasingly with the West, with the result that it has been subject to Western economic movements and recessions, and this has played a part in lessening the economic growth rates. Admired by Andropov and Gorbachov, Hungarians yet fear for their own experiment.

Czechoslovakia

Czechoslovakia resembled Hungary in gaining independence at Versailles, but in other ways its historical experience is wholly different. It was an industrial country with a remarkable engineering tradition *before* state socialism was established. Perhaps because its middling elements were greater, Czechoslovak politics in the inter-war years saw the establishment of successful social democracy. In 1938 the Western powers allowed Hitler to carve up Czechoslovakia in the hope of appeasing him. This is not something the Czechs forgot, and it probably played a vital role in the period between 1946 and 1948 when the communists finally took power. To have chosen the West for most Czechs would have been to choose powers which had betrayed or invaded it; in these circumstances Russia really did seem as if it were a benevolent brother.

This feeling did not last. Just as there had been show trials in Hungary, so there were in Czechoslovakia; the trial of Slansky and his supposed supporters was probably *the* most repulsive of all such trials. Perhaps this accounts for Czechoslovakia not noticeably participating in the move towards greater freedom that swept through Eastern Europe in the years immediately after Stalin died. The forces which were then held down erupted with all the more strength in the 'Prague spring' of 1968.

Two points must be made about the Czech attempt at liberalisation. Firstly, the demand for liberalisation had several facets. There was a demand for greater freedom of expression, and it was probably this, especially when it overflowed into attacks on the role of the Party, that doomed the liberalisation attempt as a whole. Equally important were economic demands. In a particularly sophisticated manner, Pavel Machonin and his colleagues argued that the Czech economy was falling behind the more dynamic ones of the West because it was *too* egalitarian and bureaucratic in nature.[7] Machonin did not deny that egalitarian communism was the goal of his country in the long run, but he insisted that more inegalitarian market measures in the shorter run would allow for improved economic performance. It is a measure of the complexity of the whole liberalisation process, to be emphasised later, that it is excep-

7 E. Gellner, 'The pluralist anti-levellers of Prague', *European Journal of Sociology*, vol. 12, 1971.

tionally difficult to tell how self-conscious such a strategy was. In particular, was the long-term goal of egalitarianism *seriously* maintained? Was the desire to decentralise the economy and to put it more into the hands of professionals only a *means* whereby, in the eyes of many reformers (it certainly was in the eyes of some), power could be taken away from the exclusive control of the party? Secondly, however, we must note that even the very harsh regime of Gustav Husak under which Czechoslovakia has suffered since the Warsaw Pact tanks intervened is by no means as bad as any of the Eastern European neo-Stalinist regimes of the 1948–53 period. This can be illustrated by a joke that circulated in Czechoslovakia a few years ago. It concerns the first Czech space venture. A policeman and a monkey are to man the same capsule. The officer is told that his instructions are in an envelope, to be opened only after successful take off. All goes well, and the envelope is duly opened. It simply tells the policeman to feed the monkey. The point to be made is simple: laughing at the police force suggests a very different level of repression from that which existed 30 years ago.[8] Nonetheless, it is equally clear that Husak is no Kadar, using his re-established authority to reform by stealth. At present, in consequence, Czechoslovakia remains in an unpleasant climate of restriction and repression.

Poland

Poland is the most tragic of the Eastern European societies. The dates of national history are the measure of daily life, and the list is long: 1772, 1793, 1795; 1830, 1863; 1919/20; 1939; 1944/45; 1956; 1968; 1970; 1976; and 1981/2. Some understanding of Polish society can be conveyed simply by discussing the events of these years.

The first trio of dates refers to those treaties which divided Poland between Prussia, Austria and Russia, something made possible by her failure to continue rationalising society in order to be able to compete in European warfare. Division did not prevent the growth of Polish nationalism throughout the nineteeth century. Thus in 1830 and 1863 risings were attempted against Russian rule, both of which were put down brutally. It is important to realise that Russia never developed her Polish lands and that historically low levels of agricultural investment help account for the current crisis in Polish agriculture. Poland regained nationhood as the result of the Treaty of Versailles. But anti-Russian feeling was partly at work in the years 1919/20 when Poland, under the military leadership of Pilsudski, attacked the fledgling Soviet Union, only

8 E. Gellner, 'Getting along in Czechoslovakia', *New York Review of Books*, vol. 25, 1978.

to be nearly defeated herself. In the inter-war years, Poland did not have a successful social democracy; instead the army under Pilsudski created an authoritarian and militant state naïvely devoted to Polish nationalism. This regime was destroyed by Hitler in 1939.

It is probably fair to say that Poland suffered more in the Second World War than any other national society. The excesses of the Nazis were obvious. The Poles also remember that 19,000 Polish officers were massacred at Katyn by Russian troops, and that Stalin did not push forward his advance in order to save those who rose in Warsaw in 1944. In 1982 a joke emerged from liberalising Poland that neatly sums up the national hatred for Germany *and* Russia. A soldier asks his officer who to shoot first should Poland be invaded by German and Soviet troops of the Warsaw pact. The officer pauses, and then says that the answer is obvious: 'Shoot the German'. The soldier asks why this should be so, and receives the answer that duty must come before pleasure.

The key to recent Polish history lies in the inability of the Communist Party, once it was established under Gomulka in 1948, to restructure society. Poland's losses in the war made any sort of collectivisation impossible since there simply was not the human material to allow this to happen. There was no will to impose a new trauma on a society that had suffered so much. In consequence, the Communist Party *did* rather little. It served as a capstone to a society that had changed little from the nineteenth century. Poland possessed a rather outspoken intelligentsia and a large and illiterate peasant mass, although it has increasingly had a working class based in industrial towns and no longer, of course, has an entrenched landlord class. Fundamentally this state was and remains weak. It cannot collectivise agriculture, nor has it the strength to undermine the Catholic church. Incredibly high attendance figures of up to 90 per cent show instead that the church has become a non-party, national symbol.

Poland very nearly followed the Hungarian course in 1956, and was in fact only prevented from doing so by seeing what happened in Budapest. The relative clampdown that followed did nothing to solve Poland's structural problems since the Party again refused to undertake basic reforms. This has been the background to the most recent series of troubles and risings. In 1968 students and intellectuals tried to force through some sort of change, but were not supported by the working class. The movement was easily put down and some intellectuals, most notably Leszek Kolakowski, were forced into exile. In 1970 and 1976 the working class struck, without the co-operation of the intelligentsia, against rises in the cost of living, and on both occasions strikers were killed. As the result of the first set of strikes Edward Gierek took over the leadership of the Party. It was under his auspices that Poland embarked on further heavy industrialisation financed by foreign loans, many of which were used to buy imports. Gierek wished to have everything; he sought to increase production and consumption at the same time. His policy undoubtedly reflected the rigidities, the power stand-off between different social groups, that characterise Polish society. Little serious attempt was made to deal with the agricultural problem.

In 1980 a highly disciplined working class, having learnt much from its previous defeats, at last *joined* the intellectuals in a drive for liberalisation. The intellectuals who played the greatest part in this movement, in Western eyes, are those who have international prominence such as the film-maker Andrezj Wajda or the members of the Committee to Defend Workers' Rights (KOR). However, probably of greater importance were the very large numbers of educated labour (especially engineers) over-produced by Polish universities. Without political connections to help them to decent careers, they were forced to work in factories at jobs well below the level that their training had led them to expect. This organised intelligentsia played a considerable part in the movement that was seemingly ended by the declaration of martial law by General Jaruszelski in 1981.

We can conclude this cursory glance at Polish society by noting that Jaruszelski had probably *already* wasted his chance to reform the structure of Polish society, and has thus continued true to the rather passive traditions of the Polish Communist Party. Nevertheless, it may be too simple to see Jaruszelski as a repressive and authoritarian figure; it is utterly misguided to see him as some sort of fascist. After all, the turn to the military is a traditional one in Polish history. And the centralisation of power under the military may yet provide the authority by means of which Polish society can finally be reformed. In this connection we must always remember the case of Kadar. Who would have thought in 1956 that within 15 years he would be leading the most successful and liberal of all Eastern European societies?

Liberalisation

The concept of liberalisation is a slippery one, and it will be our purpose to investigate it closely. Some preliminary guidance can be given by recalling the generic notion of liberalism that occupied the minds of Adam Smith, David Hume and many of their contemporaries. Such writers considered *all* of Europe to be liberal as it enjoyed the rule of law, and was thus not subject to the arbitrariness they considered characteristic of oriental societies. My contention has been that forced industrialisation, necessarily done at speed because of external pressure, ruled out a more liberal route to the modern world in the Soviet Union. A more liberal route might have been possible *from the start*, in contrast, in East Germany and Czechoslovakia as they were largely industrialised before becoming socialist. However, this is merely a hypothetical matter since the Soviet model was imposed on both societies, regardless of local circumstances. But is a measure of liberalism possible *after* the great transition to modernity has been successfully achieved by state socialism as a whole? The argument to be made is that it is extremely unlikely, and it is therefore foolish to expect, that state socialist societies are likely to adopt parliamentary institutions similar to our own. Nevertheless, there *are* reasons to hope for a relative softening of these societies.

Before portraying the social forces likely to press for, and those which are likely to oppose, liberalisation, it is as well to go somewhat further in describing the very confusing nature of Eastern European politics, especially as this will allow further insight into what is meant by 'liberalisation'. I propose to advance the argument by means of the footballing metaphor much beloved by British journalists, following Harold Wilson, when describing British politics. According to this metaphor a political line-up can be considered in terms of outside left, inside left, centre forward, inside right and outside right. In these terms I would pick the following Hungarian intellectual forward line, but only on the basis of one visit and some general understanding of the situation:

> Ivan Szelenyi
> Mihaily Vajda
> Alexander Szalai
> Zsusza Ferge
> Imre Pal

No attempt has been made to show which is left and right. That this is no accident will become evident once the characteristic positions of each of the five figures are outlined.

Ivan Szelenyi is perhaps the most famous recent Hungarian exile. A sociologist who did excellent empirical work on class factors in state housing, Szelenyi made the mistake, not so much of writing, but of printing and distributing the book he wrote (with Gyorgy Konrad) entitled *The Intellectuals on the Road to Class Power*.[9] The thesis of the book is the one well known in Eastern Europe since Trotsky and, above all, Djilas, namely that a new class is coming to rule state socialist societies.

Mihaily Vajda (a pseudonym) differs from Szelenyi in not explicitly sharing this diagnosis, and also in not having been expelled. He argues that real socialism must mean popular participation; such participation

---

9 Harvester Press, Brighton, 1978.

cannot be obtained without an extension of citizenship and democratic rights, and this is therefore the first task in his eyes.

Alexander Szalai, the founding father of Hungarian sociology, imprisoned by the Nazis and by the communists in the late forties and after 1956, deserves to be considered a centrist since he carefully tries to balance the demands of liberty and equality, and presses for the maximum of both that he considers to be politically feasible.

In contrast, Zsusza Ferge, his pupil and an expert in social policy, argues that Hungarian society can be improved only by the extension of state activity. She considers herself something of a social critic in seeking to make the state more enlightened.[10]

Finally, these figures may be contrasted with the traditional Bolshevik, Imre Pal (again a pseudonym), who believes that Marxism-Leninism, especially when it is seen as a moral creed, has all the answers to social problems, and that this creed should be enforced by a powerful party.

This world is one of extremely self-conscious and sophisticated decisions and these are often very, very hard for an outsider to interpret. The details of my picture and my understanding of these figures may be wrong, but for general reasons I do not doubt the nature of the liberalisation process even though the 'rules of the game' have yet to be established.[11] A typical instance of the difficulty in comprehending what is happening faces a visitor when he comes across a supposedly hard-line Marxist who is head of an institute which houses many *unconventional*, indeed questioning spirits. Is this to be interpreted as pragmatic conformism designed to allow such limited dissent, or is it a genuine position in its own right? Western visitors usually have little chance of finding the answer to such questions, and I have the distinct suspicion that many of those inside Eastern Euopean countries cannot answer them either. Perhaps the people who are of least interest are those who become open dissidents, in this case Szelenyi. Such people fail to change the system because they break hidden understandings to an extent that requires the state to step in to repress. These people are clearly brave, indeed staggeringly so, but in this particular sense they are failures. They do not help to establish rules of the liberalisation game. More interesting and important are those who remain, and it is here that we come to the central point that needs to be made. It is difficult, or rather it is inappropriate, to apply Western concepts of left and right to this political spectrum. In British terms an extension of state control in the interests of more sophisticated welfare policy would be seen as leftist, and it is thus

10 Z. Ferge, *A Society in the Making*, Penguin, London, 1977.
11 The pioneering article on liberalisation is Ernest Gellner's 'From the revolution to liberalisation', *Government and opposition*, vol. 11, 1975.

no accident to find that Ferge's thought derives one half of its impetus from the work of Peter Townsend. In Eastern European terms, however, Ferge is an inside *right* figure because she argues in favour of an extension of state action. All this can be put in rather different terms. It is chronically hard to know how to reconcile liberty and equality. In fact, these ends probably cannot be reconciled, although trade-offs between the two can be more or less defensible. At times it has been possible in Eastern Europe, as in Czechoslovakia in the years just before 1968, to cope with problems of inequality, but rather little hold has been gained on the problem which Marxism is blind to, namely that of the control of political power. Liberalisation is precisely about the possibility of placing some bounds upon the unfettered exercise of political power.

Interest in the possible future of state socialism has always been intense, and it would be possible to draw on a number of debates in order to illustrate optimistic and pessimistic positions. For our purposes, these positions are ideally illustrated by a recent exchange between Ernest Gellner and Raymond Aron. We may begin with the optimism of Gellner:

. . . an advanced industrial society requires a large scientific, technical, administrative, educational stratum, with genuine competence based on prolonged training. In other words, it cannot rely on rigid ideologues and servile classes alone. It is reasonable to assume that this kind of educated middle class, owing its position to technical competence rather than to subservience, and inherently, so to speak professionally, capable of distinguishing reality and thought from verbiage and incantation, will develop or has developed the kind of tastes we associate with its life-style – a need for security, a recognition of competence rather than subservience, a regard for efficiency and integrity rather than patronage and loyalty in professional life . . . This class is large, and it cannot be penalised effectively without a cost to the economy which may no longer be acceptable. The main body may sacrifice or even disavow its own 'dissident' advance guard, whilst benefiting from its courage, though it may perhaps secure some moderation at least in the price exacted for that courage by the old authorities.

Furthermore, relative economic success, national pride, and the legitimacy conferred on any regime by sheer longevity, may make it easier – because less risky – for the rulers to make concessions to this class. As material resources become more plentiful, competition for them may become less acute. Affluence, if not classlessness, may at least reduce antagonisms and thus, for good Marxist reasons, diminish, though it cannot eliminate, the need for a repressive state. The end of ideology, erroneously predicted in the West, may yet get its second chance in the East. Could it not perish from sheer boredom? So, as the system gains in authority through stability, it may afford to relax without putting itself intolerably at risk.[12]

12 E. Gellner, 'Plaidoyer pour une libéralisation manquée, *Government and Opposition*, vol. 14, 1979, pp. 63–4.

The communist parties of every Eastern European state may be seen as internally divided between those who wish to liberalise along Hungarian lines and the old Bolshevik section which is very nervous of any such process. Gellner's optimism concerns the technical and educated intelligentsia, alienated by a rigid ideology which goes against their work style, and yet increasingly important to a late industrial economy. The whole process of liberalisation may, to put the matter in a more theoretical manner, be forced upon the party by the logic of late industrialism. Consider one example. If computers are to be successfully used they need to be plugged into data banks and to have their own word processing facilities. Yet this would make the production of *Samizdat* publications easy and automatic. One can see why old Bolsheviks are worried! Gellner's hope is for open recognition of a scarcely concealed pluralism. Such a recognition would almost certainly entail admitting more of the market principle and much greater technical efficiency in the running of industry. It is by no means clear how far such a process might go. Would it merely mean greater enterprise autonomy? Would individuals be able to invest their earnings in the classical capitalist manner? There is no doubt however about the hope that can be entertained, and it is one curiously reminiscent of the views of the Scottish moralists. It is that as more technical and neutral criteria come to the fore, the more will legality and the absence of arbitrariness be recognised by government. Optimism in this matter is easier when one notes that Eastern European liberalisers seem to learn from their mistakes. In order to liberalise it is necessary to find a middle way between asking for too little and asking for too much, and it is the attempt to learn of this art that is so generally impressive. One may again characterise Gellner's position with reference to the thesis that a new class is coming to dominate state socialist societies. His optimism is based on this class gaining functional importance so that power can be taken out of the sole control of the Party and be somewhat dispersed. Power is likely to be concentrated in industrial society, but it may be placed in more than a single location.

Perhaps the most general consideration underlying the near Manichaean pessimism of Aron's last writings on Eastern Europe is the belief that the surrender of power by a revolutionary party is almost inconceivable. He argued that the ceding of power has only ever been made by a very small number of highly intelligent traditional elites, most recently in Greece and Spain *before* and *in order to* avoid a modern revolution.[13] Pessimism in this matter rests on more than just general historical and psychological grounds. The party has very considerable reasons to fear giving away any power. If it admits that its ideological claim to power is flawed, how can it expect such liberalisation to be somehow limited and

13 R. Aron, 'On liberalisation', *Government and Opposition*, vol. 14, 1979.

self-contained? An inflationary process of demands *has* occurred in every liberalisation attempted so far. Lech Walesa could not control all the members of Solidarity, let alone all the members of a whole society, for very long. Moreover, it is possible, perhaps likely, that a certain self-hatred among the intellectuals consequent on years of lip-service to a dogma they no longer believe in leads to an inability to discipline themselves for long.

Optimism is rather heavily dependent upon the pressure to be exerted by the new class of educated labour. This is perhaps a precarious group on which to base much hope, even if it *is* growing in size and functional importance. For any policies based on this group would quite probably, at least in the short run, disadvantage the traditional working class. The hard-liners in the party are likely to be able to improve their position if any economic liberalisation leads to the introduction of open inflation and a loss in the position of the working class. Furthermore, one highly intelligent analysis from Eastern Europe itself, that of Marc Rakovski, a pseudonym for a Hungarian who publishes in London, suggests that too much hope should not be placed on the taste for liberty among the technical intelligentsia. A more open system might allow the workers to undermine certain special privileges that still characterise the lot of technical middle classes.

Rather than go so far as to break the ties of dependence which chain them to the central management apparatus, they submit to it voluntarily in order to prevent the workers beneath them from breaking free. Their aim is not a society in which opposing social groups have the means to conduct an organised struggle against each other, in order to advance their particular interests in economic and political conflicts. What they want is to get a better position within the existing system, where everything is gained by means of the amorphous pressure which the conflicting groups can bring to bear on the central apparatus.[14]

The technical intelligentsia may yet be bought off by an extension of special privileges.

History has not as yet given any firm judgement on the likelihood of liberalisation. This can be seen most clearly when considering the three Eastern European satellites discussed above, and their respective attempts at liberalisation. At first glance the years 1956, 1968 and 1981 seem to prove that liberalisation is simply impossible, certain to fail. The evidence is more complex than this. Hungary has in a most remarkable manner *achieved* a measure of liberalisation, and this can be set against the defeat in Czechoslovakia. A great deal at this point depends upon how much one expects from liberalisation, and the Hungarian case is

14 M. Rakovski, *Towards an Eastern European Marxism*, Alison & Busby, 1978, p. 28.

crucial here. In one sense much has been achieved, but still it must be admitted that this liberalisation is fragile: even the much discussed economic reforms have not yet finally been carried through with such determination as to make them absolutely secure. Finally, Poland is so idiosyncratic, especially in having failed to modernise its agricultural sector, that rather few conclusions about liberalisation should be drawn from it. Reflecting on Poland is, however, disconcerting in one way. It may be that a *greater* centralisation of power is necessary in order to firmly establish a successful industrial society. In general the very best hopes for liberalisation result when an already industrialised economy is subtly held back by the limitations imposed by the manner in which the polity is organised.

This debate over liberalisation seems to me high powered, and exceptionally useful in indicating the types of social force at work. However, the terms of the debate should not be adhered to slavishly. Eastern European countries may not find any *clearly* defined solution to their position. A constant oscillation between liberalisation and repression is perfectly possible. Indeed this scenario is in part suggested by what has been said. The inability to control a whole population once liberalisation has begun 'calls for' repression. This then breeds sufficient self-restraint for the liberalising process to begin once again. This is once again defeated by excessive demands, and so on in a vicious, inescapable circle.[15]

Such a cycle would of course reflect upon limitations to liberalisation imposed by being part of a larger whole. Just as America keeps certain states close to its borders 'in line' for geopolitical reasons, so the Soviet Union through the Red Army keeps Eastern Europe firmly in its sphere of influence. Indeed, the need for the Soviet Union to control its satellites if it is to remain a great power is probably greater than the American need to involve itself in the Caribbean, Central and Latin America. The United States would remain a great power because of her economic strength even without such hegemony. If the Soviet Union lost its satellites, it would *not* remain in the same class. A reunited Germany might well end up a larger military and economic power than the Soviet Union, and this is the fundamental reason why such a reunification is unlikely to happen. This is crucial since it necessitates asking about the possibilities of liberalisation inside the Soviet Union itself. Only if liberalisation occurs in the Soviet Union, even if the lesson as to how to do it is learnt in part from elsewhere, will state socialism as a whole firmly cement the changes that have already taken it away from Stalinism.

15 Dr George Schöpflin suggested such a cyclical theory to me in conversation.

The Soviet Union and the Arms Race

It is quite clear that the social forces identified in the satellites are quite as much at work inside the Soviet Union. However, no secular trend can yet be observed showing one side or the other gaining control. Thus Khruschev's reforms of the late 1950s and early 1960s were abandoned, though this was more because some of the reforms were inept and inefficient rather than because a loss of control was feared. Similarly, the introduction of market mechanisms by Brezhnev only lasted until 1971 when full central planning was restored. Andropov probably favoured something like a Hungarian style of managing the economy, and his first major speech might easily have been given by Mrs Thatcher, so ruthlessly did it attack overmanning and inefficiency. However, the Politbureau, perhaps scared of the consequences this might have had for corruption among their own clients, did not then choose to continue this line, preferring to elect a traditional Bolshevik, Chernenko. Perhaps the election of Gorbachov means a move towards the more liberal pole; certainly the present leader is impressed by the Hungarian experiment. It is impossible to predict with certainty what will happen.

Just as the satellites exist within a larger whole, so too does the Soviet Union. This larger arena is that of international political rivalry. The capacity to engage in such rivalry affects, and is in turn affected by, economic relations. The first parts of this chapter have stressed how much military factors shaped the pattern of Soviet industrialisation and state formation. Are such pressures still present, and if so, what effect may they have on the evolution of Soviet society?

The Soviet Union emerged from the Second World War a great power not only because it had played the major role in defeating Hitler, but also because it gained an empire as a result. The desire to act as a great power was suppressed for many years in the face of overwhelming American superiority in nuclear weapons. This situation did *not* prevent Moscow covertly agreeing to the Korean war, but it did curtail the freedom of action which Soviet leaders felt to be rightly theirs. It seemed as if a fundamental change had taken place as the result of Russia beating America by sending the first man into space, and it was indeed only a matter of years until Khruschev boasted of his intercontinental missiles. In fact, however, the Soviet Union had very few effective intercontinental missiles, and the freedom of action claimed by Khruschev was soon put into abeyance when it became clear that the Americans knew this all too well. However, the Soviet Union has increased and improved its weapons dramatically in recent years so that, by the middle 1970s, it finally achieved the freedom of action, demonstrated most clearly in its policies in Africa, which its leaders had always felt should be the reward to the Soviet Union of its position in world politics.

There are vast debates about various issues that derive from these baldly stated facts. One of them concerns the driving force of Soviet foreign policy. Is this policy *in the last analysis* the result of the desire to spread socialism? It is perhaps worth noting that very strong reservations must be placed on any easy acceptance of this view. Much Soviet action results simply from it being a great power. Just as the United States is unwilling to share control over, and information about, its nuclear arsenal, so too is the Soviet Union. The break with Peking in 1957 occurred because the Soviet Union wished to maintain its sole control over nuclear matters. National interest proved more important than international socialist solidarity. More generally, the Soviet Union participates in international power politics in ways which traditional conceptual approaches can very easily understand. In the international political arena business proceeds as normal. This is not to admit that there *is* a total divorce between a foreign policy, amorally pursued, and the socialist aims of society. We may, however, risk the formulation that socialism may result from Soviet success or hegemony wherever it is achieved but that diplomatic and strategic actions have their own autonomous logics.

The determinants of Soviet action are sure to be debated endlessly, but a crucial point related to them is often ignored and is of great importance in the present context. The Soviet Union is a highly militarised society. It spends perhaps double the amount of its great rival upon armaments, necessarily so given the smaller size of its economy. This was particularly true of the late 1960s and early 1970s,[16] although this expenditure has apparently dropped in very recent years. This is to say that the military occupies a key position in Soviet society, largely because it has been *successful*. Its power, moreover, also rests upon the undoubted fact that participation in the armed forces is both more regular and for greater duration than has been common in the West since the days of Rome. Such citizen armies, easily exportable to countries such as Vietnam, are a crucial means of mobilising the people for the modern world.[17]

The conclusion to be drawn from all this is obvious. High rates of expenditure on arms entail consumer deprivation. It is impossible to know whether this is endorsed by the Soviet people, or whether this type of militarism is only made possible by single-party rule. In either case, the Soviet economy is distorted as a result of the great intellectual efforts going into research and development for military purposes. Pressure for

16 Holloway, *The Soviet Union and the Arms Race*, ch. 6.

17 I am indebted here to an unpublished paper by Michael Mann on 'The roots of modern militarism'.

liberalisation derives from a generalised strata of middle-class professionals, and it is to that extent unlikely to come about in the Soviet Union so long as it feels it necessary to devote a great part of its energy to international competition. Liberalisation inside the Soviet bloc depends upon developments in the international context.

What *are* the current perceptions of Soviet leaders? Do they feel sufficiently secure to switch expenditure from arms towards civilian expenditure, with all the consequences for liberalisation that might follow? The answer to this last question must regrettably be firmly in the negative.

In large part this is merely a continuation of the former position. The increase in Soviet military strength was never sufficient to completely wipe out the edge held by the United States. Thus it was always entirely misleading to imagine that the Soviet Union, since the late 1970s, felt itself to have a 'window of opportunity' because its intercontinental ballistic rockets could carry more warheads, and this for the simple reason that most American nuclear weapons are launchable from submarines. However, some recent developments have contributed to a climate of genuine fear on the part of the Soviet leaders. At a local level, it does seem that the Soviet Union regarded the SS20 programme as merely the modernisation of theatre nuclear weapons already in place, and it certainly feels threatened by nuclear weapons capable of reaching Moscow in a matter of minutes. More generally, Soviet foreign policy has not been conspicuously successful in recent years, either in Africa or in the Middle East. Perhaps the most sinister development in this regard, in Moscow's eyes, is the closer linking of Peking and Washington, a move which makes the Soviet Union feel increasingly encircled and more than ever forced to face in two directions at the same time. Finally, the threat that the arms race may enter into a new stage in which it will prove necessary to develop space weapons terrifies the Kremlin. Soviet technology remains behind that of the United States in most fields, and the militarisation of society that would be necessary to compete at a new level would be intense. It would rule out any hopes for liberalisation inside the Soviet Union.

None of these comments should be misunderstood. It is not being claimed that the relations between the superpowers is becoming drastically unstable. On the contrary, what impresses is the level of agreement about spheres of influence, appropriate signalling devices and so on. Clausewitzian principles do lead one to worry about a Soviet Union that lives in fear since stability in the nuclear age depends so much upon common understandings. Nor is it being claimed that the Soviet Union is in all respects an innocent victim of an arms race which it has itself never escalated. This is not so and the Soviet Union is, in addition, seemingly as incapable of making bold gestures as is the United States. In 1979 Soviet withdrawal of large numbers of SS20s might, for example, have prevented the stationing of cruise missiles. What is being claimed, however, is simply that participation in an escalating arms race will rule out liberalisation inside the Soviet Union, and thereby diminish the chances of more liberal practices throughout Eastern Europe.

Conclusions

The central argument of this chapter has been straightforward. The Soviet Union gains its historical importance from having industrialised by means of a single party armed with a Promethean ideology. Economic development has been real, but it has been at the expense of political liberties. One of the issues of the age is that of whether state socialist society can find a way beyond the Soviet model to a softer, more liberal system. Nobody is in a position to answer this question with certainty.

The Soviet Union is a militaristic society. There is less historical novelty here for the Soviet Union has merely repeated the Prussian route to international prestige. The character of the Soviet state results from its participation in international power politics. Only if this international arena proves less threatening will there really be significant chances for liberalisation within the socialist bloc. It is impossible to resist a general reflection at this point. The balance of terror between the superpowers could be run at a lower level. If the West wishes to create change in the socialist bloc, it must seek to arrange such a lessening of tension. The power of bunker Bolsheviks is likely to be diminished by affluence. Socialism may perish by spreading the Magyar mode of production. By and large Europeans, well informed about liberalising trends inside Eastern European parties, are more aware of this general strategy than are their American allies, who are tied to a rather old-fashioned general picture of state socialist society.

The control of nuclear weapons is an issue of greater import than that of the liberalisation of Eastern Europe societies. There is, however, no reason why progress cannot be made in both issues; progress in military/political matters is in fact a *precondition* of internal liberalisation. Nevertheless, if the arms race escalates, it still seems likely that there will remain sufficient uncertainty in strategic policy to make a nuclear war unlikely.

This suggests a final reflection. The measure of agreement between the two superpowers is what strikes those who are outside the advanced world altogether. The 'South' realises that their interests do not feature significantly in the game in which the blocs of the 'North' engage. It is now time to outline the characteristic problems of this 'Third' World, and to see how they affect the generalisations that have been made to this point. Moreover, it is absolutely vital to concentrate our attention in this way. The Third World, caught in the painful transition to the industrial world, is more likely to occasion instability in world politics than is competition between the superpowers.

8

The Third World

The notion of a Third World following those of liberal capitalism and state socialism was first coined in post-Second World War France. It is a problematical notion. It is hard to discuss a world on the basis of such a short time span: what is 40-odd years within the larger time scale of human history? Moreover, the Third World is much less a monolith than was once thought, and indeed once hoped. The attempt to create a unity of such countries via the organisation of non-aligned states (the brain-child of Nehru and Tito) has now collapsed, and it is necessary to talk of Third World countries allied to either of the first two worlds. (In passing, it can be noted that the West has, despite much breast-beating, managed its alliances with great efficiency in recent years, whereas Egypt, Indonesia, China, and Algeria have all been lost to the Soviet Union, while Libya remains a permanent embarrassment.) Further, a certain confidence enshrined in the notion of the developing societies has now gone; the belief that development was simple and *automatically* going to be achieved is now open to question. There is no doubt that some Third World countries have made astonishing progress. They are properly classified as 'newly industrialising countries' with growth rates notably higher than those of the advanced societies, and in this category fall Brazil, the 'Confucian capitalist' states of SE Asia, and Egypt. Other countries, bereft of minerals and natural advantages of all sorts, have, however, sometimes been lumped into a new residual category, that of the 'fourth world', the prospects for which are not held to include much significant development. Classical instances of this in recent years have been Ethiopia and the Sudan. African states, with the possible exceptions of Nigeria and South Africa, have noticeably slower growth rates than other non-advanced countries. Finally, there are very different problems at work in various Third World countries. African states are fortunate in *not* suffering from the massive overpopulation – an overpopulation, it should be noted, that did not characterise the emergence

of the first and second worlds – that plagues India and China, and which
is of sufficient salience in Latin America and Egypt often to wipe out the
gains otherwise made by economic development.

If there are complexities at work that need to be at the forefront of our
minds, there remains sufficient shared reality behind the notion for it to
be retained. 'Development' and 'underdevelopment' are essentially relative notions: Germany and Tsarist Russia deserve to be considered the
first underdeveloped countries, and their experience will prove relevant
here. Both these countries were European and the generalisation of the
desire to become industrialised only fully took place as the result of the
Second World War. It is appropriate that the concept of the 'Third
World' was created only at that time.

The hidden thread running throughout this chapter is that of complexities at work in Third World countries. The discussion must be focused
by addressing three analytic questions. A full discussion of nationalism is
needed in the first place in order that something can be said about the
likely characteristic polity of Third World states. Beyond this, however,
attention is turned more to matters economic, as indeed it has in many
Third World countries which have themselves realised that political
freedom does not automatically bring in its tail economic development.
In recent years, there *has* been a general theory which has argued that the
situation of the Third World can be seen in essentially straightforward
terms, and it serves as the background to the remainder of the chapter.
The theory in question is dependency theory which, in the full-blooded
version considered here, states that the fate of the Third World depends
upon what happens in the advanced capitalist world. Capitalism is held to
control the destiny of the Third World. Now there is no doubt that this
approach at the least has the merit of drawing our attention to the
extraordinary episodes of exploitation by the West. Nine million Africans
died for example in the 'middle passage' between West Africa and the
Caribbean. It is very difficult to draw up some general account of loss
and gain – between, say, the removal of minerals and precious metals and
the provision, notably by the British, of infrastructures such as railroads –
and a tally simply cannot be attempted in the space available. Nevertheless, some light can be thrown on the matter as a whole by making certain
distinctions. The second part of this chapter considers what is often only
an implication, albeit an implication that lends emotional weight, in
dependency theory: that capitalism *needs* (and is itself in this sense
'dependent' on!) poor areas of the globe, whether in the form of actual
empires or 'economic colonialism'. With some reservations, this picture
will be rejected. It then becomes important, however, to ask in the final
section of the chapter the extent to which the fate of countries in the
Third World depends upon their involvement in the world market. This

is a very difficult issue to confront. It is vital to make distinctions here, but it can be said immediately that there is only limited truth to dependency theory in this context as well.

The Birth of Nations

The European enlightenment of the eighteenth century had no time for national loyalties. They were regarded as atavistic and primitive, and were sure to be soon forgotten. The future was to correspond more to their own habits; it would be cosmopolitan and civilised. This world view can be seen very clearly in that latter-day enlightenment figure, Karl Marx, most particularly in his central and unquestioned contention that class would prove to be a greater source of social mobilisation than national loyalties. This theory met with sudden death in August 1914. One can and must go further than this. Nationalism is *the* world historical force of the twentieth-century, however surprising that might have been to the thinkers of the eighteenth century. Its only rival is socialism. Russia ended with socialism in one country. The conflicts between Russia and China, or between China and Vietnam, suggest that the more socialism spreads the more national flavours it develops. The logic of inter-state rivalry continues to place its mark on the historical record.

It is a remarkable fact that nationalism has not attracted the amount of attention its importance deserves. Perhaps the proliferation of studies of classes and class conflicts represents the impact of human hope on academia, while the refusal to consider nationalism reflects an attitude, in some ways unjustified, which sees in the spread of nations merely the spread of war and conflict. Our main purpose must be to explain and to reflect upon nationalism. Roughly speaking, there are three 'periods' of nationalism: the original birth of European nation-states discussed in chapters 5 and 6, central European nationalism from 1848 to the Treaty of Versailles, and decolonialising nationalism. As our interest here is only in the last period, we can confidently draw heavily for the explanatory part of the argument on Ernest Gellner's treatise on nationalism.[1]

Nationalism is often defined as the doctrine which insists that political and cultural boundaries should coincide, and that authority should be exercised over a culture by those belonging to it. This definition is static and fails to draw attention to the crucial processual, nation-building character of modern nationalism. Before accentuating this, however, we must first explain why traditional societies change and why this change takes a national form.

1 *Nations and Nationalism*, Basil Blackwell, Oxford, 1983.

Traditional agrarian 'societies' typically comprise distinct and sepa-rated ethnic and tribal units, unable to communicate much with each other, bound together by a small elite, often of professional rulers possessing their own culture and, by definition, considering the sheer number of cultures beneath them, not co-cultural with their subjects. Such social formations (for they do not, as argued, truly deserve to be called societies) can and do work. The daily tasks of social reproduction are so obvious when facing hostile nature that high-level communication between different groups is not really necessary. These comments are very general, but this does not matter much (especially given that varia-tions within agrarian societies were analysed in the first part of this book) since it is absolutely clear that a total change in social organisation is necessary for the emergence of industrial society. It *is* entirely appropri-ate to talk here of a necessary logic of the industrial age. Consider the spectacular example of the division of labour. For this principle of productivity to work, it is necessary that people involved along the social and geographical production line are able to communicate with each other. Where the logic of a fight against nature had been clear, labour on particular parts of a single product is necessarily much more abstract. This need for a shared culture has very radical social implications. The creation of such a culture means that several of the tribal and ethnic loyalties, hitherto allowed to coexist by a rather remote and powerless elite, *have to be destroyed* in order that one of them become the national culture. In Algeria, independence led to a crash Arabisation programme. French could scarcely take this role since it was the language of the imperial power, but neither could Berber as it is a spoken not a written language. The reaction of the Berbers to the extirpation of their culture, for that was what was involved, may readily be imagined. And the Algerian case is a simple one. The creation of a common culture, or more precisely, the creation of a society in Nigeria from the various separate ethnic units arbitrarily assembled within those incredibly straight lines drawn by the imperial powers, has proved far more com-plex. There were over 50 languages in existence at the time of indepen-dence, more than one of which could have become dominant. It is not necessary to *imagine* how the losers felt during the politics of modernisa-tion: the Ibos refused to accept the loss of their culture and fought a vicious and bloody civil war to try and reverse the situation.

The creation of the single language community spectacularly makes the point as to the societal building necessary for the modern world. Perhaps the creation of a single language community is not necessarily *the* key to the situation. The more general factor is the creation of an education system capable of turning tribesmen and peasants into clerks able to function in modern society. This functional imperative *does* seem to be well observed in Third World countries. The character of the experience involved is familiar to us also from the superlative early novels of the Nigerian writer Chinua Achebe, and these novels also have the virtue of pointing to a danger involved in the whole process. Educational achievement can lead to a job in the new state's bureaucracy that is secure and long lasting, and thus capable of defeating necessary innovations. Problems characteristically associated with bureaucracy may be *greatest* in the Third World.[2]

The argument so far can be summarised by saying that tribal groups are too *small* to allow the communication necessary for a modern industrial society. To establish the necessary social infrastructure of industrial society does not, however, say anything about nationalism. Why was it that the social infrastructure became fixed at the *national* level? There was, in principle, nothing preordained about this. The French sought occasionally to build a social infrastructure in its colonies, and in so doing sought to spread their own language. The plan to create a fully French-speaking empire able to enter the modern world met with defeat. Why was it that great empires were, in distinction to tribal or ethnic units, too *large* as units for social development?

The crucial mechanism at work seems to be that of the blocked social mobility of the native intelligentsia. The reasons for acquiring empires were not always economic, but once an empire had been acquired it seemed to make sense to profit from it. A natural consequence of this was that administration was placed in the hands of professionals who ruled in the interests of the mother country, something which in part explains the extraordinary predominance of the 'public' schools within British life. This system in the end led to an obvious anomaly. The longer that empires were in place, the less was it possible to prevent the education of some natives of particular colonies; indeed, sometimes education was positively encouraged, and it was made available in Paris, London or Brussels. These native intellectuals on their return home found that they were not treated as equals, despite occasional attempts to do so, as E.M. Forster brilliantly understood in *A Passage to India*. Here then was a situation full of dynamite. Native intellectuals were denied the jobs and influence to which their education made them feel entitled merely on the basis of their colour or creed. It is scarcely surprising that such intellectuals – the Gandhis, Nkrumahs, and Zhou Enlais of modern world history – were attracted to nationalism. Thus ideology ensured that their worth would achieve recognition.

Unemployed or poorly appreciated intellectuals may not at first glance

2 On this point, see R. Dore, *The Diploma Disease*, George Allen & Unwin, London, 1978.

seem of sufficient salience to win wars of independence. A moment's reflection brings two points to mind explaining how crucial is their role. The first point is negative. Wars of national liberation are not, in the end, hard to win. Imperial powers did not typically make very much from their colonies, and profits were anyway dependent upon social peace. Few administrators were sent out from the mother country, and rule was often conducted through local potentates of one sort or another. The maintenance of a large administration and an army, considerable numbers of which had suddenly to come from the mother country, cancelled out profits very quickly indeed. This was pointed out with great elegance by Raymond Aron in 1957 in *La tragédie algérienne*. France could not stand the drain of resources that an armed presence required, nor could it afford to rapidly raise the living standards of the colony without considerably lowering those in metropolitan France. In these circumstances, the logic of the situation leads to the imperial power seeking to confer a spurious mantle of legitimacy on one particular group of nationalist leaders so that it can divest itself of an embarrassing burden.

The second consideration is that intellectuals are by no means the only members of nationalist movements, nor is the rectification of their own material grievance the sole point at issue. Nationalist movements are able to draw upon all sorts of support. Some of this is purely instrumental. In North Africa, for example, Muslim tribesmen often supported nationalist parties because they had so disliked the replacement of their custom by legally enforceable contract. Such support proves to be 'blind' since nationalist parties in power concern themselves with nation-building to such an extent as to make the interferences of the imperial state appear puny; certainly nationalist governments do not restore tribal custom. Indian nationalism was different in having some base among those textile entrepreneurs hostile to Great Britain for economic reasons. However, there is a more general point to be made which goes well beyond such instrumental and occasional support. Some development is undertaken by the imperial power itself, and in the process many are uprooted from their traditional local communities. The later years of imperialist rule typically witness the emergence of a new working class. Nationalist intellectuals do not just have their own grievances but are also able to create more general creeds to 'capture' the socially dislocated. This great ideological appeal has real force behind it since it is 'true'. A working class may remain such but at least it will work for its own nation and not at the behest, and in the interests of, a foreign power.

The claims being made can be highlighted. The central argument is that nationalism results from the uneven diffusion of industrialism in world history. It was more or less natural that the part of the globe which led in power terms should expand its domain. Nationalism results when

Third World areas begin to gain *something*, notably when some education trickles down. As Tocqueville stressed, rising expectations provide the dynamite for political change, or, to use another of his formulations, 'old regimes' are safe from social change just so long as they remain absolutely conservative in character, allowing no hope whatever of any social reform.[3] Nationalism is the key agent of social change for most people in the world in the twentieth century, and it fits badly into the traditional Marxist philosophy of history. Social change results from the interference of external forces rather than from the development of internal ones. There are, however, more 'modern' Marxist views and one of them, conceiving of the world as the appropriate unit of analysis, is at the centre of attention throughout the rest of this chapter.

It is very important to stress the creative, nation-building character of nationalism. Despite its 'truth' in regard to its audience, nationalist doctrine should not be taken too seriously. Such doctrine often stresses that 'the nation' has always been in place and that the imperialist power is a late and unwelcome intervention. To accept this view leads to misunderstanding nationalism as atavistic loyalty, a type of thinking with one's blood. There are two reasons for rejecting this view based on nationalist self-images. Firstly, the very straight lines of the borders of many Third World states show the artificial rather than the organic quality of such states. There are apparently something like 8,000 known languages and currently something like 200 states. Insofar as people did have strong loyalties in the past, it was to those small-scale ethnic and tribal units; these are abandoned during the drive to modernity. One cannot explain Nigerian nationalism (as one might the nationalism of an older state like Japan) in terms of a previous loyalty *for the state had no previous existence*. This leads to the second general consideration. The best way to judge the character of nationalism is by what it does rather than what it says; here actions do speak louder than words. Nationalist leaders in power do not preserve traditional culture, or cultures, but rather they destroy them. Populism may be inscribed in doctrine, but factory-building and development dictate actual practice – although here too there is perhaps an important exception in modern Islam, which is discussed below. All this can be summarised by saying that nationalism is the creation of nations, and its actual practice is that of nation-building.

Nationalism is such an important phenomenon that attention to it is justified in its own right. However, the purpose behind the discussion here is slightly different, namely to say something about likely political development in Third World countries. The central point is simple, brutal and banal. It has been argued already that forced development is

3 A. de Tocqueville, *The Old Regime and the French Revolution*, Fontana, London, 1968.

likely to have some affinity with the centralisation of power in some non-democratic regime. When we consider the situation of the Third World this affinity is hugely reinforced. The tasks that faced a Stalin – the building of industry and the removal of the peasantry from the land – are mild compared to those of creating a society for the first time. As such creation involves literally the wiping out of a myriad of local cultures and allegiances, it is almost inconceivable to see how the process can be managed without recourse to dictatorship. Mr Robert Mugabe is sometimes considered evil or misguided; in fact his desire for single-party rule is historically normal.

The generalisation that must regrettably guide us initially is that Third World countries are most unlikely to concern themselves with the extension of formal democratic rights, even if their very *raison d'être* is that of mobilising the people in a new nation. There has probably even been a growing distrust of democracy. Where the Young Turks felt that a parliamentary regime, combined with secularisation, would lead to development, virtually nobody now believes that this combination holds the secret to development. This should not be misunderstood. I am not advocating the extension of dictatorial regimes to Third World countries. Insofar as such regimes can develop their societies, they *must* be seen positively for the absence of development probably entails in the long run greater suffering than that undoubtedly involved in forced modernisation. This is not to say that such a mode of development is perfect. On the contrary, problems of placing controls on political power, familiar from the previous chapter, are likely to gain ever greater-salience in societies that develop under dictatorial aegis of any sort. Further, this equation between dictatorship and development in the Third World is suitable only as an *initial* guide. For there are many further questions to be asked. Do dictatorial regimes always manage to develop their societies? Is development in combination with democracy ruled out? What difference does involvement in the world market make? The modernisation 'mix' of different countries can vary very greatly, and this may prove to have very great importance for the future. Countries such as Algeria and Eire, having witnessed long and bloody nationalist campaigns, are likely to create intense, one-dimensional societies. In contrast, a country such as Tunisia, which received independence almost without effort, is able to retain such pluralism as previously existed, and has in consequence the possibility of a much more varied polity. Such diversity cannot properly be investigated within the confines of this short chapter, but we can throw some light on the causal processes at work in the economic development of the new nations. In order to do so it is necessary first to take a step backwards to consider imperialism before analysing claims that the Third World, even now that formal imperial structures have been removed, is still controlled by advanced capitalist society in general and by American capitalism in particular.

Capitalism and Imperialism

The theory of the relationship of capitalism to imperialism has diverse strands to it, but classical formulations, upon which modern dependency theory still rest, were those of Lenin and Rosa Luxembourg. Both these theorists stressed that the internal contradictions of capitalism *necessitated* involvement in the rest of the globe. These thinkers went beyond the obvious and banal fact of superior Western power leading to involvement to insistence that there was a *logical* connection between capitalism and imperialism. Imperial possessions were held to be necessary for Lenin as markets for excess goods, and for Luxembourg as areas in which capital could be invested. To these claims have often been added others, such as that which stresses the importance of Third World raw materials for the Western world. It can be noted too that a part of the theory of great import was that competition for imperial possessions only temporarily hid the problems of capitalism. These problems were exacerbated by unsatisfied claims and these tensions, once transferred to the European scene, caused the war that began in 1914. The equation that capitalist competition leads to war remains at the centre of most modern Marxist accounts of the modern world economy, and in particular of the connection between capitalism and the Third World.

My scepticism about Marxist claims that capitalism *needs* an underdeveloped Third World, and that capitalism and imperialism are *logically* connected, proceeds in this manner. Attention is first directed towards classical imperialism to establish whether state action can really be reduced to the needs of the capitalist system. This leads to reflections upon modern 'economic' imperialism. An amplification of the stance adopted is then made by analysing American involvement in Vietnam. Finally the negative criticism of Marxist claims is abandoned, and a positive characterisation of imperialism is put in their place.

The origins of the First World War are sure to be debated *ad infinitum*, but the Leninist view that it was caused by an overspill of imperial conflicts back onto the European stage can be discounted. Lenin's theory falls for obvious chronological reasons. The scramble for Africa had been at its peak in the 1880s and was effectively over long before 1914. It is true that there had been certain conflicts, often involving Germany and France, at the turn of the century, but these had been settled by 1914.

The occasion for the war was nationalistic pressure in the Balkans. The war at its inception was not really very much different from any traditional European war, and there is no reason to seek an explanation for it much beyond the normal fact of inter-state competition. That such explanations are now often sought is merely the result of the war becoming something other than that which had been planned or was expected.

There are other important criticisms of the arguments of Lenin and Luxembourg, and they can usefully be made by concentrating on the French situation.[4] It sometimes seems as if imperialism had economic motives because the politicians, using the language of their age, made much of profits to be won. This was largely rhetoric. Politicians really had a poor idea of the needs of the capitalist system, and in fact acted for their own reasons. Other considerations are even more striking. It is not possible to argue that colonies were required as places in which to invest capital for the simple reason that capital outflows from France went overwhelmingly to Russia, where good profits could be made, rather than to her own colonies. The same is true in the British case where much investment went to Argentina. Nor did French industry send a massive amount of exports to its colonies, most of which, being poor, were not able to afford them. Nor should a presupposition of Lenin's and Luxembourg's arguments, that the home market cannot absorb goods through insatiable demand with consequent possibilities for capital investment, be accepted for a moment. David Hume's view of the growing internal market is a far better guide, both historically and contemporaneously. Finally, one last 'materialist' theory of imperialism can be considered briefly, namely that imperialism is caused by a need for *Lebensraum*. Insofar as this notion has sense, it refers to pressure caused by population growth. Population pressure *did* encourage the Greeks to found colonies. This has no truth in the French case because population in the late nineteenth century was falling.

The positive case to be made about imperialism can be anticipated by saying that this phenomenon is essentially *political*. This is especially true of such imperialism as had military/strategic origins.[5] More generally, one state after another in Europe acquired colonies simply because these were the rules of state competition.[6] Other banal but forceful considerations flesh out the view that the capitalist drive for profits cannot explain imperialism. Most obviously, it is very hard to explain why advanced

4 I am drawing here on arguments often made by Raymond Aron, perhaps most accessibly in *Imperialism and Colonialism*, Montague Burton Lecture, Leeds University Press, Leeds, 1959.

5 R. Robinson, J. Gallagher, with A. Denny, *Africa and the Victorians*, Oxford University Press, Oxford, 1961.

6 A. Smith, *State and Nation in the Third World*, Harvester, Brighton, 1983.

capitalist societies, if they truly needed the Third World, did not use their military superiority in a no-holds-barred manner to retain their colonies, rather than accepting inevitable 'winds of change'. In fact, the advanced capitalist societies experienced their greatest period of economic growth in the years after 1945 when they were divesting themselves of their colonial possessions. If capitalism depends upon the Third World, how was such economic progress possible?

There is a Marxist answer to this question. It insists that capitalism needs to exploit the Third World, and that it still does so successfully without maintaining *formal* imperial rule. Economic imperialism is held to have replaced the actual political rule of empires. Now there are famous occasions when the West *has* interfered in the internal affairs of Third World countries. America destabilised Mossadeq in Iran in 1953 and Allende in Chile in 1973. Clearly some concern with the protection of economic investments was a part of the motivation at work in these cases, but so too were geopolitical considerations which had little to do with economics. It is very hard to separate these factors. No claim is being made that economic motivation is *always* absent. Nevertheless, even a fairly cursory analysis of the situation as a whole makes for extreme scepticism as to the extent to which advanced capitalist societies need the Third World.

We can begin with investment. The simple fact of the matter concerning American investment (and it is America which since 1945 has provided the bulk of capital export) is that Europe, from about 1955, has been far more favoured than has the Third World. Europe houses IBM, General Motors and Fords. There are those on the extreme left and the extreme right who argue passionately that Europe *is* economically exploited by America. There are good reasons for doubting this case. In recent years there has been an increasing gap between European and American political and military interests and it is scarcely plausible to maintain that current European politics are controlled by the presence of American multi-nationals. We shall see in a moment how little trade there is between America and Europe. Furthermore, it is highly implausible to argue that American economic involvement, formal and informal, had deleteriously affected the European economies. On the contrary, a growing number of American politicians have begun to wonder whether the Marshall Plan was *too* successful, and this is certainly one underlying factor in the increasing tension between Europe and the United States examined in chapter 6. It is perhaps true that the presence of IBM has slowed down the creation of any European computer industry; that company certainly repatriates its profits. Nonetheless, in general terms it is very hard to see the American economic investment which has been made as being anything other than beneficial.

Table 1 The Direction of World Trade 1983

	Industrial countries		Oil-exporting countries		Non-oil developing countries		Asia		Europe		Middle East		Western hemisphere		Socialist bloc		EEC	
	Exp.	Imp.	Exp.	Imp.	Exp.	Imp.	Exp.	Imp.	Exp.	Imp.	Exp.	Imp.	Exp.	Imp.	Exp.	Imp.	Exp.	Imp.
Industrial countries	779932	806819	122281	102730	183014	216913	74164	92439	17417	28400	8488	25630	57622	39307	31048	35372	422602	437239
Oil-exporting countries	93192	134679	3482	4126	22531	55340	9719	20713	6479	9837	1806	4530	3450	17581	1956	625	46155	53107
Non-oil developing countries	210001	202723	57485	27386	79190	75055	46087	41507	6798	6698	3435	5715	16392	12827	17724	21745	81068	73488
Asia	83507	76260	22422	13134	43961	42183	36522	33960	1129	1241	1185	2579	3239	1462	3091	3556	18826	19336
Europe	28683	19525	8970	7368	7216	6712	1413	1313	2566	2232	1155	1785	1153	241	11924	13219	19346	14613
Middle East	24119	9309	4574	1812	7304	3330	3467	1186	1901	1094	386	342	1134	73	1201	574	12850	5832
Western hemisphere	44888	68841	18874	3795	12638	16844	1965	3491	246	1193	99	596	9664	10218	740	3782	11534	17061
Socialist bloc	32195	34105	656	2194	21953	17184	3489	3117	13662	11505	561	934	3543	817	–	–	15983	22581
EEC	430529	421894	48844	50742	66319	85065	18717	21540	13061	18995	5143	13731	15608	10950	20577	17556	299273	296896

Figures shown in millions of US dollars
Source: Direction of Trade. Annual 1977–83, International Monetary Fund.

Whether the same is true for American and European investment in Third World countries is another matter, which is investigated below. But one general warning can be repeated. This section has a very specific theme, namely that the advanced capitalist countries tend *not* to need, to 'depend' upon, the Third World. This is not to say, however, that the impact of capitalist societies upon Third World countries may not be very great. A large multi-national may have operations in a small Third World country that are not essential to the functioning of the firm but which comprise a vital part of the economy of the state in question. This reservation also holds in the matter of trade between North and South, to which we now turn, in order both to examine the markets for advanced capitalism and to review 'necessary' imports. We can proceed by highlighting certain relationships shown in table 1.

What is most striking about exports for our purposes is the fact that the advanced world is its own market. A moment's reflection lessens the surprise. These are the richest countries in the world and hence the most capable of buying goods. America is its own home market and its exports are very small in relation to the size of its economy. There is only a limited amount of trade between Europe and America. But Europe as a whole is in a very similar situation to the United States, and this is an increasing trend reflecting the practices of the Common Market. At present all European Community exports to the Third World comprise less than 7 per cent of GNP. When colonies were first given up, much wailing was heard that European capitalism would collapse. But capital is mobile, and not necessarily fixed to any particular market; its ability to adapt is shown very clearly by these figures. None of this is to say that adapting has been easy and painless, nor that it will be so in the future.

What of imports? Even if most imports come from other advanced countries, is it not the case that those which do come from the Third World consist of vital raw materials? Here too distinctions are necessary. In some crucial areas any such reliance has *lessened*. The Common Agricultural Policy of the European Community now ensures that Europe is a net food exporter. This policy, judged by some politicians to be *strategically* necessary, is extremely expensive. Food can be produced more cheaply in Third World countries for whom restrictions on the European market are a grave matter. There are strong reasons to doubt that advanced capitalist societies depend upon minerals from the Third World. American policy-makers do not seem to discuss such matters, and one doubts that they are sufficiently technically sophisticated to be aware of the importance of, say, manganese to the American economy. This matters since it reinforces the picture of a foreign policy dictated by non-economic goals. Perhaps, of course, it is because foreign policy makers *are* unaware of the needs of their economies, that capitalism may in the long run suffer. It may be claimed that capitalism will eventually be deprived of crucial raw materials or, in a more sophisticated version, of important raw materials *at the right price*. What evidence is there for this contention? This is a complex matter on which to adjudicate, but some points are clear. Many Third World exports are of non-essential goods, from fruit to coffee, the absence of which would not cripple capitalism, although the inability to export them would cripple the producing countries involved. There are *few* raw materials of crucial importance for advanced capitalism.[7] If they were cut off by some sort of embargo, or repriced at a crippling level, would capitalism then collapse? This is a hypothetical question of great complexity, but one can doubt that the answer is positive. Advanced science when pushed may well be capable of following in the shoes of Napoleon. He pioneered the production of sugar beet when sugar cane was denied during the Continental Blockade. Science may create substitutes for supposed necessities, and there have been recent examples of this. Much the same purpose may be achieved by a combination of further exploration and recycling.

There is one obvious exception to these generalisations, namely oil. The rises in producer prices by the oil cartel of OPEC in 1973 and 1975 *did* lead to some stumbling within advanced capitalist societies. Certainly Europe, but not America, is currently dependent upon Middle Eastern oil. One imagines that foreign policy actors at the time of decolonialisation, armed with decent historical prophecies, might well have resisted nationalism far more thoroughly had they realised the full importance of 'black gold'. It is still possible that political intervention in the Middle East may result from capitalism's need for this crucial raw material. Nevertheless, here too important qualifications must be made. The oil reserves of the Middle East only amount to about 55 per cent of the world total. Most reserves throughout the world are likely to be exhausted within 30 years, and faster, of course, if the Third World *does* develop rapidly. Ironically, capitalist society may yet have cause to thank OPEC for easing the transition to other energy sources by raising the price of this one early enough to allow time for adaption. Further, it is important to recall that the emotional core of the argument made by Marxists concerning the relations of capitalism and imperialism concerns the exploitation of the Third World by advanced capitalist states. How much validity does this picture now have for the relationship between OPEC countries and the West? Are these terms of trade now so unfair

7 Minerals imported into the United States *either* have diverse sources of supply *or* are non-essential. The United States fears only for its crucial imports of chromium and ferro-chromium, at present largely imported from South Africa. On this question see, *World Mineral Trends and US Supply Problems*, research paper R20, project director L.J. Fischman, Resources for the Future, Inc., Washington, DC, 1980.

that it is proper to continue to talk of capitalism *exploiting* the oil states? Here too there is variation, but some oil states are now among the richest in the world, although the division of such riches inside those states is extremely uneven.

Let us turn attention away from the banal reasoning occasioned by a consideration of the needs of the capitalist system as a whole, and consider the most spectacular example of foreign interference by a capitalist state in the period since the ending of the Second World War. Two highly intelligent authors, Raymond Aron and Barrington Moore (a man of the political left, although an empiricist first), have considered at some length the claim that the American involvement in Vietnam resulted from the needs of American capitalism. Both reject the claim as unfounded.[8] Some of their arguments echo those already made concerning the limited importance of external trade in the minds of American foreign policy makers as a whole. Certainly there were no crucial raw materials or markets to be protected in Vietnam, or indeed in SE Asia as a whole. Moore goes somewhat further by investigating the slightly more specific claim that *certain* firms with access to government and involved in the production of weapons did make money from the Vietnam venture. This is something that has to be claimed as the American economy suffered from financing the war via inflation rather than by the raising of taxes.

This more specific claim about the economic causes of imperialism was at the centre of John Hobson's classic *Imperialism*. Aware that the British economy did not benefit from involvement with South Africa, he charged international Jewish financiers with unduly influencing politicians. There was no truth to that contention in the case of the Boer War, but a moment's reflection on this general theory is in order. Pressure may be exerted on governments by particular capitalist firms whose profits may depend upon operations in a Third World country. The argument made to this point that the capitalist system, or indeed national capitalist economies, do not depend upon the Third World may, in other words, be accepted, yet this more specific claim may still be advanced, and indeed there is some truth to it. The United States government is influenced by its corporations, and at times its external action can be moulded by such forces. ITT certainly made its views about Allende felt to the Nixon cabinet. That corporation did not in fact even depend upon Chilean copper for the mass of its profits, but modern banks are currently dependent upon Third World involvement, and their role is discussed

8 R. Aron, *Imperial Republic*, Weidenfeld & Nicolson, London, 1978; B. Moore, *Reflections on the Causes of Human Misery and upon Certain Proposals to Eliminate Them*, Allen Lane, London, 1977, esp. ch. 5.

below. Nonetheless, it is very hard to believe that American foreign policy in Vietnam was determined by the arms industry. Moore notes that 40 of the largest 100 American firms at the end of the 1960s were involved in military production, but he nonetheless refutes the easy equation of militarism with capitalism.

The real issue is: *how important is the military market to the big corporation?* Big corporations can be among the largest providers for the military and *still* be in a situation where military contracts constitute only a small proportion of their total output. The action situation, it turns out, is one where a very few big firms are indeed almost entirely dependent upon the Pentagon market. On the other hand, for many big military contractors this portion of their sales is very small. Twelve of the fifty largest industrial companies, even though they are among the 100 biggest military contractors, have ratios of military contracts to sales of .04 or less. Within the 50 largest industrial corporations as a whole there are 33 whose ratio of military contracts to sales is .04 or less. These figures hardly support the notion that the loss of the military market would be a mortal wound to corporate enterprise.[9]

To this one might well add a further question by way of reservation. Why should actively going to war be necessary for the expenditure of large sums of money on the military machine?

A consideration of Vietnam leads to the final point concerning a positive characterisation of much of imperialism. What is striking about involvement in Vietnam can easily be seen in traditional power political terms. The war was not one controlled by the generals but rather by intellectually inclined state actors who badly miscalculated the size of the stake involved for both sides. Interestingly, the popular view of the Vietcong as nationalists is probably mistaken; they were rather the partisans of a regime, and the war against them was not, in Aron's eyes, inherently unwinnable. Why were such miscalculations made, and why was America present in this part of the globe in the first place? The answer is simply that great powers like to enjoy dominance and gain *amour propre* from this even if on occasion, as in the Soviet Union at present, this is economically expensive. The reverse face of such ambition is hubris, or, to use the late Senator Fulbright's expression, 'the arrogance of power'. All this deserves summary. The view being developed is that held by American liberals in the late 1960s. Their argument against American foreign policy in Vietnam and elsewhere depended upon the assertion that such involvement was not in fact *necessary*. Their complaint was against the stupidity of their country which was so misguided as to make it more, rather than less, likely that American influence would eventually be diminished. For this foreign

9 Moore, *Reflections*, p. 141.

policy encouraged Third World citizens who witnessed the propping up of aged dictators to equate the United States with reaction.

Varieties of Development

The argument to this point can be summarised very briefly. Perhaps *the* danger that faces the Third World is not that advanced capitalism will exploit them – interestingly many underdeveloped countries cry out for what Western Marxists consider exploitation – but rather that they may be ignored altogether. This formulation overstates the case somewhat for all that has been defended so far is the simple proposition that advanced capitalism does not, with some exceptions, itself 'depend' upon the Third World. It is now time, however, to turn to the other side of the coin. Is it the case that relationships of no vital importance for Western countries and companies nevertheless have determinate salience for the Third World itself? It is important to be clear what is meant by 'determinate' in this context. Discussions of an active process of 'underdevelopment' sometimes gives the impression of an absolute increase in poverty, that is a process whereby blockages are placed on the very possibility of economic advance. There *is* an element of reality to which this notion draws our attention, but, given the growth rates in newly industrialising countries, it is largely without empirical justification. More limited versions of dependency theory stress *relative* disadvantages. These seek to draw our attention to the different situation facing late developers entering into an established, and largely integrated, world market. Such developing societies cannot build upon craft traditions, as did those of the West, while their pattern of growth is held to be determined and dictated by demand from the large markets of advanced capitalism. Nobody would wish to deny this, although we must also remember that certain *advantages* accrue to late industrialisers. The core of dependency theory does not simply claim that there is an international context within which developing countries must operate. It argues the strong thesis that the fate of the Third World is determined by and depends upon what happens in the advanced capitalist world. This theory deserves to be called Marxist since it sees the motor force of change in forces of international economic competition. It is difficult to deal with a complex and intangible question, but an historically based line of argument allows for key distinctions to be drawn so that a more differentiated theory can be created. *Pace* Marxism, this theory must allow for the geopolitical realities of international state competition.

Dependency theory has recently received a considerable boost from the work of Immanuel Wallerstein and it is useful to highlight his position.[10] Europe in the early modern period was comprised in his view of core areas in England, the Netherlands and northern France, and peripheral areas, notably Prussia and Poland, whose fate was determined by their place in the world economic order. The presence of a large market *does* give a chance for landlords and entrepreneurs in the periphery to concentrate on a type of primary commodity production. This led in Eastern Europe to an attack on towns and independent peasant communities; the connection posited by Adam Smith between commerce and liberty was thus ruled out of court. It is worth noting that this way of expressing the matter is slightly more positive than is Wallerstein's account for it stresses the active decisions of those with productive power, often landlords but sometimes peasants.[11] Wallerstein's general theory has been challenged insofar as it rules out *any* independent impact of political developments, particularly those concerning contests in war. Some of the characteristic developments in Poland were clearly caused by geopolitical competition, and changes inside Polish society *antedated* the emergence of wide-scale international economic relations, in any case rather smaller in the sixteenth century than Wallerstein allows.[12] However, these reservations do not alter the correctly perceived fact that from the late sixteenth century much of Eastern Europe did provide corn and rye to the Western core, and was 'dependent' upon this relationship. Is it then true that this relationship determined the future of Eastern Europe and prevented its economic development?

This is a complicated question, but the answer is certainly negative. In the late nineteenth-century, imperial Germany developed with spectacular success. Industrialisation was capitalist internally, but involved for crucial periods the protection of nascent industries by means of withdrawal from international capitalism behind tariff walls, a policy which also characterised American economic development. But imperial Germany contained part of the European core along the Rhine and is, to this extent, perhaps not truly representative of the problems at issue.

The history of Russia *is* surely exactly suited to examine dependency theory. For in the late nineteenth century a society with a single export commodity began to develop by means of foreign capital. For dependency theory this meant that it was not the master of its own fate. There is, of course, a massive debate as to whether the revolution was inevitable or whether a German type of revolution from above might, under slightly

10 I. Wallerstein, *The Modern World System*, Academic Press, New York, 1974, and various other volumes, including some directly on the developing countries.

11 R. Brenner, 'Agrarian class structure and economic development in pre-industrial Europe', *Past and Present*, vol. 70, 1976.

12 T. Skocpol, 'Wallersteins's world capitalist system: a theoretical and historical critique', *American Journal of Sociology*, vol. 82, 1977.

different circumstances, have been successful. It is hardly for me to adjudicate on this debate, but it is noticeable that much recent historiography has stressed that Russia's developmental problems were by no means all externally imposed, as dependency theory would have it. On the contrary, the power stand-off between landlords and state placed a formidable obstacle in the way of the creation of real modernisation, including, perhaps vitally, the creation of a decent home market, although it did not prevent the emergence of a small industrial sector. Further debates concern the extent to which the Bolsheviks speeded up economic development, and the costs of the Soviet model have been made clear above. However, we need not even consider these debates here for there is *total agreement* on the outcome. Russia did modernise. The international market was not the master of the fate of Russian society. And there are still further debates, on which some light can later be cast in general terms, as to the reasons for this economic success. Was complete withdrawal from the world market, including the ending of all foreign capital investment, absolutely necessary for Russian development? Could the strong state of the Bolsheviks not have allowed some involvement in international economic relationships, supposing that investment had been forthcoming, sure in the knowledge that its creation of modern citizens, a social infrastructure and heavy industry had made the development of Russia anyway fundamentally autonomous? I suspect that the answer to this last question is positive. But what matters is the general point: no greater hole could be placed in dependency theory than the ability of a society, albeit one well endowed with all sorts of ecological and natural benefits, to break out and become one of the two superpowers.

Perhaps even this is not quite correct. Raymond Aron remarked somewhere that the key event of the twentieth century is not the Russian but the Chinese revolution, presumably because of the sheer number of people involved. Whatever the reason for his claim, and indeed whether or not it is justified, the argument to be made about China is exactly the same as that made about Russia. China was also able to break its ties of dependency. There is absolutely no doubt that these ties were extremely strong, involving at their peak massive foreign interference and the creation of treaty ports for advanced nations. It seemed as if China would be dismembered. One interesting reason why this did not take place was that the weak Chinese state was protected by its enemy's enemy. America, fearful of Japanese military and industrial strength sought to prevent its further growth by protecting China.[13] At present, rather little

13 Dennis Smith, 'Domination and containment', *Comparative Studies in Society and History*, vol. 19, 1977.

is known with very great certainty about the Chinese manner of development.[14] An initial introduction of the Soviet model proved, given the size of the population and the regional character of Chinese markets, disastrous. More pragmatic Liuist policies which replaced them appreciated the market and allowed the peasantry to own private plots, and this had great success. They are dominant again now, after the interruption of the Cultural Revolution. Chinese leaders now have sufficient confidence to consider speeding up their growth by means of some involvement in the world market. More importantly, there is now a little evidence that population growth is beginning to come under control, and fears have even been expressed that an unbalanced population pyramid in the near future will place very considerable burdens on the young. This control is vital, for such economic development as there has been so far has not done much more than keep pace with the huge growth in Chinese population since the revolution. Here, one must judge the revolution a success by an entirely different standard. It proved capable of creating a state strong enough to survive militarily, and thus able to prevent the dismemberment that might have overtaken China. Two crucial theoretical points already made when considering Russia need reiterating. Firstly, most historians of modern China suggest that development from above was prevented by a power stand-off between state and gentry that proved far too entrenched for Chiang Kai-shek. Only when this *internal* problem was solved was development possible. Secondly, there can once again be no doubt that Chinese development is beginning to take place and that relations of dependency were not sufficient to prevent it taking its own course.

Before turning to societies which are from choice or necessity part of the world market, a digression is called for on the situation of model Islam. In both China and Russia at the end of the nineteenth-century, intellectuals felt torn between introducing Westernising ideals which impugned their birthright and hanging on to the latter at the cost of an ineffectiveness which might mean dismemberment as a state. The conflicts between Westernisers and Populists were the subject of Chinese and Russian novels of the period, but the outcome was clear. In the final analysis, one of the Westernising currents, that is Marxism rather than liberalism, won in both cases. The adoption of such a Western creed meant, especially perhaps in the case of China, the extirpation of local culture and this made modernisation correspondingly difficult. The historic interest of modern Islam is that it stands in stark opposition to all

14 I learnt a great deal from a conference in Frankfurt in July 1984, organised by Jiri Kosta, which compared the fate of the Soviet model of industrialisation in Poland, China, Yugoslavia and Cuba.

this. A regeneration of the local tradition can serve as a suitable ideology by means of which the infrastructure of industrial society can be created. This world religion adapts itself with ease to the requirements of modernity, and allows many Islamic intellectuals to have their cake and eat it as well. Such intellectuals can stress their 'custom' *and* accept modernity. The reason for this should be familiar from the earlier discussion of Islam where its concern with literacy, discipline and egalitarianism, those key components singled out by Max Weber as vital for the industrial productive system, were stressed. These concerns were those of the city-based great tradition of Islam; tribal Islamic observance was altogether more particularistic. In classical Islam there was something of a pendulum swing between these two poles, but the needs of modernity have unhinged the pendulum in favour of the great tradition. Though there is great variety among Islamic states, fundamentalist reform is spreading fast among all Islamic states. This is strong evidence of its efficacy in mobilising the people for modernity.[15]

The advanced societies once hoped that the Third World would become like themselves. The world historical importance of the ability of Islam to fit the modern age is the absolute demonstration of the falsity of this position. This part of the Third World wishes to be itself. Of no one is this more true than of the Ayatollah Khomeini, a leader whose influence it is impossible to exaggerate. Some words about the revolution associated with his name can only add to the general argument being made. It may be proper to see the late Shah of Iran as dependent upon America for the type of development that he undertook, although one would have to add that most of the aid he received was given for geopolitical rather than economic reasons. Nobody can say that of the Ayatollah whose concern for *independence* has bought him the united enmity of both superpowers. Of course, it remains to be seen whether Islamic clerics can run a modern state. It is worth recalling that Islam is a doctrine which sees as normal the sacral functioning of everyday life. Such evidence as is available suggests that the ulama *are* proving quite successful in managing the oil sector of the economy.

This is a good place to digress for a moment on the wars which characterise Third World society. The Ayatollah Khomeini's hope was that a Shi'ite version of Islam would unite the vast majority of the Iraqi population with Iran, that religious loyalty would prove stronger than loyalty to a state. This has not happened. The salience of the national principle in the Third World is strong and the wars that are fought there are certainly classically Clausewitzian.[16] Yet the point that needs to be

15 E. Gellner, *Muslim Society*, Cambridge University Press, Cambridge, 1981, ch. 1.
16 R. Aron, *Clausewitz*, Routledge & Kegan Paul, London, 1983.

made about them is rather more simple. Real dependency of Third World countries would be demonstrated if leaders of their states uniformly took their orders from Washington, or perhaps from Moscow. There are many famous occasions when *exactly the opposite* occurred. Kissinger and Nixon tried strenuously to prevent the Indo-Pakistan war of 1971, but in vain. It seems that there is a certain autonomy for Third World states in these matters and, given the importance of war in history, this is of vital importance. A revolution attacked, as has been that of Iran, grows in strength and is occasionally capable of producing a citizen army society. If Iran does develop in this way, might she not yet have military success in the area which would prove destabilising to the whole of the modern world order?

The general approach so far has been that of casting doubt on dependency theory by citing societies and civilisations which have broken from the world system and which have been able to develop. It is as well to spell out the implicit view as to how that development was possible. Development was achieved by the creation of a strong state capable of ending the power stand-off within such 'societies', and thereby to begin the creation of a modern citizen body. The crucial force at work is judged to be the ability to deal with internal problems rather than the actual isolation from world market forces. Some measure of involvement with the latter may well help. This general view follows naturally from the first part of the book where internal blockages were seen to have prevented development in three of the world civilisations. Before the argument is continued and amplified, however, three comments of a cautionary nature must be made on the 'socialist' style of development.

The central claim made about the societies cited is that development has been successful. Firstly, however, the mere fact that a socialist style does try to create the social structure for modernity means only that it fulfils a *necessary* condition for industrialisation and development. The achievement of social progress does not necessarily guarantee economic progress just as some economic indicators showing progress in capitalist developing countries may mislead if they only involve the creation of bank accounts abroad for an elite. Disasters have occurred under the Soviet model. The Cuban economy is often no longer considered dependent because it has broken out of the capitalist world order, but it remains so, possibly to a greater extent than hitherto. Its economy survives only as the result of the Soviet Union paying at least three or four times the world price in sugar to prop up the economy. This subsidy is absolutely necessary as sugar production in Cuba is no longer profitable in purely economic terms. This is not, however, to ignore the decided indicators of social progress, merely to insist that Cuba, especially when Che Guevara demonetised the economy, has seen extraordinary economic failure under Castro. Once again, this is not to deny a certain expensive success in power-political terms. Further, in China rigidities of the Soviet model caused disastrous failures in the period of the Great Leap Forward and during the Cultural Revolution. In the former of these periods very many millions starved, while heavy accumulation produced *less* growth than did smaller levels of accumulation under more pragmatic policies. Chinese leaders are clearly trying to learn from these mistakes, and the foremost among their economists are deeply interested in the 1965–8 reform policies of Czechoslovakia (about which the re-formers learn from their adviser Ota Sik) and the Hungarian reforms since 1968. The situation in Kampuchea is even more serious. Here fanatical ideological commitment, bereft of all economic and social sense, led to the loss of at least a third of the population. Kampuchea is unlikely to recover from this. This returns us to the matter of the characteristic polities of Third World states.

Secondly, it is worth recalling the debate as to whether full collectiv-isation and central planning is necessary for socialist economic develop-ment. The balance of evidence suggests that something like this *was* necessary in the Soviet Union but that Chinese circumstances were by no means so suited to this approach. This is an important matter since a *fully* centralised state (and *nobody* doubts that centralisation is necessary if the traditional power stand-off between state and society is to be re-moved and decent land reform and industrial plans to be pushed through) is perhaps more likely to suffer excesses when it seeks to rule out the market altogether, and tries to control every social process. In this matter, it is important to emphasise once more the considerable degree of divergence between the agricultural systems of the socialist states. One can at least hope that some measure of market forces may dilute the Soviet model, and with it the dangers of Stalinist excess. The hope of some is that a liberal socialist economy, based on strong market incen-tives, can characterise a socialist developing society from the start with all the likelihood of political softness which that would entail. There has been no such society. Market forces probably have their moment of salience in attempting to dilute a failing Soviet model already in place. But even this may be possible *only* when agricultural reform and indust-rial planning is not linked with the actual nation-building. That package seems so massive as to rule out anything other than complete centralisa-tion of power. In any case, thirdly, the total centralisation of power is not endorsed, despite its historic successes, in any uncritical way. There were sometimes options in the process of development that might have allowed a slightly more liberal society, and which advocates of total central power chose to ignore. The centralisation of political power, even in some more market-oriented strategy, is very hard to undo and is always dangerous. This legacy will present terrible and long-lasting problems to the members of such societies until the rules of the liberalisation game are somehow systematically created and then generally learnt.

It is now time to turn to those countries which seek to develop as part of the capitalist world. It is not true to say that this strategy is forced on countries without raw materials given that Cuba gets her oil direct from the Soviet Union. Nevertheless, the absence of significant raw materials encourages the adoption of this path. The key hope behind the policy is that the exceedingly costly and not always impressive process of socialist accumulation can be avoided by loans and investment from abroad which will create faster economic development through participation in the world market. In order to evaluate this whole approach it is necessary to make further distinctions, and we can begin to generate them by first of all noting that some Third World states are *minimal* and others *maximal*. The former may be dictatorial, but they do not penetrate their society in order to create a modern social infrastructure. The latter possess strong bureaucracies, a real drive for autonomy, and prove capable of mobilising the people.

Minimal states such as Guatemala and Chile were effectively dominated for long periods by a single company often concerned with the export of a single crop or raw material, and repatriating a high proportion of high profits. This is naked exploitation. Capitalism may not need to behave in this way, but it certainly does so, and this can sometimes be ascribed, especially in the United States, to the ability of capitalists to affect the external action of particular nations. If one considers countries such as Egypt and Nigeria, which broadly follow the minimal state model, one notes that growth rates can be high. But this should not deceive. These are less 'societies' than dual systems. An enclave of modern economic relations, largely foreign-owned and often housed in a tax-free Export Processing Zone tied to the world market, *coexists* with a peasant base which the minimal state does not bother to touch. Such states are often only a combination of capitalist and officer groups who amass fortunes which are sent abroad. This seems to have occurred to such an extent in modern Nigeria that the benefits of oil money may have been lost forever. The United States has a deplorable and short-sighted record of having supported such dictatorial governments, and of having intervened to destroy attempts made internally to change this situation. Dependency theorists are right in such cases to say that 'development' for the mass of the population is systematically blocked by relations with the advanced Western world. This latter sentence is carefully formulated to allow for those relations being either economic or geopolitical in character. The United States' refusal to recognise strong states in

Central America probably has more to do with perceived geopolitical than perceived economic interests.

To admit that this is so in some very notable cases does not mean that blockages in all Third World capitalist societies should be laid at the door of external factors, whether economic or military. Consider modern India. The situation there is more complex than the single notion of a minimal state allows, but the label remains justified given the inability of the state to deeply penetrate its society, to destroy caste and to mobilise the population. Highly regrettable though it must be to say so, and profoundly as one hopes the situation will change, Indian democracy is largely an elite pastime. There may in fact be something to the notion that the alteration of political parties *hinders* those fundamental reforms that are necessary for modernisation. But what changes are necessary? There seems to be some measure of agreement among those who have recently written on Indian society that vital changes are required in the landholding system. This is unlikely to come from Congress given the position of the landlord strata within that party and in society as a whole. Certainly the attempts at land reform which have been made have been defeated by landlord power in the localities.[17] The 'Green Revolution' *has* very remarkably made India self-sufficient in food. The fundamental obstacle to India's *further* advance remains internal. Reforms cannot be made from the outside, and the advanced societies can no longer be blamed if they are not implemented.

There are, however, strong states that have chosen to develop within the international capitalist arena. Some of these, notably Finland and Denmark, *have* managed to combine democracy with development. Both these countries had strong egalitarian peasant communities which created a large home market sustaining local industry. Finland was extremely resistant, for nationalistic reasons, to the idea of foreign investment in productive industry despite being prepared to act on the world market. In addition Finland benefits from its geopolitical situation. It is granted special favours from both the major power blocs without having the burden of full entanglement in either of them. Few generalisations can, however, be made from such small countries – which are anyway European and so not heavily involved in nation-building – whose adaption to the modern world was much helped by the nearby presence of large markets.

Larger strong states within the capitalist world come to mind which

17 D. Selbourne, *An Eye to India*, Penguin, London, 1977; D. Hiro, *Inside India Today*, Routledge & Kegan Paul, London, 1978; B. Moore, *Social Origins of Dictatorship and Democracy*, Penguin, London, 1969, ch. 6; R. Cassen, *India: population, economy, society*, Macmillan, London, 1978.

are not democratic but are instead harshly authoritarian. Considerable attention was given in chapter 6 to imperial Germany, and further attention could have been devoted to Japan.[18] Perhaps the most striking state of this type in the current world scene is that of South Korea which combines great respect for market forces with a repressive state possessed of a bureaucracy capable of mobilising society. The other 'Confucian capitalist' states of SE Asia – for the model of bureaucracy is a beneficial historic legacy distinctive of the area – are smaller; they are city states rather than nation states. There are idiosyncratic features at work in all of them, notably strong anti-communism and the favourable access to the American market, given, one suspects, for geopolitical rather than economic reasons. Nevertheless, the case of South Korea does bring to our attention the question as to the very nature of development. Is it proper to speak about development if it creates as politically repulsive a society as is South Korea? I suspect that for the majority of the population the fact of economic growth does outweigh, as it does for the majority under state socialism, the political consequences. But to raise this question is to bring back to mind the long-term evolution of such regimes. Is there something about the industrial productive system that means that this combination of hierarchy and modernity is unstable? Can we hope for no more than the weak thesis of progress in the Third World, as Ernest Gellner insisted? In chapter 6, consideration of this question was limited to probabilities since defeat in war cut short the evolution of imperial Germany and Japan. But the key question as to the likely politics of modernity can now be considered further. Again history has not yet brought in any final judgement, but analysing Latin America, where dependency theory was created, rather than South Korea, can advance the argument.

Argentina, Brazil and Mexico have become strong states, although important reservations about this will be made below. These states were not content to remain single-crop or product-enclave economies and sought to introduce import substitution policies. These policies were largely financed and run by foreign multi-nationals with whom bargains of varying but increasing degrees of efficacy and advantage were struck. Moreover, these societies are no longer directly involved in nation-building for national liberation was achieved some considerable time ago, and it is this that makes it at least possible that there may yet be some truth to Adam Smith's equation of commerce and liberty. Finally, these societies have notable trade union structures and traditions of democracy. However, no clear alignment of workers against employers results since both these forces can be seen as split into two camps – the

18 For an interesting discussion, see B. Moore, *Social Origins of Dictatorship and Democracy*, esp. chs 5 and 8.

former between the established working class and a newer working class of recent peasant origin prone to populist tendencies, and the latter between an older landholding aristocracy and a new industrial bourgeoisie. The inability of these groups to work together has often led the military to intervene and establish 'order'. Yet it remains a mistake to see Latin American politics as being inherently prone to military coups, just as it has proved incorrect to see them, unlike peasant societies such as Nicaragua, as any longer inherently revolutionary. The situation is much more complex. The only generalisation that can be risked at this point is that these polities have witnessed an oscillation between dictatorship and democracy.

What are the *exact* theses of dependency theory in relation to these societies? Early import substitution is held to concentrate on light, labour-intensive industry with production for the home market. In contrast, later import substitution depends upon large capital-intensive multi-nationals which produce capital goods and cars, but only for the luxury market. Political repression is necessary in the latter state in order to compress wages. Although this is only the briefest outline of a theory that can sometimes be bewilderingly complex, it is not hard to see gross empirical failings at work. These have been nicely captured by J.G. Merquior:

... automobile and domestic consumer durables booms have taken place in Latin America well *before* the establishment of authoritarian rule. The motor-car industry in Brazil was launched in the Kubitschek years (1955–60). No doubt the Brazilian *Wirtschaftswunder* from the late 1960s to the early 1970s (and the country still managed to achieve an 8 per cent GNP growth rate on the eve of the second oil price rise!) greatly benefited from wage compression, hence, indirectly, from the authoritarian politics of the period; but it would be sheer nonsense to present such an economic *consequence* as if it had been the cause or motive of the 1964 coup. Incidentally, the height of Brazilian populism (1960–64) has a poor showing in terms of wage protection: by 1963, the real minimum wage was already lower than in 1952. Dependency theorists claim that wage rises under Goulart (the President toppled from power in March 1964) significantly reduced the industrialists' profits; yet there is no statistical warrant for such a trend.

Authoritarianism in uniform got the upper hand in Brazil and the Southern Cone (Argentina, 1966; Uruguay, 1971; Chile, 1973) in spells of sluggish growth, wild inflation and political stalemate. More and more, in the years preceding the military takeover, governments began to realise that the social contract of liberal populism – the compromise which transferred income to industry without taxing the farmers, by a skilful combination of easy credit, overvalued currency and protectionism – was highly inflationary and eventually growth-inhibitory.[19]

19 J.G. Merquior, 'Power and identity: politics and ideology in Latin America', *Government and Opposition*, vol. 19, 1984, p. 244.

There is a further, extremely important criticism to note about dependency theory, and it is one which concerns the possibility of mass liberal politics in this area. If international capitalism controls the Third World, it is difficult to see why many Latin American states are currently involved in attempts at liberalisation. This is the harder to explain as the theory suggests that a world recession should lead to the strengthening of authoritarianism in Latin America. Some words about this liberalisation process are necessary. Both an enlightened elite and a discontented mass press for liberalisation. The Brazilian liberalisation process was designed by the elite, interestingly including the military, in order to gain a new legitimacy which would, among other things make Brazilian access to international loans that much more easy. The elite's attempt to control the process of liberalisation through manipulation of electoral rules has come unstuck, and there is now considerable pressure for change from below. This brings the position much closer to that in Argentina where a transition to democratic rule, after the disastrous handling by the military of the economy and the Malvinas/Falkland Islands dispute, has been achieved as the result of pressure from below.

The politics of liberalisation in these societies remain as complex as they are in Eastern Europe, and it is still much too early to say whether the transition to democracy can be finally established. As in Eastern Europe, the rules of the game are not yet established. One such rule is likely to be the necessity of gaining consent from several vested interests. Thus in Argentina, Raul Alfonsin would be well advised not to tamper too quickly or deeply with corrupt trade union structures. The socialist ventures of Allende in the different circumstances of Chile were perfectly legal, but were nonetheless mistaken in attracting the united hostility of professional and capitalist classes. 'In Gramscian terms, Unidad Popular was a minority government trying to make social revolution without having in the least acquired hegemony within Chilean society at large.'[20] Beyond these general comments one can detect the possibility of negative and positive scenarios. Hopes ultimately rest upon the development of the logic of industrialism such that a more complex division of labour creates a larger middling stratum devoted to a more open society. In this connection, a certain optimism may be held about Brazil. The middle element there seems to be growing while more authoritarian parties, sometimes led by the old coffee plantation capitalists, rest upon the declining social base of the rural poor in the north-east.[21] But to

20 Ibid., p. 248.
21 My views here have recently been much strengthened by reading a Marxisant manuscript of great power by Nicos Mouzelis dealing with early democracy and late industrialisation in the Balkans and Latin America entitled *The Politics of the Semi-Periphery* (Macmillan, forthcoming). His argument stresses that the establishment of a civil

mention the north-east of Brazil is to point to the more pessimistic case. A reservation was made above about the strength of the state in Argentina, Mexico and Brazil, and this point has its relevance here. The extent to which what might be termed the social liberalism of such states is more liberal than social is an open question, but clearly the process of building social infrastructures is by no means finished. Until it is, there remains a great deal of potential social dynamite inside Brazilian society, and this may yet disrupt the whole liberalisation process. To this may be added Adam Smith's point that market forces are likely to be liberal when large numbers of people are capable of participating in the market; this also has the benefit of creating a large enough home market to absorb industrial growth.

This last point is particularly important since it returns us to the question of the international economy. In a sense, it is the failure to develop home markets which necessitates export-led industrialisation. Broadly speaking, the argument that has just been made is that dependency theory is often open to question because the creation of a strong state, whether with or without a more liberal internal polity, may well allow for successful activities in the larger capitalist society. The international market is a constraint but it leaves room for the creation and autonomous action of a strong state. This receives daily confirmation from the protectionist policies of rich countries towards newly industrialising countries. But are there any ways which have so far been overlooked in which international capitalist relations create terrible difficulties for Third World countries such as Brazil, Argentina and Mexico? The answer to this question, albeit with several important reservations, is broadly positive. Since the late 1970s international indebtedness has come to plague Latin America. This is very bad news for liberal hopes as indebtedness may occasion crises capable of destroying the new-found affinity between commerce and liberty which has concerned us.

It would be a mistake to blame all this indebtedness upon international capitalist lending agencies. The great surge in indebtedness occurred because the rise in oil prices proved far more serious for newly industrialising countries than it did for advanced societies in the capitalist world. These developing countries chose to borrow some of the vast sums of money put into the international banking systems by the newly enriched OPEC countries, so as to avoid rapid deflation and to continue a policy of state investment. It is very hard to untangle responsibilities for

---

society, that is of strong and autonomous social groups (i.e. liberties in the terminology of the present volume), is possible in these societies. He sees an affinity between democracy *and* capitalism, in this nicely echoing Adam Smith and David Hume.

the creation of this indebtedness. In Brazil, most borrowed capital was invested productively, and indebtedness therefore will not vitally matter in the longer run. This was not true of Argentina. In this connection it is always important to remember that Latin America as a whole remains a net *exporter* of capital, a large part of which is invested in the property market of the United States. A significant part of the responsibility for this this indebtedness must be ascribed to *internal* factors.

Nevertheless, there are two important ways in which international factors may be held to blame. It is first important to note the debate, upon which this author cannot adjudicate, which argues that the terms of trade between the advanced and the Third World are systematically set against the latter. Commodity prices for manufactured goods, which are required by Third World countries, and in particular by their multi-nationals for fast growth, are held to be less flexible than those for primary exports which continue to comprise the bulk of Third World exports. Even if this is true it does not account for all international indebtedness which is mostly of recent origin. Secondly, however, modern international banks do represent one section of the capitalist community which increasingly relies upon the Third World for its profits.

From 1970 to 1976, for example, Chase Manhattan, New York's second largest bank, saw its domestic profits plummet from $108 million to $23 million. During the same period, however, Chase's international earnings rose at a steady rate of 17.8 percent per year, from less than $31 million to 1970 to over $108 million in 1976 ... The top ten US banks registered no growth in their domestic operations, whereas their foreign profits were growing at 33 percent per year.

In less than a decade, America's biggest banks had become acutely dependent on foreign profits. The growth of international earnings outstripped domestic earnings and quickly rose to half or more of banks' total profits.[22]

This situation has led to an exceedingly competitive situation. In the words of Richard Weinert of the New York investment banking firm Leslie, Weinert & Co.,

Indebtedness is a two-sided relationship. It depends not only on a willing borrower, but equally on a willing lender ... L[ate] D[eveloping] C[ountry] indebtedness results as much from the need of lenders to lend as from the need of borrowers to borrow ... a full analysis of lending to LDCs must take account of both the demand and supply of lending, and see the volume and pattern of loans as a result of their dynamic inter-relationship.[23]

Bankers have been interested purely in their own profits and have had no compunction about lending to military regimes, even if the irregular behaviour of some such regimes, notably the Argentinian, has led some

22 M. Moffitt, *The World's Money*, Michael Joseph, London, 1984, p. 51.
23 Cited in ibid., p. 98.

bankers to welcome the return of democracy. Bankers were stupid not to realise the total indebtedness that was thereby being created, just as Third World countries were at fault in not recognising that interest rate increases in the United States would make their debts unbearable. Objectively, the resulting situation is one in which a country recently returned to democracy can find itself saddled with debts sometimes contracted by an irresponsible elite. Insofar as bankers encouraged such irresponsibility, it behoves us to ask how long they can expect the producers of the Third World to continue paying them dramatic profits. These payments now threaten to absorb all of the gains made by economic growth. It is important to note certain differences between the lending of money to such countries and to those in the advanced world. Insolvency in Third World countries has led international bankers to encourage the calling in of the IMF to restore financial credibility before they themselves either lend more or reschedule the debts. Clearly the IMF is no development agency and tends rather to specialise in short-term financial measures creating very considerable deflation which accordingly cuts growth rates. When the IMF insists on deflationary policies in, say, Britain, any suffering caused is mitigated by welfare provisions. When similar demands are made of Third World countries, there is no equivalent cushion More importantly, the British people have the possibility of removing governments whose economic policies they reject. Citizens in the Third World frequently do not have this option. The consequence is exploitation, although a banking collapse would cause at least a temporary crisis in the economies of the advanced countries!

Conclusions

The argument of this chapter has been that the development of the Third World as a whole *is* taking place, both in the socialist and the capitalist arenas. Nation-building was seen as a necessary condition without which development was impossible, and this was judged a process likely to lead to despotism. Advanced capitalism does not 'depend' upon the Third World, and a considerable part of a state's development strategy rests in its own hands; the most significant exception to this general rule is the important one of international banking, which does give international agencies a measure of control over national societies. The most significant hope entertained was that some Third World countries within the capitalist arena may be able, once the period of nation-building is over, to liberalise their polities.

These findings amount to saying that international capitalism encourages development and is not usually to be blamed if this does not take place.[24] However, further qualifications to the generally positive picture of international capitalism must be introduced at this point, the second of which has important policy implications for Third World countries themselves. Firstly, the capitalist character of the world economy is beginning to lead to substantive irrationalities. Though this case is often made with regard to the usage of raw materials, it is in fact strongest in the case of food production. America is responsible for more than half the world's food exports, and this weapon may yet be more powerful than any that Third World countries have to their name. Yet this forced food production in America is globally irrational. 'Asian wet rice cultivation yeilds 5 to 50 food calories for each calorie of energy invested. The Western system requires 5 to 10 calories to obtain one food calorie.'[25] Secondly, a strong *negative* case can be made that omissions on the part of the advanced world make development harder than it need be. Although dependency theory is largely untrue, there is no reason why the international context could not be organised so as to make life *easier* for the Third World. Table 2 shows that an expansionary economy in the advanced world would very significantly aid the development of the Third World.

Obviously, this expansionary economy is at present missing, and the Third World suffers in consequence. High American interest rates of the Reagan years make debts harder to repay and growth more difficult to achieve; and limitation on demand from the advanced world consequent on increased protectionism would depress those export earnings upon which development so often depends. The situation at the moment has much in common with that of the inter-war years, and those were disastrous, especially for Latin America. The sin of omission of the advanced Western world is that of failing to put our own house in order. Our imagination has failed to realise the long-term political benefits to be achieved by governments both by writing off large portions of international indebtedness in the spirit of the Marshall Plan and by opening our markets on preferential terms to Third World economies. This is to argue in favour of politics controlling and regulating the workings of the international capitalist system. Such a policy is desirable because of

24 Only after completing this chapter did I read Bill Warren's *Imperialism: pioneer of capitalism*, New Left Books, London, 1982. This renegade Marxist account overlaps considerably with my own, although I have questioned, for some 'societies', the relevance of notional state figures upon which Warren always relies.

25 L.S. Stavrianos, *Global Rift: the Third World comes of age*, Morrow, New York, 1981, p. 437, cited by P. Worsley, *The Three Worlds*, Weidenfeld & Nicolson, London, 1984, p. 165.

Table 2   The year 2000: two scenarios

| | 1975 GDP per capita (1970 $) | 2000 | | | |
| | | High growth scenario | | Breakdown in North-South relations | |
		GDP per capita (1970 $)	Annual growth in GDP per capita (%)	GDP per capita (1970 $)	Annual growth in GDP per capita (%)
North America	5,080	9,775	2.7	7,780	1.7
Japan	2,870	10,280	6.0	3,590	1.7
European Economic Community	2,752	7,960	4.3	4,730	2.2
Other OECD	1,252	4,170	4.9	2,088	2.0
USSR, Eastern Europe	1,700	5,330	4.7	4,730	4.1
Developing countries, including China	256	860	5.0	656	3.8

Total world output, 1975: $3,800 billion

Total world output, 2000:
High growth scenario: $12,970 billion; annual growth rate of 5.0 per cent
Breakdown in North–South relations: $8,980; annual growth rate of 3.4 per cent

Source: Facing the Future: Mastering the Probable and Managing the Unpredictable (OECD, 1979). Cited in *Rich Country Interests and Third World Development*, ed. R. Cassen, R. Jolly, J. Sewell and Robert Wood, Croom Helm, London, 1982, p. 24.

interrelatedness of the modern world. The economies of advanced societies in the capitalist arena may not *need* the Third World. Nonetheless, the future of the advanced world may well be determined by the manner in which development occurs in the Third World. Our motivation for advocating help in the process of development should be that of fear rather than of generosity. Such a policy seems idealistic, but is in fact *realistic*. In the longer run control of solar energy and in the shorter run possession of nuclear weapons will mean that what happens in the Third World may determine the future of the advanced societies.

Although political wisdom dictates generosity along these lines, it is important to warn Third World countries, if they need warning, that this path is not likely to be taken. Perhaps this is simply because politicians of the advanced societies do not have sufficient steering room to encourage the destruction of old labour-intensive industries, now more suitable to the Third World, so that they may build up a high-technological profile of their own. A more likely explanation is simply that of selfishness, as increases in protectionism, in agriculture, and in industry (most recently American tariffs against Brazilian steel) so clearly demonstrate.

Many of the difficulties that face Third World countries on their path to development are in fact internal, and are not amenable to external treatment. Internal problems must the more urgently be solved if the export of such problems – for this is what the policy of seeking markets abroad rather than developing social infrastructure and social mobilisation at home amounts to – increasingly loses its efficacy. This is not for a moment to say that trade and external relations should somehow be curtailed. But perhaps wisdom for Third World leaders resides in trading more with each other and less with the selfish, unreliable and unimaginative advanced societies of the capitalist world.

Conclusions:
Options and Constraints

This book has sought to map modern social evolution. The rise of the West pioneered human progress in the strongest sense, by combining commerce and liberty in a wholly miraculous manner. Recent social evolution is more problematic. Involvement in the international political and economic forces of the modern world *has* brought progress, but forced development tends to place a liberal political style at a discount. The uncoupling of the commerce *plus* liberty equation may not be absolute in the modern world, as various liberalising options inside Eastern Europe and in certain strong states inside the capitalist part of the Third World indicate. If the overwhelming necessity for centralising politics in the face of modern realities is the fundamental reservation as to the progressive character of modern social evolution, a second doubt has also been voiced. National societies in the advanced capitalist world may be coming to a point where the flexibility they need in the face of international competition is very hard indeed to achieve. This is a very important point because protectionist, beggar-my-neighbour international competition can diminish the size of the world market as a whole in a way that adversely affects development in the Third World. Such policies will not be able to prevent the emergence of industrial power outside Europe, but I fear the social and political dynamite that may be generated if that process of transition is prolonged and vicious.

It is now time to conclude the second part of this book, and indeed to present some conclusion to the whole. The first section addresses the former of these tasks. It does so principally by looking at the three general sources of power that have been distinguished and discussed throughout rather than again considering the three parts of the modern world. This approach encourages concentration on the constraints engendered by the inter-dependency of each part of the modern world; it stresses, as chapters on each of the worlds of modernity could not, that modern society is world society. The section offers conclusions to the whole, and concentrates on options rather more than on constraints. All speculation on the future tends to the polar extremes of gloomy pessimism or optimistic moral uplift, and it is a standard ploy to have both in a single volume. These radical polar alternatives enhance the sex appeal of the prophet involved, but add little to the understanding of reality. A conscious attempt is made here to avoid such posturing. I do not believe that the analysis of social reality should always lead to concrete proposals for policy. Thus when Adam Ferguson criticised Adam Smith (quite wrongly as it happens) on the grounds that *Wealth of Nations* led nowhere, my sympathy is firmly with Smith. Social science is very weak in comparison with natural science. Theory is needed rather than praxis. The point can be made forcibly by reflecting on Marx's career. Would another revolutionary on the barricades really have had anything like the impact of those years of intellectual labour in the British Museum? Intellectuals should confront problems in their work, and I have tried to do so in this book. The second section of this concluding chapter does not contain a list of options for every part of the modern world, hard to achieve given modern independencies, and anyway implied in the first section. Instead it presents options for one part of the advanced world, that of Western Europe, and one of these *is* endorsed and advocated. This policy suggestion follows from the logic of the book, but there is no historic logic as such which says that it will be adopted. The best-laid plans come to grief and mine, perhaps desirable, may well be no exception. Life is hard.

Progress and its Discontents

Political, economic and ideological power have left their mark on the historic record. Each of these types of power have been autonomous over others at particular moments, but no general theorising has been offered as to the circumstances explaining why and in what circumstances such moments of autonomy arise. While continuing to remember both that power has arbitrary and enabling faces and that the sources of power are 'made up' of particular actors, intellectuals, state servants and economic agents of various types, let us begin to account for such 'perfect moments' of autonomy.[1]

Ideological power is based on an ability to pass messages and thereby to unite people over a large geographical area into a community. There are two great autonomous periods of ideology, two great occasions when intellectuals have affected the historic record. The first of these is the

---

1 We can look forward in future years to the third volume of Michael Mann's *Sources of Social Power* which will reflect systematically on this type of issue.

obvious one of the creation of the world religions and ethics. The first part of this book has explained how the monopolists of the word interacted with other elite actors to block or to enable economic development. The second moment of great salience for ideological power occurs when intellectuals can offer great ideologies to explain and organise the speedy transition from the agrarian to the industrial era. This is the world of nationalism, Marxism, Islamic fundamentalism, Comteanism and various combinations of these elements. Such ideologies are not, as might be argued in the spirit of Elie Kedourie,[2] accidents unleashed upon the world by those ideological fanatics who invented such theories. Structural circumstances called for inventiveness. Great ideologies have been called for by the uneven diffusion of industrialism around the globe, and they are probably necessary to make the transition to the industrial age at all. Finally, it is worth reiterating that ideologies have been approached throughout the book in terms of an approach best dubbed 'organisational materialism'. Stress has been laid upon the concrete services that intellectuals can provide at particular points in history. Nevertheless, Weberist arguments have been accepted when this seemed warranted. The impact of Islamic doctrine was given some place in the first part of the book, and one can add to this that making the transition to the industrial age under Marxism meant accepting a doctrine which gives industrial citizens a weak conceptual apparatus to control power thereafter. Similar points may have to be made in the future about national societies that industrialise under the auspices of other, less familiar ideologies.

It is as well to be clear as to a key presupposition at work here. The revival of Islam shows that ideology has great force in the modern world, perhaps sufficient power to decisively affect the future of advanced Western societies. Nevertheless, such power is here restricted to a transitional phase. This *is* deliberate. Max Weber was correct in arguing that modern science, requiring machine-like explanation and attention to empiricism, undermined traditional belief systems but did not, as Comte had fondly hoped, create any new 'positive' beliefs. Science destroys a life world but it cannot create a new one. In the advanced countries we live in a colder world.[3] There is a certain wobbling in my characterisation

---

2 E. Kedourie, *Nationalism*, Hutchinson, London, 1960. For a critique, see E. Gellner, *Nations and Nationalism*, Basil Blackwell, Oxford, 1983.

3 For a more detailed defence of this position, see my 'Habermas and Gellner on epistemology and politics, or need we feel disenchanted?', *Philosophy of Social Sciences*, vol. 12, 1982, and 'The intellectuals as a new class: reflections on the British case', *New Universities Quarterly*, June 1985. I have been influenced here by Ernest Gellner. Disenchantment is *the* central theme of his work, as can be seen in his *Legitimation of Belief*, Cambridge University Press, Cambridge, 1974, and in my discussion of his work in *Diagnoses of Our Time*, Heinemann, London, 1981.

which may well be apparent to the observant reader. Should the absence of a shared ideology be seen as a 'discontent' brought about by progress? Is the passing of the availability of shared ideologies capable of uniting human beings something to be regretted, especially when we recall the lack of cohesion in the liberal polities of advanced capitalist society?[4] That *is* one way of looking at the matter. But one can *joyously* embrace the colder world both for Protestant, Kantian reasons (we are alone, free to make our world), and for reasons of sheer disgust (every neo-salvationist recipe currently on offer is repulsive). My wobble between these alternative assessments scarcely matters as long as the basic point, that total ideologies are no longer available, remains true. One reservation should be made here. Most nation states do possess *one* ideology of importance. They can rely upon their citizens to fight for them, if not because of rabid nationalism then at least because of continuing national loyalty. Yet the world is complex, and even this may change. Perhaps the revival of Islam will create a permanently religiously mobilised society in which ideology will have no end. Perhaps it is further possible that, after a nuclear exchange which the world survives, intellectuals might link citizens, against their states, in a new form of society. These are speculations, however, and neither of them seems in the least plausible. A reservation should, however, be made here. I believe that feminism *is* beginning to succeed in uniting women in an historically novel way; the full implications of it are unclear and indeed are still to be felt.

It is possible to detect evolution within ideological power because all humanity has come to be included in the terms of modern ideologies. The most powerful of these also deserve to be considered 'advanced' because they manage without any religious foundation. In politics, evolution and advance is equally apparent, as is most obvious from the key arm of the state, the modern military. The impact of state competition (via preparation for or participation in war) upon society played in a vital role in the rise of the West, and it unquestionably characterises the world that the West has made. There can be no doubt that war in its classical sense plays a critical role in the evolution of the Third World, as recent conflicts between India and Pakistan, and Vietnam and Kampuchea, very clearly indicate. However, evolution of military affairs is ultimately historically novel because it has endowed two great superpowers with the capacity to destroy humanity (although it has also left them relatively powerless to control allies such as Egypt and India). The rules of the

---

4 Modern social theory is largely dominated by thinkers prone to reject industrial society out of hand, yearning for total meaning. They suffer from, to use Freud's evocative expression, the search for an 'oceanic feeling'. Jürgen Habermas, Alasdair MacIntyre and Charles Taylor leap to mind as instances of this phenomenon.

game played by America and Russia have destroyed the rationality of war. We cannot help but feel discontented with this aspect of progress. At first glance, there seems here to be a resemblance with the evolution of ideological power: both types of power end up by undercutting part of their rationale. Deeper reflection, however, causes some scepticism about any such similarity. Although the recourse to war is now irrational, there is everything to be said for using the traditional concepts devised by the greatest theorist of war, Clausewitz, to understand the signals and gestures that allow the superpowers to communicate with each other.[5] The interesting dilemma that Clausewitz poses for liberal theory has also been noted. Clausewitzian understandings are complex and hard to achieve, and the demand for restraint does not go well with democratic passions. The understandings that exist are the property of enlightened elites in the Soviet Union and in America. In this whole matter, though it would be stupid to be over-sanguine and while it is possible to envisage running the system at a lower level, it is not unreasonable to believe that conflict between the superpowers will *not* occur. For what strikes most is the extent of shared understandings over spheres of influence, warning signals and so on, and the ability to manage rationally a two-power system. In contrast, the thought of nuclear proliferation is altogether terrifying. In pure strategic theory, the possession of a few nuclear weapons, say, of first-strike capacity only, is dangerous and irrational: knowing one's enemy *must* launch first forces a necessary pre-emptive strike. Theories are only much good if their terms of reference are shared. There is some doubt as to whether Russia shares American strategic thinking: it apparently doubts (with good reason!) that a nuclear exchange could be limited to any one level. Nevertheless, the superpowers are unquestionably involved in the same sort of game. A Third World power actually prepared to use a nuclear weapon, perhaps transported by hand to a foreign capital, and so to break the rules of the game completely would have tremendous power of blackmail. Just as the ideological passions of the Third World may determine the future of the West, so too may its capacity for military/political blackmail. The two factors reinforce each other.

What of internal politics? Here there has been a massive increase in the power of the state. This is clearly visible in the ability of modern states to penetrate and organise their society, to do away with those laterally insulated groupings that characterised the model of the agro-literate polity. Modern revolutions involve the creation of societies that do begin to accord with the sense of classical sociological theory.

5 A brilliant defence of this position is contained in R. Aron, *Clausewitz*, Routledge & Kegan Paul, London, 1983.

Nevertheless, this should not be exaggerated and the concept of liberties continues to give us much purchase in modern conditions. A part of the uniqueness of the West lay in the capacity of different social actors, strongly organised and in possession of rights, to co-operate willingly rather than to oppose each other in some sort of power stand-off. Modern Western societies seem to be facing a situation in which a power-stand-off is being created between key groups, and the internal politics of these societies revolve around ways in which this rigidity can be avoided. This steering problem may be resolved at a superficial level by the capacity of the state to discipline particular groups, most obviously its working class. Yet this is no *real* solution. Late industrial society, even more than early capitalist Europe, needs the voluntary participation of its citizens, and the removal of liberties may bring order without efficiency. The problem of maintaining social flexibility *together with* high citizen participation ratio is shared by Eastern and Western variants of industrialism. Certain arguments about potential strategies have been noted, but the key fact of the current situation remains that nobody possesses a recipe to ensure openness in combination with efficiency.

Finally, let us turn to economic power. Here the expansion of human power is obvious and fabulous, and the creation of industrialism remains the most important fact about the modern world as a whole. Our discussion has been of the two means of running the industrial/political economy, and of routes to industrialisation in the developing world. Nevertheless, the industrial society theorists were criticised in one fundamental way: the dynamism of the modern industrial world remains that of the international market, that is of international capitalist relationships. This economic competition brings progress, not least to the Third World, and the price of progress remains the absence of a tranquil life. That price tag seems to be worth paying in the eyes of most people, except for those intellectuals hostile to modernity – not that any but the largest and most self-sufficient have much option other than to accept the price tag whether they wish to or not.

It is important to be specific as to what exactly is being claimed. The rise of the West involved a complex interaction between capital and nation. Capitalist society was larger than and consequently constrained nation states. Furthermore, the absence of a single controlling polity was a necessary condition for the existence of capitalism, and competition between states greatly affected, often beneficially, the fortunes of the capitalists of particular national societies. Has all this changed in the modern world? It is sometimes claimed that the vast increases in state power already noted extend everywhere. It *is* the modern nation, rather than some larger cultural organisation, which gives people their identity. It is true that a certain nationalisation of economic life has occurred, and this is beautifully captured by the presence of multinationals owned by particular nation states. Yet the fundamental situation in economic matters remains the same. Capitalist society is still larger than national societies and competition in that society calls for the removal of internal social rigidities more urgently than ever. There is a whole series of issues here about which we have as yet far too little evidence, and I still find it difficult to adopt a consistent language when discussing them. To what extent do the owners and managers of various multinationals continue to have loyalty to the state to which they repatriate their profits? We do not really know the answer to this fascinating question, and it is time we tried to discover the truth of the matter.

Certain worries about the workings of the modern international economy have been expressed. They centre less upon 'discontents' with progress than upon fears that the political economy may not work so as to provide the goodies that are possible. An international economic system can operate at a zero-sum level or at a higher level in which a growing cake allows for all to share in a more general prosperity. The modern international economy is American-dominated, and that domination is currently causing the capitalist system to run on a zero-sum basis. The abuse of leadership is seen by Europe in the inflation that the United States has passed on, but it is apparent to the whole world, catastrophically so in the developing sections of the world economy, in the high interest rates employed by President Reagan to protect the American dollar. Any change is likely to be towards protectionism and this will scarcely improve matters, especially for the Third World.

There are important and difficult questions that follow from this, and clear answers to these would make our immediate futures that much more certain. The most notable such question is whether capitalist society is bigger even than the United States. Some considerations, notably that 'American' international banks and corporations are prepared to speculate against the dollar, suggest a positive answer; others, especially that the American state has guarded against – and will probably continue to – a banking collapse, lead to a more negative assessment. It is *impossible* to judge, for the situation is new and volatile. Nobody is yet sure how America's new debtor status will affect the modern world. My guess has been that American military power will enable it to claim and to abuse leadership of the economic system for a considerable, and dangerous, period.

One conclusion is forced upon us, and it leads to the final section. Developing countries suffer from high interest rates and are otherwise ignored by advanced nations within the capitalist world. Only five advanced nations are spending more than 0.7 per cent of their GNP on aid to the Third World. This is bound to create resentment. The developing part of the world has ideological force and military means, and to this we must now add a resentment currently being enhanced by the advanced societies, most notably by American policies but with the European Community lagging not far behind the superpower in its protectionist drive. This is a situation full of social dynamite. Two general and abstract considerations suggest themselves. Firstly, the international market needs to be *depoliticised*. The distortions to the market imposed by American leadership need to be changed. Secondly, however, long-term political wisdom would suggest that the terms on which the international market works need to be changed. The international market should be *politicised* so as to allow the period of transition to development to be less painful. The most important of such changes would be in international monetary policy, the deflationary style of the International Monetary Fund, the opening of markets to the Third World, and in terms of trade as a whole. Is it possible to establish such changes? Let us turn to matters of policy, and concentrate our attention on the options, rather than on the constraints, that face us.

The Decline of the West: a European Perspective

Several facets of the situation facing modern Europe have already been sketched in. European nations exist within a larger context comprised of international political competition, and they inhabit that section of the world dominated by international capitalism, itself led by one great power, largely because of its military strength. The involvement of European national societies within this larger society means that, to be blunt, no single nation can act without regard to these international constraints, and is certainly in no position to change the terms of constraint. The question that concerns us is whether a more unified Europe might be able to do what is beyond the power of any single European nation.

It is as well to admit that the history of concerted European action does not give rise to much optimism as to an alternative strategy. The European Community evidences a measure of economic co-operation, but it has signally failed to destroy national autonomies and create a genuinely unified organisation. The community is *international*. It is a place where heads of nations meet to bargain about their different national interests. It is not genuinely a *transnational* phenomenon. The fact of disunity is one important reason why the United States has been able to continue to treat these European states as its clients through a policy of divide and rule, even after they have gained very remarkable economic strength. Is the situation changing in front of our eyes? Militarily, the difference in perception of interests, always present but revitalised by the debate around the introduction of theatre nuclear weapons, has gained in salience. This led recently to a meeting of European members of NATO at which European plans for defence were discussed; the exclusion of an American representative is unprecedented and would have been unthinkable some years ago. Economic differences, essentially resulting from the failure of the United States to balance its budget, have been emphasised. It is worth reiterating that in American eyes there remains a link between these economic difficulties and its military role. The United States still sees its abuse of the international market as the price for the umbrella of defence it casts over Europe. Nevertheless, here too an increase in acrimony is obvious, and the strengthening of the European Monetary System together with increased European banking in Deutschmarks is witness to this. Concentrated European raids on the dollar are striking, perhaps hugely significant. Finally, the political divergence between the superpower and its European allies is now considerable, since most key events – the Arab-Israeli conflict, the Third World, and the need for detente towards Eastern Europe – are perceived through very different lenses.

In this situation, one of two options is to do nothing. There are sophisticated reasons for adopting this position. The most subtle rationale argues that, to use Sir Robert Walpole's phrase, it is best to 'let sleeping dogs lie'. Europe caused two great conflagrations in the twentieth century, and perhaps the world would benefit from it taking a back seat in world history for some considerable period. Moreover, it is added, those prophets of doom who predicted great disturbance as the result of the ending of dollar convertibility to gold in 1971 have been proved wrong. The system has survived, somewhat poorly perhaps, although considering the huge problems it had to face, survival is not to be lightly dismissed. The world has been safe in American hands, the argument continues, and if the cost of the Pax Americana is now slightly higher, it remains more rational to live with the devil one knows than to unleash new and untried forces.

This is a powerful case, especially in its call to understand carefully what it is that we might do. I do *not* fully understand the logic of the situation that I recommend, and therefore advocate the second option with some caution. It needs much more thought and consideration. However, there are two striking reasons why fundamental change is necessary. Firstly, the military/political competition between the superpowers is supremely dangerous, and any way in which the competition can be made to run at a lower level ought to be adopted. What is most worrying, in the last analysis, is the fears of the Soviet Union that it is being encircled, especially as these fears block liberalisation and encourage the retention of a bunker mentality among the Soviet elite. The second option would allow for some contribution to relieving these tensions, and also to making Europe itself slightly safer (even though fears of it being used as a nuclear battlefield have been exaggerated). Secondly, stepping back from the flux of history allows us to see the decline of the West over the last 50 years. In one sense, this decline is something to welcome, for it means that there has been significant evolution elsewhere, and there is no reason in principle why, to consider the economic sphere, a falling share of world trade should lead to regression of any sort. Nevertheless, there are unique elements of permanent historical value about Western civilisation. The most fundamental of these is a concern with liberal political rule. If the transition to the modern world is made more painful than it must necessarily be anyway, the fate of the world may be grim indeed, and there will certainly be few chances of the liberal inheritance proving important elsewhere. Modern American policy runs the world economy as a zero-sum game, and the Third World, even more than Europe, suffers in consequence. It should be stressed that the European Community is also essentially a single protectionist block, and it has little to congratulate itself on in its own relationship with the Third World. Nevertheless, the second option may be able to contribute to the transitional problems of the Third World.

The policy option at issue centres upon Europe taking control of its own destiny. The nations in this powerful economic area could cease to be the clients of a superpower, and could become a collective historical actor. The advocacy of this position should not be seen as crude anti-Americanism. There is every reason to be appreciative of the services of the United States since the Second World War, most notably in the form of the Marshall Plan. In historical terms this superpower has, despite significant blemishes on its record, a very significant record of success and achievement. Moreover, American criticisms of Europe seem to me essentially justified. If Europe does not have its own defence it will *deservedly* continue to be treated occasionally in an off-hand manner for the brute reason that it *is* a client of a great power. There is justification too to bemusement in Washington at the demand for a balanced American budget since American Keynesianism under Reagan has been responsible for much of the recent improvement in the world economy.[6] However, the United States *is* overextended militarily, and this is having extremely deleterious effects upon its economy. A diminution of respon-

---

6 Europeans would be wrong to ask for deflationary measures; but a budget can also be balanced by raising taxes, and they are right to ask for this.

sibility for Europe would help the American economy, and this is desirable since it would help to create a more stable world order.

Change will not come from the United States. It cannot see beyond the fact of its own supremacy, and there is no reason whatever to imagine that it will relinquish this without autonomous actions by Europeans. Such action is in the interests of Europe and America. Crucially, however, it can be made to help the Third World. And here a moment of anti-Americanism is in order. It has been argued that the Third World would benefit both from *depoliticising* the world economy of American influence, and *politicising* it so as to systematically favour the developing societies. There is insufficient evidence here to be certain, but it seems to be the case that America, a state overwhelmingly influenced by capitalism in economic life, would systematically oppose the latter as well as the former. It is, for example, hard to imagine the United States really gaining firm control of its 'international' banks.

The second option has two elements. Firstly, European control of its economic destiny can only be achieved by creating a European defence system. There is uncertainty as to whether such a defence capacity could be non-nuclear, but defence would be possible without the presence of American nuclear weapons. This autonomy would allow proper control of the European economy. It would allow for detente with the Soviet Union of a more extensive type. The Soviet Union needs troops to be able to control its client states, and there is *no* likelihood of this changing. However, the Soviet Union might well be prepared to limit both conventional and nuclear forces if it did not feel threatened by American missiles inside Europe. Such a European policy would require co-operation not just of European states in NATO, nor of those in the EEC but those of Scandinavia as well. Such internationalism will be extremely hard to achieve, and much intellectual labour is needed on the exact character of European defences, but this first element is graspable and achievable.[7]

The second element will be the more difficult to achieve, but it seems to me the more important of the two. The autonomy of Europe should be used to open the door to the imports of the Third World, change terms of trade to encourage their development, and lend money in a manner that does not require the deflationary policies beloved of the International Monetary Fund. Europe should encourage the creation of rules of the international economy that serve political wisdom rather than simply the interests of capital. The laws of economics should be varied to serve our

7 M. Mann, 'Nationalism and internationalism: a critique of economic and defence policies' in J.A.G. Griffiths (ed.) *Socialism in a Cold Climate*, George Allen & Unwin, London, 1983. I am influenced by, but in debate with, this argument.

political goals. The dialectic of nation and capital should systematically be tilted towards the former. The period of transition to development is creating social dynamite dangerous to the modern world as a whole, and anything that can be done to diminish this is profoundly to be recommended. Political leaders need to think of the long term rather than the short term, especially as there may be a systematic conflict between the two. This openness to the world economy requires great flexibility in national societies, and this is obviously, indeed notoriously, hard to achieve. Nevertheless, the future of the advanced societies must lie with high-technology goods for the Third World will eventually become adept at making most of the goods in which we currently specialise. Policies are needed which kill off ailing industries fast, and invest in new ones in their place; industrial policy must concern itself with regeneration rather than with protectionist propping up of lame ducks. There is a Machiavellian wisdom in all this. If we remain flexible, avoid 'errors in police' to use Adam Smith's expression, there is no reason why we should face economic decline; nor is there any reason to believe that continued supremacy would be at the expense of the Third World. We can serve them and ourselves. I am not in possession of a secret recipe as to how the social flexibility that this requires is to be achieved, nor do I think it will be easy for national economic interests to be submerged in a conception of common European aims. But if the relationship of nation to capital is to be varied, then nations themselves must first learn the art of co-operation. Some comments have been offered already as to the variety of routes that seem to be currently taken in attempts to achieve this end. It seems to me likely that any increase in flexibility will have to be brought about by integrating those who lose as a result of involvement in international economic relations.

This second option deserves summary. We need to accept openness to the capitalist world market for socialist reasons (for why should only the members of a single nation alone be considered worthy?) and socialistic measures internally for capitalist reasons (without national cohesion based on voluntary citizen participation a modern nation cannot compete in that larger capitalist society). Interestingly and ironically, this prescription is the exact opposite of the current practice of the Conservative government of Mrs Thatcher.

These are policy suggestions, but they are offered with caution because of limited knowledge and the difficulty inherent in thinking through a volatile situation. One point can, however, be made without reservation. We will need more philosophic history if we are to understand our options and to control our destiny. We need to think, urgently and deeply.

Bibliographical Essay

Anyone wishing to approach historical sociology for the first time should not neglect classics of the past which, when read rather than ritually cited, retain all their capacity to excite and astonish. Adam Smith, *Wealth of Nations* (Oxford University Press, Oxford, 1976), David Hume, *Essays Moral Political and Literary* (Longman, London, 1875) and Edward Gibbon, *The Decline and Fall of the Roman Empire* (Dent, London, 1905) should not be forgotten; they are well introduced by D. Winch, *Adam Smith's Politics* (Cambridge University Press, Cambridge, 1978), D. Forbes, *Hume's Philosophical Politics* (Cambridge University Press, Cambridge, 1975) and J. Burrow, *Edward Gibbon* (Oxford University Press, Oxford, 1985). Equally important, of course are the works of Marx and Max Weber which we know at once better and less well; A. Gidden's *Capitalism and Modern Social Theory* (Cambridge University Press, Cambridge, 1971) remains a distinguished introduction to their thought. Despite the decline in the popularity of philosophic history, there are modern historical sociologists of great verve and power, and the following should not be missed: M. Mann, *The Sources of Social Power* (Cambridge University Press, Cambridge, vol. 1, 1986, vols 2 and 3 to follow); the work of W.H. McNeill in general, especially his classic *Rise of the West* (Chicago University Press, Chicago, 1963); P. Anderson, *Passages from Antiquity to Feudalism* and *Lineages of the Absolutist State* (New Left Books, London, 1974); F. Braudel, *Capitalism and Material Life: 1400–1800* (Methuen, London, 1967); J. Baechler, *The Origins of Capitalism* (Basil Blackwell, Oxford, 1975); the work of B. Moore as a whole, especially *Social Origins of Dictatorship and Democracy* (Penguin, London, 1969); and T. Skocpol, *States and Social Revolutions* (Cambridge University Press, Cambridge, 1979).

Beyond these philosophic histories, a historical sociologist approaching the agrarian era is better advised to consult and think about detailed historical monographs than to rely on synoptic views presented by historians; extraordinary richness is to be discovered by means of this approach. The works on which I have principally relied are noted in the first half of this book, but some comments may still be of use. M. Elvin, *The Pattern of the Chinese Past* (Stanford University Press, Stanford, 1973) is fundamental, but marvellous insights are contained in studies of Chinese taxation, most notably in R. Huang, *Taxation and Governmental Finance in Sixteenth Century Ming China* (Cambridge University Press, Cambridge, 1974). Although studying the state makes sense in China, it has much less relevance in India and Islam; the works of modern anthropologists in these civilisations are correspondingly of greater importance: L. Dumont's *Homo Hierarchus* (Weidenfeld and Nicolson, London, 1957) and *Religion/Politics and History in India* (Mouton, The Hague, 1957) are classics of modern Indology, and E. Gellner's *Muslim Society* (Cambridge University Press, Cambridge, 1981) is an exhilarating interpretation of Islam, which brings to life Ibn Khaldun's great *Muqaddimah* (Routledge and Kegan Paul, London, 1978). It is likely that Indology will always be relatively backward given the state of its source material. More can be hoped for from Islamicists, and path-breaking work has been performed by P. Crone and M. Cook, notably in *Hagarism* (Cambridge University Press, Cambridge, 1977), P. Crone, *Slaves on Horses* (Cambridge University Press, Cambridge, 1980), M. Crook, *Muhammad* (Oxford University Press, Oxford, 1983) and several forthcoming works by P. Crone. The literature on the West is immense, high-powered and exciting. Those concerned with the origins of modern Europe should consult the works of M. Finley, especially his *Ancient Economy* (Chatto and Windus, London, 1973); K. Hopkins, *Conquerors and Slaves* (Cambridge University Press, Cambridge, 1978) and *Death and Renewal* (Cambridge University Press, Cambridge, 1983); G. de Ste Croix's magnificent and idiosyncratic *Class Struggles in the Ancient Greek World* (Duckworth, London, 1981); and P. Brown, *St. Augustine* (Faber, London, 1967) and *The World of Late Antiquity* (Thames and Hudson, London, 1971). Important works on the medieval and early modern European world include: J. Goody's marvellous example of the 'historical turn' of modern British social anthropology, *The Development of the Family and Marriage in Europe* (Cambridge University Press, Cambridge, 1983); M.M. Postan, *Medieval Economy and Society* (Penguin Books, Harmondsworth, 1972); G. Duby, *The Early Growth of the European Economy* (Weidenfeld and Nicolson, London, 1975); *The Formation of National States in Western Europe* (Princeton University Press, Princeton, 1975), a distinguished, inter-related collection of articles edited by C. Tilly; P. Burke, *Tradition and Innovation in Renaissance Italy* (Fontana, London, 1974); and E. le Roy Ladurie, *Montaillou*

(Scolar Press, London, 1978). E.L. Jones, *The European Miracle* (Cambridge University Press, Cambridge, 1981) strikingly compares world civilisations. Basil Blackwell will publish the proceedings of a conference dealing with the rise of the West in comparative perspective, and this will be edited by M. Mann, J. Baechler and J.A. Hall.

The literature on the modern world is vast, but a few comments are in order. P. Wiles, *Economic Institutions Compared* (Basil Blackwell, Oxford, 1977) is a general interpretation of great power. The works of R. Aron retain importance, most notably *Democracy and Totalitarianism* (Weidenfeld and Nicolson, London, 1968), *Imperial Republic* (Weidenfeld and Nicolson, London, 1978) and *Clausewitz* (Routledge and Kegan Paul, London, 1983). E. Gellner, *Nations and Nationalism* (Basil Blackwell, Oxford, 1983) offers an explanation of nationalism and this is critically assessed by A.D. Smith in *Theories of Nationalism* (Duckworth, London, 1981). There are many works now that argue for the controlling power of the international market over the destiny of national states, but a classic remains I. Wallerstein, *The Modern World System* (Academic Press, New York, 1974). T. Skocpol's *States and Social Revolutions* (Cambridge University Press, Cambridge, 1979) adds an understanding of international political pressures to this. Skocpol argues that international pressures constrain rather than control, allowing a measure of autonomy for states; this position is expounded at a theoretical level by M. Olson in *The Rise and Decline of Nations* (Yale University Press, New Haven, 1982) and in greater empirical detail in J.H. Goldthorpe (ed.), *Order and Conflict in Contemporary Capitalism* (Oxford University Press, Oxford, 1984), a collection which is also of great use in assessing the nature of corporatism. We know far too little as yet about the role of America as a leading economic and military power, and of the inter-relationships between these sources of power, but the works of D. Calleo, notably *The Imperious Economy* (Harvard University Press, Cambridge, Massachusetts, 1982), are a good place to begin any assessment. M. Moffitt, *The World's Money* (Michael Joseph, London, 1984) and L. Tsoukalis (ed.), *The Political Economy of International Money* (Sage, London, 1985) are important treatments of a volatile but vital matter. Those wishing to think about the West will benefit from general and philosophical works such as F. Hirsch, *Social Limits to Growth* (Routledge and Kegan Paul, London, 1977); A. Ellis and K. Kumar (eds), *Dilemmas of Liberal Democracies* (Methuen, London, 1983) presents various representative views on Hirsch's thesis. But a full understanding of the West can only be arrived at through an awareness of different national historical patterns. The same point holds true for the socialist bloc. D. Holloway, *The Soviet Union and the Arms Race* (Yale University Press, New Haven, 1983), S. Cohen, *Bukharin and the Russian Revolution*

(Oxford University Press, Oxford, 1980) and the debate between E. Gellner and R. Aron in *Government and Opposition* (vol. XIV, 1979) should be consulted, however, in order that the general forces at work may be appreciated. Finally it is important to note that our understanding of the situation of the Third World is still at a most unsatisfactory stage. Here too an appreciation of differences is vital. For the general issues at stake, B. Warren, *Imperialism; Pioneer of Capitalism* (New Left Books, London, 1982) remains an exciting and powerful study.

Index

Abbasid, 89–91, 103
absolutism, 160
Achebe, 219
Africa, 27, 211, 212, 223
agrarian society, 5–6, 18, 27–32, 151–2, 218
Akbar, 105–6
Alfonsin, 8, 242
Algeria, 215, 218
Ali, 87
Allende, 225, 229, 242
Almohad, 90
Almoravid, 90
Althusser, 173
Ambrose, 117, 119
America, *see* USA
Anderson, 97, 104, 107, 129, 130
Andropov, 200, 210
anti-society, 80, 118
Arabs, 86–91, 94, 183
arbitrariness, *see* power, blocking
Argentina, 8, 224, 240, 242, 243, 244
Arius, 118–20
arms race, 210–13
Aron, 4, 9, 156–7, 206–9, 220, 229, 230, 233
Arthashastra, 66, 77
Aryans, 58, 59–63, 91, 120
Asoka, 66–7, 68
Atlanticism, 180–1
Augustine, 117–19

Aurangzeb, 106
Austria, 207
Ayatollah Khomeini, 8, 235
Ayer, 45

Bacon, F., 6
Bacon, R., 122
Basques, 169
Belgium, 148, 165
Bell, 7
Berbers, 94, 217
Berlin, 4, 9
Bernier, 72
Bethlen, 198
Bhagavad Ghita, 72
Bismarck, 164
bolshevik, 171, 174, 192, 207, 213, 233
Brahman, 31, 58, 61, 62, 64–77, 80, 83, 91, 110, 126, 142–4
Brahmanas, 62, 63
Brazil, 188, 240, 241, 242, 243, 244, 247
Brenner, 129–30
Bretton Woods, 180
Brezhnev, 210
Britain, 8, 15, 16, 42, 62, 160–3, 170, 175–9, 187–8, 220
Buddhism, 28, 39, 40, 52, 59, 64–70, 82, 113, 119, 131
budget deficit of America, *see* USA

Bukharin, 193–4, 195, 196
bureaucracy, 36, 38–57, 88, 90, 97,
  139, 151, 152, 240
Burke, 20, 161
Buyid, 90
Byzantium, 16, 87, 120, 133

Caesaropapism, 62, 89, 118, 120, 133,
  135
Calleo, 182, 184–6
capital flight, 178, 179, 245
capitalism, 14, 17, 33, 45–54, 81,
  99–103, 109, 151, 153–5, 158–88,
  189, 207–8, 223–48, 249, 250,
  254–60
Caribbean, 216
Carthage, 86
caste, 58, 59–63, 73, 74, 78–83, 91
Catalans, 169
centralisation, 151
Ceylon, 70
Charlemagne, 124, 126, 131, 134
Charles the Bald, 127
Che Guevara, 236
Cheka, *see* KGB
Chêng–Ho, 50
Chernenko, 210
Chiang Kai–Shek, 168, 193, 234
Chile, 225, 229, 238
Chi'n, 33, 36, 40
China, 12, 16, 18, 28, 30, 33–57, 59,
  62, 66, 68, 69, 70, 82, 87, 92, 94–5,
  102, 109, 112–13, 114, 116, 120,
  123, 128, 129, 132, 133, 134, 135,
  149, 152, 166, 193, 214–15, 217,
  233–34, 237
Chinese script, 40
Chou, 35
Christianity, 14, 18, 20, 21, 28, 30, 44,
  52, 53, 60, 67, 72, 78, 79–80, 93,
  95, 97, 99, 102, 111–44, 158
circulation of elite, 93–8, 102
cities, 47, 48, 49, 61, 64, 92–4, 126,
  129, 136, 159

citizenship, 166, 171–9
civil society, 137, 170, 190
class and class struggle, 10–14, 31–2,
  44, 92, 153–4, 155, 162–79, 195,
  197–8, 204, 217, 220
class, working, 153–4, 162–79, 202–3,
  208
Clausewitz, 161, 165, 182, 212, 235,
  253
collectivisation, 156, 160, 193–4,
  198–202
Combination Acts, 162
commerce, *see* capitalism; merchants
Common Agricultural Policy, 227
community, 21, 79–80, 83, 86, 162
competition, 56, 148, 175, 178, 189
competition, economic, *see* capitalism
competition, military, 46–7, 56, 64,
  102–3, 133–40, 154, 160, 162, 164,
  189, 193–4, 210–13
Comte, 150, 251
Confucius and confucianism, 21,
  38–45, 69, 135, 139, 187, 240
Connally, 181
Constantine, 117–18
convergence, 152–3
corporatism, 178–9
Crimea, 166, 191
Cuba, 236–7
Czechoslovakia, 190, 200–1, 206, 208

Dahrendorf, 171–2, 175
Danegeld, 173, 176
Dasas, 60
Decembrists, 190
deflation, 174, 176–7
democracy, 152, 161, 165, 177–9,
  182, 187
Denmark, 148, 239
dependency, 15, 216, 223–48
Deutschmark, 184, 257
development, forced, 148, 155–7,
  163–70, 203
devshirme, 107

Diocletian, 122, 117
disenchantment, *see* rationalisation
division of labour, 61, 78, 150, 218
Djilas, 204
dollar, 180–6, 243–7, 255, 257
Domesday Book, 120–3
Donatism, 118–19
Dostoyevsky, 191
Dumont, 58, 67, 68, 69, 71
Durkheim, 1, 29, 70, 75, 79, 89, 125, 176
dynastic cycle, 42–3, 55

Ebionite, 116
ecology, 33, 68, 92, 99, 111
education, 151–2, 177, 218–19
Edward I, 129, 138
EEC, 147, 170, 180, 183, 227, 259
Egypt, 18, 86, 98, 113, 214, 238, 252
Eire, 222
empire, 14–15, 33–57, 64–70, 74, 97, 102, 135–6, 210–13
Engel, 34
Engels, 121, 192
equality, 18, 80, 88, 129, 143, 201
Ethiopia, 215
eunuchs, 42, 50
Europe, Eastern, *see* state socialism
Europe, Western, 158–88, 225–9, 256–60
Eusebius, 118
evolution, 17–19, 147–57, 188, 249, 249–55

Falklands, 8
fascism, 4, 163–70, 114
Fatimid, 90, 98
Ferge, 204–5
Ferguson, 250
feudalism, 11, 13–14, 31, 35–6, 38, 43, 74, 81, 83, 126–8, 164
Finland, 239
First World War, 165, 191, 223
Forster, 219

fourth world, 215
France, 13, 42, 52, 138, 139, 157, 160–1, 188, 191, 217, 219, 223, 224
Franco, 169–70
Frederick II, 161
free trade, 164, 179
Fulbright, 230

Galbraith, 171
Galtieri, 8
Gandhi, 59, 74, 78, 219
GATT, 147
Geary, 162, 164–6
Gellner, 28–9, 36, 39, 92, 116, 151, 206–9, 217, 240, 251–2, 253
gentry, 37, 39, 41–4, 51, 55
Germany, 42, 156–7, 163–70, 177, 179, 180, 181, 187, 188, 189, 191, 195, 196, 199, 200, 201, 202, 209, 216, 223, 232, 240
ghost acres, 99
Gibbon, 14, 119
Gierek, 202
Gneisenau, 161
gnostic, 72, 116
Gomulka, 202
Goody, 131–2
Gorbachov, 200
Grand Canal, 36, 49
Great Wall, 36, 82
Greece, 31, 92, 113, 114, 207, 224
Green Revolution, 239
Guatemala, 238
gunpowder, 19, 33, 47, 91, 103–9, 112–13

Hagar, 87
Han, 33, 36, 38
Hardenburg, 161
Hegel, 5, 12
hierarchy, 61, 78–80, 151, 152, 161–2, 175
Hinduism, 9, 21, 30, 59, 63, 72–7, 105, 125, 129

Hirsch, 187
historical materialism, *see* Marxism
Hitler, 1, 134, 167–8, 196, 200
Hobbes, 121
Hobson, 229
Hodgson, 90–1, 103–4
Holland, 16, 187
Horthy, 198
Hume, 3, 8, 13, 14, 15, 16, 21, 142,
    158–62, 163, 173, 174, 186, 203,
    224
Hungary, 190, 192, 197–200, 207,
    208–9, 210, 237
hunters and gatherers, 17, 27
Husak, 201

IBM, 225
Ibn Khaldun, 9, 91–8, 102, 105, 107
idealism 20, 74
ideology, *see* power, ideological
IMF, 178, 180, 245, 256, 259
imperialism, 10, 168, 223–31
India, 15, 16, 18, 28, 58–83, 91, 103,
    104–6, 112, 120, 121, 132, 142–4,
    239, 252
Indonesia, 215
Indus, 59–60, 86
industrial society, 5–6, 18, 147–57,
    159, 171, 177, 190–5, 206–7,
    208–9, 254
inflation, 167, 175, 176, 181, 183
intellectuals, *see* power, ideological
interest rates, *see* dollar
internal colonialism, 143
international indebtedness, *see* dollar
inventions, 19, 33, 121–3
iqta, 91, 99
Iran, 86, 225, 235
Iraq, 85, 90, 98, 235
irrigation, 27–8, 36, 60, 76, 90, 111
Islam, 16, 17, 18, 21, 30, 60, 62, 72,
    80, 84–110, 112, 121, 125, 132,
    134, 142–4, 169, 234–6, 251, 252

Italy, 168, 187
ITT, 229

Jainism, 65, 72
Japan, 166, 177, 179, 187, 189, 191,
    221, 233, 240
Jaraszelski, 203
Jenkins, 175
Jesus, 115, 116, 118
Jews, 113, 115, 116, 164, 191, 198,
    229
Johnson, 13
Julian, 114, 119

Kadar, 199–200, 201, 203
Kama Sutra, 73
Kamenev, 196
Kampuchea, 237, 252
Kant, 252
Kasatriya, 61
Katyn, 202
Kautilya, 66, 77
Kedourie, 251
Keynes, 143, 160, 167, 171–9, 180,
    198, 258
KGB, 196
Khruschev, 190, 197, 210
kingship, 63, 69, 76–7, 80, 127, 135
kinship, 41, 63, 64, 67, 87, 88, 101,
    129–32, 135
Kirov, 194
Kissinger, 181, 184, 236
Kohl, 176
Kolakowski, 202
Konrad, 204
KOR, 203
Koran, 84
Kun, 198

Labour Party, 163, 175, 178
laissez–faire, 13, 154–5
landlord, 30, 41, 42–3, 44, 48, 54,
    55–6, 73, 80–3, 99–100, 108,

112–13, 126–8, 130, 160, 164, 190–1, 233, 241
land use, 122
Latin America, 156, 170, 240–5, 246, 247
Lattimore, 36
law, 13, 82, 101, 113, 127, 132, 138
Laws of Manu, 73
Lebensraum, 224
legalism, 40
Lenin, 11, 165, 166, 196, 223, 224
Lewis, 107
liberal, 23, 93–4, 144, 148, 154–5, 158–88, 189, 202–10, 241–5, 249, 254
liberalisation, 8, 157, 200, 203–9, 212, 213, 241–5, 258
liberties, 23, 147, 158–9, 176, 187, 188
literacy, *see* power, ideological
Luxembourg, 223, 224

Machonin, 200
MacIntyre, 187
McNeill, 16, 139
Magadha, 64, 66
Maghreb, 90, 97, 113
Mamluks, 90, 100, 107
Manchu, 33, 43, 53
mandarins, 40–57, 72, 114, 174
Manichean, 113, 114
Mann, 19, 36–7, 44, 75, 140
Mannheim, 198
Marcuse, 173
market, *see* capitalism
Marshall Plan, 180, 181, 225, 258
Marx, 1, 3, 4, 8, 9–14, 15, 17, 18, 35, 38, 59, 74, 89, 142, 165, 175, 192, 217, 250
Marxism, 4, 5–6, 7, 8, 9–14, 21–2, 31–2, 34–5, 37, 38, 44, 92, 128–30, 153–4, 165–6, 168, 169, 175, 192, 193–7, 205, 206, 221, 223–31, 234, 251

Mauryans, 59, 62, 66, 68, 77
Mecca, 86
Medina, 86
Mediterranean, 28, 37, 91, 99, 112
Megasthenes, 73
merchants, 46, 48, 49, 50, 64, 80–2, 93–4, 95, 102, 112–13, 124, 136
Merquior, 241
Mesopotamia, 86, 91
Mexico, 240, 243
middle class, 163, 164–70
militarism, *see* power, military
Ming, 33, 41, 42, 50, 52–3, 55, 126
Mithraism, 114
Mitterand, 177
mode of production, 5–6, 11, 12, 31
monasteries, 52, 69, 82, 132
monetarism, 176
Mongol, 33, 43, 45, 46, 92, 98, 100, 107, 120
monopoly, 54
monotheism, *see* world religions
Montagne, 92, 96
Montesquieu, 13
Moore, 1, 148, 150–1, 156, 162, 229, 230
Mossadeq, 225
Mugabe, 222
Mughals, 59, 105
Muhammad, 85–7
multipolarity, *see* competition, military

Nagy, 199
Nandas, 62, 66
Napoleon, 134, 161, 164, 190, 228
nationalism, 4, 148, 169, 201, 202, 211–23, 239
nation-building, 148, 164, 217–23
nations, 138, 154, 178–9, 249, 254–5
NATO, 147, 180–6, 257, 259
nazism, *see* fascism
Needham, 49
Nehru, 215

New Economic Policy, 192–4
Nicaragua, 241
Nietzsche, 150
Nigeria, 215, 218, 221, 238
Nixon, 181, 183, 184, 185, 229, 236
Nkrumah, 219
nomads, *see* pastoralists
North-West Frontier, 58, 82
nuclear weapons, 182, 247, 253, 259
Nuremburg, 187

Obshchina, 191
occupational structure, 172, 198
oil crisis, 175, 176
Olson, 6
Omayyad, 90
OPEC, 228, 243
oriental societies, 11–14, 35, 203
Ottomans, 91, 97, 100, 104–9

Pal, 204–5
passions, how to control, 13, 173–4
Pasternak, 192
pastoralists, 18, 30, 36, 43, 46, 50, 60,
    84–110, 112
Paul, 116
Pax Americana, 179–86
peasants, 27–8, 30, 36, 42, 43, 44, 53,
    55, 81, 100, 113, 121–2, 128–30,
    149–50, 153, 159–60, 190–4
persecution, 117, 118
Persia, 16, 28, 58, 87, 98, 103, 104–5,
    112
Petronius, 114
Philip II, 136, 139
philosophy of history, 3–23, 35–6, 92
Pilsudski, 201
Pirenne, 3
plough, 60, 121–2
Poland, 140, 190, 201–3, 209, 232
Popper, 4, 5–6, 9, 50
population, 54–6, 123, 131, 214–15
populism, 191, 221, 234

positivism, 150
Postan, 129–30
post-capitalism, 172
power, 22–3, 30, 147, 160, 249–56;
    blocking, 23, 31, 34, 55, 77, 78, 80,
    85, 89–91, 97–8, 102, 109, 112–13,
    137–44, 160, 176, 178, 191,
    232–48; economic, 10, 21–2, 37,
    64, 77–82, 150, 181, 254–6;
    enabling, 23, 34, 140–4, 160;
    ideological, 10, 16–17, 19–22, 30,
    32, 62–3, 74–7, 80, 89–91, 95–6,
    97, 131–5, 169, 187, 220, 217–23,
    234–6, 250–2; military, 19, 37,
    42–4, 46–7, 52, 62, 91, 93–8, 108,
    112–13, 151, 181–8, 196, 210–13,
    252–3, 257–8; political, 10, 14–16,
    21–2, 32, 33, 34, 37, 62–3, 76–7,
    79–80, 89–90, 91, 133–40, 153,
    188, 252–4
Prague Spring, 200–1
Preobrazhenskii, 193–6
progress, *see* evolution
protectionism, 185, 247, 255, 258
protestantism, 17, 65
Prussia, 164, 189, 201, 213, 232

racism, 168
Rajk, 199
Rakosi, 199
Rakovski, 208
rationalisation, 150, 251–2
Reagan, 182, 183, 185, 246, 255, 258
Reith, 174
relativism, 72, 77
renunciation, 68
Rig Veda, 60
Rodinski, 38, 43
Rome, 31, 33, 34, 38, 43, 44, 47, 52,
    60, 66, 87, 112–21, 123, 127, 142,
    158, 196, 211
Rumania, 168
Russia, 109, 112, 156, 166, 182, 196,
    216, 217, 224, 232, 233

Safavi, 98
salvation, *see* world religions
Scharnhorst, 161
science, 49, 73, 79, 101, 109, 133, 228
Second International, 165
Second World War, 160, 166, 168, 170, 171, 229
sectoral change, 149–50
segmentation, 92–3, 94
Seljuks, 90
Serbia, 166
Shah of Iran, 235
Shang, 35, 39
Shaw, 176
Shi'ism, 87, 89, 98, 105, 235
Slansky, 200
slaves, 31, 94, 97, 98, 103, 107–9, 112–13
Smith, Adam, 1, 3, 8, 13, 14, 15, 16, 18, 127, 128, 140–4, 148, 150, 158–62, 163, 170, 174, 177, 186–7, 203, 232, 240, 243, 250, 260
social change, *see* competition evolution
Social Contract, 175
social flexibility, 155, 186–7, 254
social infrastructure, 31, 50, 55, 76–7, 81–2, 101, 102, 109, 137, 216
socialism, 11, 17, 155, 167, 177–9, 189–214, 260
Socialism in One Country, 194, 195–7
social mobility, 152, 171, 172, 197–8
society, 29, 120–1, 147, 151–2, 186
solidarity, 94–5, 102
Solzhenitsyn, 194
soteriology, 70–1
South, *see* Third World
South Korea, 240
Soviet model, 149, 153, 155–6, 156, 157, 189–214, 234, 237
Spain, 90, 98, 169–70, 207
SPD, 166, 167
Stalin, 150, 192–7, 222, 237
Stalinism, 190, 194–7, 209

Stamp Acts, 162
Standestaat, 137
state, 45, 56–7, 81, 88, 111, 112, 194, 236–48; capstone, 35, 51–3, 81, 101, 104, 108–9, 113, 135, 137, 202; custodial, 71, 76, 137; cyclical, 95–8, 137; organic, 53, 102, 133–40, 143, 158
state capitalism, 195
state socialism, 17, 54, 151, 153, 189–214
state system, *see* competition, military
Ste Croix, 31, 44, 153
Stewart, 140, 141, 142
students, 169–70, 175, 191
Sudan, 215
Sudra, 60
suffrage, 163, 164
Sufi, 84, 103
Sung, 46, 47, 48, 49, 50, 125
Sunni, 87
superpower, 171, 182–6, 196, 210–14
Sweden, 179, 188
Syria, 18, 85, 87, 100, 113
Szalai, 205
Szelenyi, 204–5

Taff Vale, 163
Tang, 33, 52
Taoism, 39
Tawney, 3
taxation, 37, 42–3, 53, 68, 81, 88, 94, 101, 127, 139, 160
Teller, 198
terms of trade, 178
Thatcher, 176–9, 210, 260
Third World, 136, 153, 170, 184, 186, 188, 214, 215–48, 249, 252, 255–60
Tibet, 70
Timur Lane, 105
Tito, 215
Tocqueville, 138, 221
totalitarianism, 169

Townsend, 206
trade, *see* merchants
Trotsky, 192, 193, 195, 204
Tunisia, 222

Ulama, 31, 72, 84–110
Ulysses, 176
Umayyad, 87–91
underdevelopment, *see* dependency
Untouchables, 61
Upanishads, 64, 65, 72
USA, 15, 153, 154, 169, 177, 179–88,
    190, 210, 211, 212, 213, 223–31,
    253–5, 256, 257, 258, 259
USSR, 153, 171, 180, 182, 186,
    189–214, 237, 253, 258, 259

Vaisya, 60
Vajda, 204–5
Versailles, 167, 198, 200, 201, 217
Vietnam, 181, 211, 217, 223, 230,
    252
Von Papen, 1
Von Thyssen, 168

Wajda, 203
Wallerstein, 231–2
Walpole, 257
Waqf, 99, 100, 101
war, *see* competition, military
watermill, 121
Watt, 86
Weber, 1, 3, 16, 19–21, 29, 40, 41, 46,
    50, 65, 70, 84–5, 101, 132, 136,
    150, 160, 235, 251–2
Weberism, 16–17, 19–21, 46, 58,
    74–5, 84–5, 105, 120, 133, 251–2
Weimar, 167, 168, 169
Weinert, 244
welfare, *see* citizenship
Westernizers, 190, 191, 234
Westminster Model, 148, 163
Wittfogel, 12, 27, 36, 38, 42
world religions, 9, 20, 28, 39, 80, 84–5,
    142–4

Yugoslavia, 197

zealots, 115

MORE ABOUT PENGUINS, PELICANS, PEREGRINES AND PUFFINS

For further information about books available from Penguins please write to Dept EP, Penguin Books Ltd, Harmondsworth, Middlesex UB7 0DA.

In the U.S.A.: For a complete list of books available from Penguins in the United States write to Dept DG, Penguin Books, 299 Murray Hill Parkway, East Rutherford, New Jersey 07073.

In Canada: For a complete list of books available from Penguins in Canada write to Penguin Books Canada Ltd, 2801 John Street, Markham, Ontario L3R 1B4.

In Australia: For a complete list of books available from Penguins in Australia write to the Marketing Department, Penguin Books Australia Ltd, P.O. Box 257, Ringwood, Victoria 3134.

In New Zealand: For a complete list of books available from Penguins in New Zealand write to the Marketing Department, Penguin Books (N.Z.) Ltd, Private Bag, Takapuna, Auckland 9.

In India: For a complete list of books available from Penguins in India write to Penguin Overseas Ltd, 706 Eros Apartments, 56 Nehru Place, New Delhi 110019.

A CHOICE OF
PELICANS AND PEREGRINES

☐ **The Knight, the Lady and the Priest**
Georges Duby   £6.95

The acclaimed study of the making of modern marriage in medieval France. 'He has traced this story – sometimes amusing, often horrifying, always startling – in a series of brilliant vignettes' – *Observer*

☐ **The Limits of Soviet Power** **Jonathan Steele**   £3.95

The Kremlin's foreign policy – Brezhnev to Chernenko, is discussed in this informed, informative 'wholly invaluable and extraordinarily timely study' – *Guardian*

☐ **Understanding Organizations** **Charles B. Handy**   £4.95

Third Edition. Designed as a practical source-book for managers, this Pelican looks at the concepts, key issues and current fashions in tackling organizational problems.

☐ **The Pelican Freud Library: Volume 12**   £5.95

Containing the major essays: *Civilization, Society and Religion, Group Psychology* and *Civilization and Its Discontents*, plus other works.

☐ **Windows on the Mind** **Erich Harth**   £4.95

Is there a physical explanation for the various phenomena that we call 'mind'? Professor Harth takes in age-old philosophers as well as the latest neuroscientific theories in his masterly study of memory, perception, free will, selfhood, sensation and other richly controversial fields.

☐ **The Pelican History of the World**
J. M. Roberts   £5.95

'A stupendous achievement . . . This is the unrivalled World History for our day' – A. J. P. Taylor

A CHOICE OF
PELICANS AND PEREGRINES

☐ *A Question of Economics* **Peter Donaldson** £4.95

Twenty key issues – from the City and big business to trades unions – clarified and discussed by Peter Donaldson, author of *10 × Economics* and one of our greatest popularizers of economics.

☐ *Inside the Inner City* **Paul Harrison** £4.95

A report on urban poverty and conflict by the author of *Inside the Third World*. 'A major piece of evidence' – *Sunday Times*. 'A classic: it tells us what it is really like to be poor, and why' – *Time Out*

☐ *What Philosophy Is* **Anthony O'Hear** £4.95

What are human beings? How should people act? How do our thoughts and words relate to reality? Contemporary attitudes to these age-old questions are discussed in this new study, an eloquent and brilliant introduction to philosophy today.

☐ *The Arabs* **Peter Mansfield** £4.95

New Edition. 'Should be studied by anyone who wants to know about the Arab world and how the Arabs have become what they are today' – *Sunday Times*

☐ *Religion and the Rise of Capitalism*
R. H. Tawney £3.95

The classic study of religious thought of social and economic issues from the later middle ages to the early eighteenth century.

☐ *The Mathematical Experience*
Philip J. Davis and Reuben Hersh £7.95

Not since *Gödel, Escher, Bach* has such an entertaining book been written on the relationship of mathematics to the arts and sciences. 'It deserves to be read by everyone . . . an instant classic' – *New Scientist*

A CHOICE OF PENGUINS

☐ **The Complete Penguin Stereo Record and Cassette Guide**
Greenfield, Layton and March   £7.95

A new edition, now including information on compact discs. 'One of the few indispensables on the record collector's bookshelf' – *Gramophone*

☐ **Selected Letters of Malcolm Lowry**
Edited by Harvey Breit and Margerie Bonner Lowry £5.95

'Lowry emerges from these letters not only as an extremely interesting man, but also a lovable one' – Philip Toynbee

☐ **The First Day on the Somme**
Martin Middlebrook   £3.95

1 July 1916 was the blackest day of slaughter in the history of the British Army. 'The soldiers receive the best service a historian can provide: their story told in their own words' – *Guardian*

☐ **A Better Class of Person** John Osborne   £2.50

The playwright's autobiography, 1929–56. 'Splendidly enjoyable' – John Mortimer. 'One of the best, richest and most bitterly truthful autobiographies that I have ever read' – Melvyn Bragg

☐ **The Winning Streak** Goldsmith and Clutterbuck   £2.95

Marks & Spencer, Saatchi & Saatchi, United Biscuits, GEC . . . The UK's top companies reveal their formulas for success, in an important and stimulating book that no British manager can afford to ignore.

☐ **The First World War** A. J. P. Taylor   £4.95

'He manages in some 200 illustrated pages to say almost everything that is important . . . A special text . . . a remarkable collection of photographs' – *Observer*

A CHOICE OF PENGUINS

☐ *Man and the Natural World* **Keith Thomas** £4.95

Changing attitudes in England, 1500–1800. 'An encyclopedic study of man's relationship to animals and plants . . . a book to read again and again' – Paul Theroux, *Sunday Times* Books of the Year

☐ *Jean Rhys: Letters 1931–66*
˙Edited by Francis Wyndham and Diana Melly £4.95

'Eloquent and invaluable . . . her life emerges, and with it a portrait of an unexpectedly indomitable figure' – Marina Warner in the *Sunday Times*

☐ *The French Revolution* **Christopher Hibbert** £4.95

'One of the best accounts of the Revolution that I know . . . Mr Hibbert is outstanding' – J. H. Plumb in the *Sunday Telegraph*

☐ *Isak Dinesen* **Judith Thurman** £4.95

The acclaimed life of Karen Blixen, 'beautiful bride, disappointed wife, radiant lover, bereft and widowed woman, writer, sibyl, Scheherazade, child of Lucifer, Baroness; always a unique human being . . . an assiduously researched and finely narrated biography' – *Books & Bookmen*

☐ *The Amateur Naturalist*
Gerald Durrell with Lee Durrell £4.95

'Delight . . . on every page . . . packed with authoritative writing, learning without pomposity . . . it represents a real bargain' – *The Times Educational Supplement*. 'What treats are in store for the average British household' – *Daily Express*

☐ *When the Wind Blows* **Raymond Briggs** £2.95

'A visual parable against nuclear war: all the more chilling for being in the form of a strip cartoon' – *Sunday Times*. 'The most eloquent anti-Bomb statement you are likely to read' – *Daily Mail*

PENGUIN REFERENCE BOOKS

☐ **The Penguin Map of the World** £2.95

Clear, colourful, crammed with information and fully up-to-date, this is a useful map to stick on your wall at home, at school or in the office.

☐ **The Penguin Map of Europe** £2.95

Covers all land eastwards to the Urals, southwards to North Africa and up to Syria, Iraq and Iran * Scale = 1:5,500,000 * 4-colour artwork * Features main roads, railways, oil and gas pipelines, plus extra information including national flags, currencies and populations.

☐ **The Penguin Map of the British Isles** £2.95

Including the Orkneys, the Shetlands, the Channel Islands and much of Normandy, this excellent map is ideal for planning routes and touring holidays, or as a study aid.

☐ **The Penguin Dictionary of Quotations** £3.95

A treasure-trove of over 12,000 new gems and old favourites, from Aesop and Matthew Arnold to Xenophon and Zola.

☐ **The Penguin Dictionary of Art and Artists** £3.95

Fifth Edition. 'A vast amount of information intelligently presented, carefully detailed, abreast of current thought and scholarship and easy to read' – *The Times Literary Supplement*

☐ **The Penguin Pocket Thesaurus** £2.50

A pocket-sized version of Roget's classic, and an essential companion for all commuters, crossword addicts, students, journalists and the stuck-for-words.

PENGUIN REFERENCE BOOKS

☐ *The Penguin Dictionary of Troublesome Words*   £2.50

A witty, straightforward guide to the pitfalls and hotly disputed issues in standard written English, illustrated with examples and including a glossary of grammatical terms and an appendix on punctuation.

☐ *The Penguin Guide to the Law*   £8.95

This acclaimed reference book is designed for everyday use, and forms the most comprehensive handbook ever published on the law as it affects the individual.

☐ *The Penguin Dictionary of Religions*   £4.95

The rites, beliefs, gods and holy books of all the major religions throughout the world are covered in this book, which is illustrated with charts, maps and line drawings.

☐ *The Penguin Medical Encyclopedia*   £4.95

Covers the body and mind in sickness and in health, including drugs, surgery, history, institutions, medical vocabulary and many other aspects. Second Edition. 'Highly commendable' – *Journal of the Institute of Health Education*

☐ *The Penguin Dictionary of Physical Geography*   £4.95

This book discusses all the main terms used, in over 5,000 entries illustrated with diagrams and meticulously cross-referenced.

☐ *Roget's Thesaurus*   £3.50

Specially adapted for Penguins, Sue Lloyd's acclaimed new version of Roget's original will help you find the right words for your purposes. 'As normal a part of an intelligent household's library as the Bible, Shakespeare or a dictionary' – *Daily Telegraph*

PENGUIN OMNIBUSES

☐ **Victorian Villainies**   £5.95

Fraud, murder, political intrigue and horror are the ingredients of these four Victorian thrillers, selected by Hugh Greene and Graham Greene.

☐ **The Balkan Trilogy Olivia Manning**   £5.95

This acclaimed trilogy – *The Great Fortune, The Spoilt City* and *Friends and Heroes* – is the portrait of a marriage, and an exciting recreation of civilian life in the Second World War. 'It amuses, it diverts, and it informs' – Frederick Raphael

☐ **The Penguin Collected Stories of Isaac Bashevis Singer**   £5.95

Forty-seven marvellous tales of Jewish magic, faith and exile. 'Never was the Nobel Prize more deserved . . . He belongs with the giants' – *Sunday Times*

☐ **The Penguin Essays of George Orwell**   £4.95

Famous pieces on 'The Decline of the English Murder', 'Shooting an Elephant', political issues and P. G. Wodehouse feature in this edition of forty-one essays, criticism and sketches – all classics of English prose.

☐ **Further Chronicles of Fairacre 'Miss Read'**   £3.95

Full of humour, warmth and charm, these four novels – *Miss Clare Remembers, Over the Gate, The Fairacre Festival* and *Emily Davis* – make up an unforgettable picture of English village life.

☐ **The Penguin Complete Sherlock Holmes Sir Arthur Conan Doyle**   £5.95

With the fifty-six classic short stories, plus *A Study in Scarlet, The Sign of Four, The Hound of the Baskervilles* and *The Valley of Fear*, this volume contains the remarkable career of Baker Street's most famous resident.

PENGUIN OMNIBUSES

☐ *Life with Jeeves* **P. G. Wodehouse** £3.95

Containing *Right Ho, Jeeves, The Inimitable Jeeves* and *Very Good, Jeeves!* in which Wodehouse lures us, once again, into the ever-green world of Bertie Wooster, his terrifying Aunt Agatha, his man Jeeves and other eggs, good and bad.

☐ *The Penguin Book of Ghost Stories* £4.95

An anthology to set the spine tingling, including stories by Zola, Kleist, Sir Walter Scott, M. R. James, Elizabeth Bowen and A. S. Byatt.

☐ *The Penguin Book of Horror Stories* £4.95

Including stories by Maupassant, Poe, Gautier, Conan Doyle, L. P. Hartley and Ray Bradbury, in a selection of the most horrifying horror from the eighteenth century to the present day.

☐ *The Penguin Complete Novels of Jane Austen* £5.95

Containing the seven great novels: *Sense and Sensibility, Pride and Prejudice, Mansfield Park, Emma, Northanger Abbey, Persuasion* and *Lady Susan*.

☐ *Perfick, Perfick!* **H. E. Bates** £4.95

The adventures of the irrepressible Larkin family, in four novels: *The Darling Buds of May, A Breath of French Air, When the Green Woods Laugh* and *Oh! To Be in England*.

☐ *Famous Trials*
Harry Hodge and James H. Hodge £3.95

From Madeleine Smith to Dr Crippen and Lord Haw-Haw, this volume contains the most sensational murder and treason trials, selected by John Mortimer from the classic Penguin Famous Trials series.